Sustainable Development, Global Trade and Social Rights

Studies in Employment and Social Policy

VOLUME 51

Editors

Professor Alan Neal (founding editor of the *International Journal of Labour Law and Industrial Relations*, and Convenor of the European Association of Labour Law Judges); Professor Manfred Weiss (past president of the International Industrial Relations Association); and Professor Birgitta Nyström (professor of private law at the Law Faculty, University of Lund, Sweden, and member of the European Committee of Social Rights).

Objective

Studies in Employment and Social Policy series seeks to provide a forum for highlighting international and comparative research on contemporary areas of significance for evaluation and regulation of the world of work.

Introduction

Launched in 1997, the Studies in Employment and Social Policy Series now boasts over forty titles, addressing key policy and development issues in the fields of industrial relations, labour law, social security, and international labour regulation.

Content

With contributions from leading figures in the field, the series brings together key policymakers, academics, and regulators, providing a unique context in which to analyse and evaluate the rapid and dramatic work and social policy developments taking place around the globe.

The titles published in this series are listed at the end of this volume.

Sustainable Development, Global Trade and Social Rights

Edited by

Adalberto Perulli
Tiziano Treu

Published by:
Kluwer Law International B.V.
PO Box 316
2400 AH Alphen aan den Rijn
The Netherlands
E-maill: international-sales@wolterskluwer.com
Website: lrus.wolterskluwer.com

Sold and distributed in North, Central and South America by:
Wolters Kluwer Legal & Regulatory U.S.
7201 McKinney Circle
Frederick, MD 21704
United States of America
Email: customer.service@wolterskluwer.com

Sold and distributed in all other countries by:
Air Business Subscriptions
Rockwood House
Haywards Heath
West Sussex
RH16 3DH
United Kingdom
Email: international-customerservice@wolterskluwer.com

Printed on acid-free paper.

ISBN 978-90-411-9235-6

e-Book: ISBN 978-90-411-9270-7
web-PDF: ISBN 978-90-411-9303-2

© 2018 Kluwer Law International BV, The Netherlands

All rights reserved. No part of this publication may be reproduced, stored in a retrieval system, or transmitted in any form or by any means, electronic, mechanical, photocopying, recording, or otherwise, without written permission from the publisher.

Permission to use this content must be obtained from the copyright owner. More information can be found at: lrus.wolterskluwer.com/policies/permissions-reprints-and-licensing

Printed in the United Kingdom.

Editors

Adalberto Perulli is Full Professor of Labour Law at the Ca' Foscari University of Venice and Visiting Professor at the University of Paris Ouest Nanterre La Défense since 2000. He is the Director of Master in Labour Law at the Ca' Foscari University of Venice. He did research and studies for the European Commission and for the International Labour Organization (ILO) of Geneva. Prof. Perulli has been rapporteur to the XVIII ISLSSL World Congress of Labour and Security Law on "Labour Law and productive decentralization" in Paris, on 2006; He is Master EMA Director at EIUC (European Inter-University Centre for Human Rights and Democratisation) and also member of the scientific and editorial staff of several Italian and foreign labour law reviews. Among his most important publications: Perulli A., Treu T., (ed. by), Enterprise and Social Rights, Kluwer, 2017; Perulli A., Sustainability, Social Rights and International Trade: The TTIP, in International Journal of Comparative Labour Law and Industrial Relations, vol. 32, 2015; Perulli A., Fundamental Social Rights, Market Regulation and EU External Action in International Journal Of Comparative Labour Law And Industrial Relations, vol. 30, 2014; Perulli A., Casale G., Compliance with labour legislation: its efficacy and efficiency, Ginevra, ILO, 2010; Perulli A., Economically dependent / quasi-subordinate (parasubordinate) employment: legal, social and economic aspects, European Commission, Brussels, 2002.

Tiziano Treu is Professor Emeritus of Labour Law, Catholic University of Milan, Law School, and President of ISLSSL – International Society of Labour and Social Security Law. Previously he has been President of the Italian Association of Labour Law and Social Security. During his political experience Prof. Treu has been Minister of Transportation and Minister of Labour and Social Security in the Italian Government, and more recently President of the XI Commission (Labour and Wefare) of the Italian Senate. Among his recent publications: Diritto del lavoro dell'Unione Europea (7th ed., with M. Roccella), Labour Law in Italy (4th revised ed.), Verso nuove relazioni industriali, (with M. Carrieri, eds.).

Contributors

Janice R. Bellace is the Samuel Blank Professor of Legal Studies, and Professor of Legal Studies & Business Ethics, and Management at the Wharton School of the University of Pennsylvania. She is president-elect of International Society of Labour and Social Security Law. Previously she has been President of the International Labour and Employment Relations Association (ILERA), and president of the American Labour and Employment Relations Association (LERA). She is a member of the editorial board of several international labour and labour law reviews. She authored books, chapters and articles on comparative and international labour law and labour relations, including Labour, Business and Human Rights (forthcoming, Elgar). She was a member of the ILO's Committee of Experts for fifteen years.

Vania Brino is Associate Professor in Labour Law and Director of the International Master Program "Global economics and Social Affairs," Ca' Foscari University of Venice.
She is editorial member of various journals and reviews. She is the author of publications in national and international labour law.

Valentina Cagnin is Research Fellow at the Venice Ca' Foscari University for a research project on Digitalization and Labour Relationship. She has a PhD in European Law on Civil Commercial and Labour Contracts and a Degree in Economics and Finance at the Venice Ca' Foscari University. Her main research fields are: Corporate Social Responsibility, Italian, European and International Labor Law, Sustainable Development, Sustainability, EU GSP, Free Trade Agreements (CETA, TTIP, TTP), and ISDS (Investor-State Dispute Settlement).

Giuseppe Casale is Deputy Director of the International Training Centre of the ILO, Director of the Turin School of Development and Secretary General of the International Society for Labour and Social Security Law. He is a visiting professor at the Cà Foscari University, Venice and lectures in international and comparative labour law in several European universities. He is an editorial member of various international journals and reviews. He is the author of several publications in international and comparative labour law, and comparative industrial and employment relations.

Contributors

Michele Faioli is a professor at Law School of Tor Vergata University in Rome (Italy). He teaches courses in the areas of labor relations and comparative labor law, including industrial relations, social security, European labor law.

Professor Faioli is a Faculty Fellow at Scuola Europea di Relazioni Industriali (SERI) where he chairs the theme project on Industrial Relations, Comparative Studies and European Labor Law. Faioli's comparative research mainly looks at collective bargaining impact on labor relations. Faioli also maintains a website on these matters aimed at colleagues and students (www.seri-fgb.eu). SERI's initiatives are also carried out with Fondazione Giacomo Brodolini.

Mario Fasani is Senior Research Coordinator at the Turin School of Development (TSD) of the ITCILO. He was a former labour lawyer at the International Labour Organization in Geneva, where he authored and co-authored several publications in the field of labour law.

Adrián Goldin is Professor Emeritus of the University of Buenos Aires and former Director of the Department of Labour Law and Social Security of its Law School. Former full professor at the University of San Andrés (Buenos Aires, Argentina) and also Professor Emeritus of that university. He's been the president of the International Society for Labour and Social Security Law (2012–2015), and he is currently its Honorary President. He is a fellow full member ("Academico de Número") of the Academia Iberoamericana de Derecho del Trabajo y de la Seguridad Social, corresponding member of the Brazilian Academy for Labour Law and former president of the Argentinean Association of Labour Law and Social Security. He is also a member of the editorial board of many international Labour Law journals. He has authored books, contributed to edited collection, and published some 150 articles and research reports in Argentina and abroad on labour law and labour relations.

Sheldon Leader is Professor of Law and Director of the Essex Business and Human Rights Project, University of Essex (UK). He focuses on bringing academics and non-academics together in collaborative projects, aiming to formulate and apply principles linking business activity and human rights standards, often with the tools of legal and political theory. Relevant publications include "Human Rights and the Constitutionalized Corporation" in Multinationals and the Constitutionalization of the World Power System edited by Stephane Vernac, et al. Ashgate Publishing Ltd. (2016); "Coherence, Mutual Assurance, and a Treaty on Business and Human Rights" in Surya Deva and David Bilchitz (eds) Business and Human Rights: Exploring the Contours of a Treaty (Cambridge University Press, 2017); "Collateralism" in R. Brownsword (ed.) Global Governance and the Search for Justice (Hart Publishing: 2005); Freedom of Association: A Study in Labor Law and Political Theory (Yale University Press, 1992).

Antoine Lyon-Caen President of the "Institut International Pour les Etudes Comparatives," he is Professor Emeritus at the Law School of the University of Paris Ouest Nanterre La Défense, Professor at the Higher School of Social Sciences (Chair: Law, Economy and Enterprise) and Barrister at the Conseil d'Etat and the Supreme Court of cassation. He is Director of Revue de droit du travail (Labour Law Journal) since its creation and Member of editorial committees of several European journals as well as author of various books in Labour Law, concerning European Social Policy, Social Policy and Competition Law, Law and Globalization. Critical approach of Law and Economics (Last book published: Multinationals and the constitutionalization of the world power system with J.-P. Robé, S. Vernac, Préface J.G. Ruggie, éd. Routledge, 2016).

Manfred Weiss is Professor of Civil Law and Labour Law first since 1974 at the University of Hamburg and from 1977 to 2008 at the Goethe University in Frankfurt. Visiting Professor in many countries. Former President of the International Labour and Employment Relations Association (ILERA). Consultant to the EU Commission, to the ILO and to foreign Governments for many years. Many publications in labour law and Industrial Relations. In 2015 he received the Labour Law Research Network's (LLRN) award for his achievements in international labour law. He holds honorary doctorates from universities in France, Hungary, Peru and South Africa.

Summary of Contents

Editors	v
Contributors	vii
Introduction *Adalberto Perulli*	1
PART I Sustainable Development and International Trade	13
CHAPTER 1 Sustainable Development, Global Trade and Social Rights: An Evolutionary Perspective *Adalberto Perulli*	15
CHAPTER 2 Sustainable Development, Social Rights and International Trade *Antoine Lyon-Caen*	33
PART II International Trade Agreements: The Linkage Between Trade and Social Rights	39
CHAPTER 3 The MERCOSUR (Southern Common Market): Argentina, Brazil, Paraguay, Uruguay and Venezuela *Adrián Goldin*	41
CHAPTER 4 The Link Between Trade and Social Clauses *Janice R. Bellace*	57

Summary of Contents

CHAPTER 5
Atlantic Transitions for Law and Labor: CETA First and TTIP Second?
Michele Faioli   71

PART III
The European Union Internal and External Action in the International Trade Relationships Context   97

CHAPTER 6
Globalization and Human Rights: Social Clauses in Trade Agreements and in International Exchanges among Companies
Tiziano Treu   99

CHAPTER 7
The EU Generalised Scheme of Preferences and the Special Incentive Arrangement for Sustainable Development and Good Governance
Manfred Weiss   121

PART IV
Investments, IMF, ISDS (Investor-State Dispute Settlement) Clauses and the Arbitral Procedures to Resolve a Conflict   129

CHAPTER 8
Social Rights and the Janus Face of International Investment: The Role of Commercial Banks and Project Finance
Sheldon Leader   131

CHAPTER 9
Stabilization Clauses in State-Investor Agreements: A Brief Overview
Vania Brino   141

CHAPTER 10
New Generations Treaties and the Attempts for a Renewal of the ISDS
Valentina Cagnin   155

PART V
The ILO Perspective   169

CHAPTER 11
An Overview of the Main ILO Policies and Tools in the Organization of Promotional Activities on Social Rights
Giuseppe Casale & Mario Fasani   171

Index   193

Table of Contents

Editors	v
Contributors	vii
Introduction *Adalberto Perulli*	1
PART I Sustainable Development and International Trade	13
CHAPTER 1 Sustainable Development, Global Trade and Social Rights: An Evolutionary Perspective *Adalberto Perulli*	15

1	Sustainable Development, Global Trade and Social Rights: The Renewal of an Historical Link	15
2	The Evolutionary Perspective of the Linkage	20
3	Internormativity and Globalization: An Evolutionary Perspective	21
4	Social Rights, Content and Regulatory Value of the Social Clause in an Evolutionary Perspective	23
5	Social Clause and Industrial Relations	26
6	Economic and Social Rationalities: The Positive Effects of Respect for Social Rights	27
7	Impact Assessment and Implementation Mechanisms	29

Table of Contents

CHAPTER 2
Sustainable Development, Social Rights and International Trade
Antoine Lyon-Caen — 33

1   Introductive Proposal — 33
   1.1   Notions — 33
   1.2   State or Inter-State Perspectives — 35
   1.3   Perspectives Centred on Enterprises — 37

PART II
International Trade Agreements: The Linkage Between Trade and Social Rights — 39

CHAPTER 3
The MERCOSUR (Southern Common Market): Argentina, Brazil, Paraguay, Uruguay and Venezuela
Adrián Goldin — 41

1   Sustainable Development and Decent Work — 41
2   On the MERCOSUR — 42
   2.1   Institutional Development — 42
   2.2   Labour Rights — 43
      2.2.1   Influences and Common Traits — 43
      2.2.2   The Authoritarian Factor — 46
3   Sustainable Development in the MERCOSUR — 47
   3.1   Analysis of Certain Social Indicators — 48
   3.2   Regulatory Level — 49
   3.3   Specific Regulatory Instruments of the MERCOSUR — 50
      3.3.1   The Social and Labour Declaration of the MERCOSUR — 51
          3.3.1.1   Its Approval and Amendment — 51
          3.3.1.2   The Principles — 52
          3.3.1.3   Regulation Contents: Rights — 52
          3.3.1.4   Implementation and Follow-Up — 54
      3.3.2   The Multilateral Agreement on Social Security — 55

CHAPTER 4
The Link Between Trade and Social Clauses
Janice R. Bellace — 57

1   Introduction — 57
2   The Specter of NAFTA — 59
   2.1   The Impact on Jobs of Trade Liberalization — 59
3   The Rights in Labor Clauses — 60
   3.1   Meaning of the ILO Fundamental Principles — 62
   3.2   The Meaning of the Rights in Labor Clauses — 64

4	Monitoring and Enforcement	65
5	The Undercutting of Any Meaning of the Labor Standards in the TPP	66
6	Next Generation Labor Clauses	67
References		68

CHAPTER 5
Atlantic Transitions for Law and Labor: CETA First and TTIP Second?
Michele Faioli   71

1	Introduction: Regulatory Distortions	72
2	For Delineating an ex post Investigation Method: Convergence and Quasi-Similarities	77
3	For Testing an ex ante Investigation Method: The EU Model Versus the ISDS Mechanisms	80
4	The CETA Labor Chapter	84
5	Conclusions: Proposal	88
References		91

PART III
The European Union Internal and External Action in the International Trade Relationships Context   97

CHAPTER 6
Globalization and Human Rights: Social Clauses in Trade Agreements and in International Exchanges among Companies
Tiziano Treu   99

1	Economic and Social Rationale in International Trade		99
	1.1	The Diffusion of Social Clauses	100
2	Social Clauses: Economic Motivations and Sustainable Development		101
	2.1	The Reactions of the Public Opinions	103
3	Different Categories of Social Clauses		103
	3.1	Different Contents and Languages	104
4	Procedures and Enforcement		105
	4.1	The Clause ISDS	106
	4.2	The Weakness of the Procedures	107
5	Uncertain Outcomes		108
	5.1	The (Possible) Pattern Setting Value of the CETA	109
6	International Exchanges among Companies		109
	6.1	Company Regulations and Corporate Social Responsibility	110
7	Transnational Agreements		111
8	Pilot Cases		112
9	Possible Innovations		113
10	Multiple Instruments and Strategies for International Social Regulation		114
References			118

Table of Contents

CHAPTER 7
The EU Generalised Scheme of Preferences and the Special Incentive
Arrangement for Sustainable Development and Good Governance
Manfred Weiss   121

1	Introduction	121
2	The Legal Basis for the Present System	122
3	The Different Schemes	123
	3.1 General Scheme of Preferences	123
	3.2 Special Incentive Arrangement for Sustainable Development (GSP+)	124
	3.3 Everything but Arms Arrangement	124
4	Sanctions in Case of Violation	125
	4.1 Temporary Withdrawal (Common to All Arrangements)	125
	4.2 Monitoring Mechanism for GPS+	125
	4.2.1 'Scorecard'	126
	4.2.2 'GSP+ Dialogue'	126
5	General Safeguards	126
6	Evaluation	127

PART IV
Investments, IMF, ISDS (Investor-State Dispute Settlement) Clauses and
the Arbitral Procedures to Resolve a Conflict   129

CHAPTER 8
Social Rights and the Janus Face of International Investment: The Role of
Commercial Banks and Project Finance
Sheldon Leader   131

1	The Basic Framework	131
	1.1 What Are the EPs?	131
	1.2 The Discipline of Project Finance	132
2	Evaluation	133
	2.1 The Impact of PF on Social Rights and Sustainable Development	133
	2.2 Risk to Basic Rights and Risk to Profit	135
	2.3 Two Examples	136
	2.3.1 Social Change as a Transition to Sustained Prevention of Serious Social Damage	137
	2.3.1.1 No-Go for a Proposed Project	138
	2.3.1.2 Lack of Transparency	138
	2.3.1.3 Competition among Banks Affecting the Categorization Process	139
	2.3.2 Social Change as Fundamental Transformation	139
3	Conclusion	140

CHAPTER 9
Stabilization Clauses in State-Investor Agreements: A Brief Overview
Vania Brino   141

1	Framing the Issue	141
2	The Increasing Role of Multinational Enterprises in the Rule Making Process at Global Level	144
3	Stabilization Clauses: Meaning and Problems	146
	3.1 Stabilization Clauses: Aims, Effects and Models	147
4	What About the Trends for the Future?	151

CHAPTER 10
New Generations Treaties and the Attempts for a Renewal of the ISDS
Valentina Cagnin   155

1	Investor-State Dispute Settlement: A Controversial Tool for Dispute Resolution	155
2	ISDS and Social Rights: The Risk of Freezing the Law	160
	2.1 *Veolia Propreté v. Egypt* Case	160
	2.2 *Centerra v. Kyrgyz Republic*	161
	2.3 *Piero Foresti & Others v. South Africa* Case	161
3	New Generation Treaties (CETA, TTIP, TPP and EUSFTA) and the Progress Made in Developing a Balanced and Forward-Looking Approach in the International Investment Policy	162
4	The Questions on the Compatibility of the Investment Court System (ICS) with the EU Law	166

PART V
The ILO Perspective   169

CHAPTER 11
An Overview of the Main ILO Policies and Tools in the Organization of Promotional Activities on Social Rights
Giuseppe Casale & Mario Fasani   171

1	Introduction	171
2	The Role of International Labour Standards	172
3	An International Legal Framework for a Fair Globalization	173
	3.1 Freedom of Association	174
	3.2 Forced Labour	175
	3.3 Discrimination	175
	3.4 Child Labour	175
	3.5 Fair Globalization	175
4	A Path to Decent Work	176
5	The 2030 Agenda on Sustainable Development and Decent Work	177

5.1		Targets for SDG 8: Decent Work and Economic Growth	177
5.2		Evaluation of the Impact of the ILO Declaration on Social Justice for a Fair Globalization	178
5.3		Priority Areas for Action	179
5.4		Productive and Decent Jobs	182
5.5		Social Protection	182
5.6		Social Dialogue and Tripartism	183
5.7		MNE Declaration	184
5.8		2014 Follow-Up Mechanism and 2016 Revision of the MNE Declaration	185
5.9		Principles Directed to Governments	187
	5.9.1	General Policies	187
	5.9.2	Employment	188
	5.9.3	Training	188
	5.9.4	Conditions of Work and Life	188
	5.9.5	Industrial Relations	188
5.10		Principles Directed to Enterprises	189
	5.10.1	General Policies	189
	5.10.2	Employment	189
	5.10.3	Training	189
	5.10.4	Conditions of Work and Life	189
	5.10.5	Industrial Relations	190
References			190
Index			193

Introduction

Adalberto Perulli

Among the more frequently discussed themes in the field of the social regulation after the advent of the economic globalization there is certainly that of the relationship, controversial but fundamental between global trade and social rights. It deals with a recurrent theme in the history of labor law, which arose from the objective of regulating competition among states and among enterprises, in an epoch in which the national economies were compared but without a regulatory framework of the rules of international commerce, and the birth of the United Nation Society had not happened yet. The links of labor law with this "hard" component of the liberal economy – centered on commerce and the philosophy of the free trade – have marked the history of the 1900s with alternative historical accounts and with different perspectives. With the birth of the International Labour Organization (ILO) the respect of social rights by leading Member States was already conceived as a condition for the advancements by other states desiring to progress in social regulation. The prospect of an institutional connection between regulation of commerce and respect of the social rights will find its consecration in Article VII of the Havana Charter, in which it is foreseen expressly that the states adherent to the new Trade International Organization must respect equitable conditions of work.

The failure of the negotiations and the conclusion of the General Agreement on Tariffs and Trade (GATT) marked a decisive setback of social conditionality as a requirement for international trade regulation. Negotiations for the birth of the World Trade Organization (WTO) would then continue to be marked by the resurgence of the issue, but it will nevertheless find the sharp opposition of the developing countries, the jealous guardians of the elements of competitiveness in a "Ricardian" logic of safeguarding the comparative advantages of nations. The failure of the insertion of a social clause in the WTO does not, however, mark the end of the idea and the practice of social conditionality in the treaties of international trade, and this for reasons linked to the philosophy that informs diagnosis of the social impact of free trade by two great powers of the global economy, the U.S. and the European Union (EU). Both of these actors have, for different reasons, made the respect for social rights a constant element of external relations, with generalized preference systems (albeit very different) or in the ambit of bilateral treaties. This stage of relaunching the historical link between international trade and social rights has been followed by the progressive realization of the social clause in the field of macro-regional treaties (NAFTA, Comprehensive Economic and Trade Agreement (CETA), MERCOSUR) and finally in the framework of the said mega-treaties, such as Trans-Pacific Partnership (TTP), Transatlantic Trade and Investments Partnerships (TTIP), CETA, with a progressive enhancement of the Sustainable Development model as a regulatory framework that can stabilize and institutionalize the link between social rights and free trade.

Today, we are experiencing a slowdown, if not a real crisis of these models of regional integration, caused by the resurgence of economic nationalisms. What is the future of global trade in the light of U.S. and Brexit neo-protectionism? What tools can be used to convey a new consensus and phase of cohesion in the international community where development policies, international business transactions and social and environmental sustainability coexist harmoniously? And what responsibilities, in this confused and fluid picture, must be taken on by the economic actors: first of all the multinational companies that move investment and productive locations globally? This Volume deals with these issues.

Social clauses, often accused of masked neo-protectionism, could be relaunched not only in the renegotiation of trade agreements between the U.K. and the EU, but also to find space and unexpected revival in U.S. trade policies to safeguard jobs that President Trump believes threatened by globalization. The crisis of commercial mega-treaties could be resolved in a new impetus for bilateral treaties, which China is practicing with great determination, assuming for the first time commitments, albeit still very temperate, in the field of the protection of social rights and environmental issues. The role of the World Bank and of institutional investors could as a result be amplified, in this context, by developing a financing project and an international cooperation where stabilization clauses prohibiting States from amending the existing regulatory framework at the time of funding will eventually contain derogations for social and environmental rights. The multinational enterprise, whose social and economic power surpasses that of individual national states, could find a new planetary legitimacy if it adopted and carried out with seriousness and commitment, throughout the production chain, the guidelines contained in the new ILO tripartite declaration. Thus, to a creeping de-globalization guided by populisms, could arise an opponent: a new, more socially oriented globalization.

In the first Part, dedicated to the general framework of the topic, Adalberto Perulli examines the link between Sustainable Development, Global Trade and Social Rights, outlining the complexity of the topic and its numerous analytical dimensions, carrying out some evolutionary considerations, with specific reference to social clause – the main instrument of social conditionality within the regulation of trade – and the linkage between global trade and social rights. The Author analyzes several different evolutionary points: the first one concerns a first theoretical profile of the social clause in its evolutionary aspects, as a way for to achieve inter-normativity (U.S. 1974 Trade Act, EU GSP + , the Preamble of the ILO Constitution), as the globalization has increased the interrelation between phenomena, between social/economic/political/environmental phenomena, and these interrelationships make the co-regulation of a complex situation a necessity. The second evolutionary aspect concerns the sources of international law and the content of the trade-labor linkage: after the identification of a nucleus of unconditioned social rights, Adalberto Perulli underlines three evolutionary elements: the normative value of the labor provisions, the protection of social standards from possible attacks in terms of guarantee about investments of multinational companies and the broadening of the sphere of rights to be taken into consideration within mega trade treaties. The third evolutionary aspect concerns the linkage between social clause and industrial relations at international level and the fourth is about the evolution of a positive relationship between economic and social rationalities, in the field of international trade. The last evolutionary point is about the impact assessment and implementation mechanisms: according to the Author, the social chapters of trade treaties should contemplate a clause requiring evaluation of the impact of a social clause in order to monitor the effectiveness of the linkage strategy. These social chapters should also contemplate an adequate mechanism of implementation of conditionality intended to monitor its effectiveness and the compliance with the obligations deriving from it.

In the same direction Antoine Lyon-Caen's essay, which underlines the existence of different levels of regulation within international competition, makes room for regulatory competition. Enterprises actually utilize these different levels as countries might be tempted to modulate the content of their norms in order to ensure economic attractiveness of their territories. The general conditions of population, the working conditions, the utilization of natural resources have become elements of international competition and we need to evaluate whether comparative advantages arising from restrictions on freedom, from the conditions of health and security of people and from the excessive exploitation of natural resources should be considered as justified or unjustified.

The expression "sustainable development," that is the research of a balance between economic growth, social progress and the protection of environment, promotes an interaction between social progress and environment protection, making sure that the development is livable. This suggests the adoption of long-term policies, in order to make sure that the incidences on the relationship among generations are integrated.

How may we subordinate international trade to the conditions required by sustainable development? This reflection entails: (i) the adoption of a State or inter-State perspective, and (ii) a perspective centered on enterprises.

(i) The promulgation of international labor norms is not enough to respond to the needs of sustainable development. In the last five decades, the framework of international trade has considerably evolved, most of all under the effect of global negotiations tending to the suppression or the reduction of the obstacles to the circulation of commodities, services and capital, raising the matter of the linkage among trade rules and social rules thanks to the social clause. This tool allows States to constitute a liaison between the facilitated access to a market and the compliance with the social and environmental norms but there are many different ways to conceive a policy of social and environmental conditionality.

(ii) Multinational enterprises have fully become actors of regulatory competition but they are not completely autonomous in the determination of their extra-economic responsibilities. We need to know: (1) who is responsible and in the name of whom (or what?); (2) To whom is a broad responsibility actually acknowledged? (3) Before whom may a report of responsibility connected to the prevention of social and environmental and to compensation via an award of damages take place?

In the second Part, dedicated to the social clauses experiences in treaties of international trade, Adrián Goldin develops an analysis of MERCOSUR, the Southern Common Market. MERCOSUR which was founded in 1994. It is actually an irregular customs union with numerous exceptions applicable to foreign trade. Argentina, Brazil, Paraguay and Uruguay are the founding members while Venezuela was incorporated in 2012 and the 2015 ratification of Bolivia is still pending. The territory of the MERCOSUR is about 13 million square kilometers, its population amounts to 293 million inhabitants and the region accounts for over 80% of the South American GDP.

There are some common traits of labor rights in this region. One of the distinctive features of labor rights in the MERCOSUR as compared to such rights in developing countries is that the former are influenced by the legal tradition inherited from continental Europe, rather than being transplanted. The social rights in the region express a weak sense of belonging to the European Social model, and a remarkable influence by the ILO's Convention and Recommendations and by Latin American orders (Chile and Mexico). Another characteristic trait of these legal orders is the broad gap between law and reality, a lack of effectiveness of such legal regimes manifest in the generalized presence of informal work and a certain tendency to establish rules that exceed the regional contexts or practices and that, therefore, are not (fully) applied. Finally, in the countries of the MERCOSUR, there has also been a growing trend towards highlighting the fundamental rights of people, including such rights established in the eight fundamental ILO Conventions and any other rights to which every human being is entitled, in this case, regarding the exercise of such rights in the work environment.

The link between labor legislation and the authoritarian regimes repeatedly prevailing within the region does not seem to have altered the protective nature of social rights, at least in the field of individual labor relations. However, an authoritarian influence was, undoubtedly, more characteristic in the field of Collective Labour Law. The social dimension of sustainable development in MERCOSUR involves fostering social integration, building stable, safe and fair societies and is based on the promotion and protection of human rights, as well as nondiscrimination, tolerance, respect for diversity, equal opportunities, security and everyone's participation, including all members of neglected groups and vulnerable sectors of society.

As for the regulatory level, the countries in the region have ratified the ILO fundamental labor Conventions almost in their entirety, a large part of priority conventions and a significant number of technical conventions but the number of claims in the countries of the MERCOSUR for infringement of fundamental conventions in connection with freedom of association (87 and 98) totals 431, out of which 185 claims have been recorded in Argentina, 64 in Brazil, 55 in Uruguay and 53 in Paraguay).

Finally, the specific regulatory instruments of the MERCOSUR in labor and social matters as approved by the States Parties are the Social and Labour Declaration of the MERCOSUR and the Multilateral Agreement on Social Security, both closely related with the realization of the sustainable development principle in the region.

Also Janice Bellace, facing the topic of the link between trade and social clauses from a U.S. perspective, underlines that since the early 1990s, social clauses, often called labor clauses, have been inserted in Free Trade Agreements (FTAs) as a sign of the signatories' commitment to worker rights and fair labor standards. But labor clauses in FTAs have not been successful in meeting this concern in large part because of vague substantive language regarding these rights and weak if not nonexistent enforcement mechanisms.

Despite being cast as the "highest" labor standards in an FTA, the Trans-Pacific Partnership (TPP) – signed on February 2016 by twelve nations, which must go through the internal ratification process of each country within two years – fails to set forth fundamental worker rights with any specificity and leaves the setting of "appropriate" working conditions to each country to decide. As a matter of fact, it is difficult to argue that the TPP's labor clause has real meaning because it is impossible to identify definitions of these rights on which the signatory nations agreed. The current text of Chapter 19 of the TPP and in particular its footnotes (where it is stated that "The obligation set out in art. 19.3 (Labour rights), as they relate to the ILO, refer only to the ILO Declaration") results in worker rights that have little meaning and places a heavy burden of proof on those seeking to prove a violation. For example, since the prohibition on "child labour" is de-linked from the core convention, we only know that children under 18 should not be permitted to engage in work dangerous to their physical or moral well-being, but we do not know at what age they are permitted to work in a factory (which is stipulated in ILO Convention n. 183).

A truly "high standard" labor clause (the next generation labor clause) should expressly state that signatories are bound to observe, apply and enforce internationally recognized labor standards and in particular the four fundamental principles set in the 1998 ILO Declaration and the linked eight core conventions, and also that, "these rights should be understood in a manner consistent with that expressed by the ILO's supervisory system." Such a statement included in an FTA would lay the basis for a justiciable claim. Without a stronger and more specific labor rights clause, there is little basis for worker rights' advocates to raise a successful complaint especially in light of the historically weak and slow dispute resolution process in American FTAs.

The contribution of Michele Faioli is dedicated instead to the mega-treaties experience.

Since 2009 the EU has concluded many trade and investment agreements. The most recent are the ones with Canada (CETA), U.S. (TTIP) and those with China, India, Japan, Latin America and MERCOSUR.

Such mega-treaties, based on bilateral negotiations for the free trade, also deal with labor and industrial relations. They are instruments to foster globalization and, to some extent, they may become an important occasion to advance better work conditions too. The problem is that the forms of labor protection they guarantee are broadly formulated standards, not directly enforceable under the domestic law, and therefore it depends on how these standards are applied by tribunals in the circumstances of each case.

Mega-treaties may also create labor regulatory distortions, which delineate the host State's right to regulate, vis-à-vis other States, situations in which standards are explicitly lowered in order to attract investments. Those distortion could be analyzed within: (i) an ex post vision – i.e., evaluating the derogations from labor standards once the mega-treaties are implemented and effective, and an (ii) an ex ante vision – i.e., creating legal frames to avoid the derogations from labor standards.

Moreover, the large majority of labor provisions that are presently in the mega-treaties try to get back to the distorting of possible effects resulting from lowering labor rights protection as an incentive to attract foreign investments. This is mostly due to the language used: there could be an aspirational language (i.e., "parties should not waive or derogate"), formulations of obligations of conduct (i.e., "parties shall strive to ensure"), or formulations of obligations of results (i.e., "parties shall not or will not derogate," or commitments for States.

The result of the aspirational language used (faced also in the 2017 CETA Labour Chapter), is that labor provisions in mega-treaties lack of an effective remedy to labor violations. Labor chapters are still ineffective, given that labor rights are not vested in individuals and / or unions for obtaining protections before judges). Meanwhile, corporations, thanks to the Investor-State Dispute Settlement (ISDS), can vest their rights and may affect labor standards by lowering or freezing them.

In order to reduce the potential of normative conflicts between domestic labor law and mega-treaty regimes, there are some theoretical proposals for "a labour chapter of new generation." The mega-treaty should stipulate, for example, that the right of establishment is connected to the mandatory application of the most favored domestic labor regime, beyond the application of the law where the worker performs his/her job activities (lex loci laboris) and/or the law of the place of origin of the worker (lex loci domicilii), or, again, it should stipulate that forms of stabilization clauses can never apply in labor.

In the third Part, the analysis continues with the Tiziano Treu's contribution, which underlines that Global trade has a growing influence on the national system and on all aspects of personal and collective life, as it puts in contact different economies but also national social and regulatory models. This challenges the traditional separation between the economic and the sociopolitical spheres and raises the conflict between the commercial logic of trade and the socioeconomic interest, promoting some protectionist policies and at the same time the diffusion of social clauses in trade agreements and other different systems and sources of social regulations (such as the General System of Preferences (GSP), the UN Guidelines, the Organisation for Economic Co-Operation and Development (OECD) Guidelines for multinational enterprises, the voluntary codes of conduct and the transnational collective agreements).

Social clauses could be conditional, promotional, or mixed, and they could contain a post-ratification conditionality, when the clauses commit the parties to respect the terms of the treaty under some penalty or a pre-ratification conditionality, when the respect of social standards is a precondition to the signing of their capacity to promote labor reforms prior to the agreement. Then social clauses are different on the language (many of them are drafted in aspirational not binding language) and on the content: the commitments vary, ranging from the respect of the "basic rights" or of the "internationally recognized labour rights" to the observance of the core labor standards of the ILO, or again, they can imply the observance of the eight ILO core Conventions. Procedures of enforcement of dispute resolution and of monitoring are multistep and activated by the negotiating parties, namely the States but the weakness of the procedures is mostly due to the vagueness of the commitments written in the agreements and to the State bureaucracy.

A new perspective is necessary to correct the weakness of social clauses and of their enforcement procedures: more precise and consistent legal norms and also a set of public policies and administrative practices adopted by the national states vis-à-vis global trade and international markets are necessary. It is important also to reconsider the role of the legislator and of the representative bodies but also of the bureaucracy and the technical agencies which are decisive in the preparation of the dossier and in the negotiations among States, involving all the stakeholders and the social actors and improving on the lack of transparency and information. A right of initiative to bring legal actions by social actors and the intervention of independent mediators and arbitrators could be a means to improve the application of social clauses. Multinationals should also accept more stringent social obligations and the ILO could contribute directly to the enforcement of these clauses as arbitrators indicated by the parties to the treaties.

Manfred Weiss, for its part, focuses on a particular aspect of EU's external relations, that is the EU Generalised Scheme of Preferences and the Special Incentive Arrangement for Sustainable Development and Good Governance. Since 1995, the European Union has granted trade preferences to developing countries under its unilaterally imposed scheme of generalized tariff preferences.

The Treaty on the European Union (TEU, Article 21, 3) and the Treaty of the Functioning of the European Union (TFUE, Articles 208 and 209) contain a whole set of rules providing a legal basis for this scheme of preferences which is now specified in Regulation n. 978/2012 of October 25, 2012.

The new Regulation (in force since January 2014) reduces significantly the number of countries addressed by the scheme (from 176 beneficiaries to 90), in order to focus on the countries most in need and to make sure that the scheme can be handled more effectively.

The Regulation distinguishes between three regimes: the general scheme of preferences (GSP), the special incentive arrangement for sustainable development (GSP+) and the everything but arms arrangement (EBA).

The GSP scheme gives a significant reduction of tariff lines to developing countries if they respect the principles laid down in UN / ILO Conventions on core human and labor rights (these are the eight ILO conventions on core labor rights and seven UN conventions referring to the prevention and punishment of crime and genocide, to the elimination of all forms of racial discrimination, to civil and political rights, to the elimination of all forms of discrimination against women and to the rights of the child). The GSP + offers even deeper tariff cuts of the same tariff lines for vulnerable countries that ratified and implemented a significant number of international conventions (twenty-seven) relating to human and labor rights, environment and good governance. According to these criteria of eligibility thirteen countries benefited from GSP + preferences in 2014 and 2015. The third category of the scheme, called EBA is a special arrangement for the least developed countries, which are granted full duty-free.

All three schemes of the EU arrangement for tariff preferences are not the result of negotiations as FTAs normally are but a unilateral system. However, it is a kind of "soft unilateralism" as it is not primarily motivated by a politics of protectionism but by the intention to provide developing countries access to the European market and combine free trade with protective standards, among them labor standards. At the same time, it should not be ignored that in the very end it has its limits in blunt economic considerations, because thanks to the safeguard rules (Articles 22–28) which protect the EU economy, the GSP can only work as long as it does not hurt the competitiveness of the EU.

Part IV deals with the topic of social clauses strictly linked to investments. Sheldon Leader focuses on the role of commercial bank and project finance, explaining how the Equator Principles (EPs) provide a risk management framework, adopted by financial institutions, for determining, assessing and managing environmental and social risk in projects. It is primarily intended to provide a minimum standard for due diligence to support responsible risk decision-making. The Principles seek to provide banks, governments, and potentially affected populations with the assurance that the projects which are funded will respect basic social guarantees, many of which match the guarantees about development policy sought in the UN's sustainable development strategies.

Those lending principles have been subscribed to by many banks financing development projects: they are the means of channeling the energies and ethics of lenders and borrowers of Project Finance.

The EPs can be considered as a particular strategy for regulating international investment in the light of the requirements of basic social rights. It is a strategy that aims to prevent investment from provoking serious social and environmental damage, intended to move societies along the path to sustainable development: implicit in the EPs is the need to draw a boundary line between projects that are viable, while risky, and those which are not viable because the risk of social damage is simply too great.

At the same time, however, this is an investment technique that threatens to aggravate some of the same social damage it seeks to limit. It is a policy with two faces: one pointed towards, and the other against, the incorporation of human rights into investment behavior. This is why we can see the Janus face of this significant species of international investments. From one side, the needs for predictability of return on project investment may encourage a particularly careful calculation of environmental / social risks, given the impact these can have on steady cash flow. On the other side, there is the possibility that risks of certain types of damage to local populations might be heightened by some of the pressures on project time and performance, as well as techniques of risk management in Project Finance. Moreover, there could also be a competition among banks affecting the categorization process, deciding if the environmental and social risks of the project are irreversible (Category A), largely reversible (Category B) or minimal (Category C). This strategy therefore has an ambiguous legacy for social rights that highlights the need for fundamental reform.

Valentina Cagnin's essay analyzes the ISDS, a neutral, private, international arbitration procedure which allows foreign investors to sue the host government for alleged discriminatory practices against them or other violations of international investment law before ad hoc tribunals. Even if it is a consolidated tool for the EU Member States, it is considered a controversial tool as over time a number of abuses have arisen through the use of ISDS because its original justification (to assist foreign direct investments to obtain compensation for direct expropriation of private property by national governments in developing countries with poorly functioning court systems) has long since departed. ISDS could lead to a freezing of the national law, or to what we called a "regulatory chill," even in the field of social rights (as demonstrated by some well-known cases: *Veolia Propreté v. Egypt*, *Centerra v. Kyrgyz Republic* and *Piero Foresti & others v. South Africa*). Concerns around ISDS have been raised particularly in the context of the negotiations of some recent mega-treaties (CETA, EUFSTA, TTIP, TPP). It was originally inserted in all of those treaties but the strong opposition to this mechanism of dispute resolution (by scholars, consumers, Non-governmental Organizations (NGOs), citizens, European Parliament, etc.) has led to a certain progress in developing a balanced and forward-looking approach in the international investment policy. This impetus is manifest in the ICS, the Investment Court System. ICS should represent an alternative dispute settlement procedure which could be better reconcile the legitimate demand of investors with the legitimate concerns of civil society but the EU Court of Justice has not yet ruled on the compatibility of an ICS system with EU law.

Vania Brino's essay covers a topic of great importance, linked to investments. It is about the use of stabilization clauses in State-Investor Agreements. In particular, it analyzed meaning, aims, effect and models of stabilization clauses. The landscape of this reflection is the controversial dilemma in managing the interdependencies between foreign direct investment and human rights. The key issue regards, in particular, the risks for human rights, including labor rights, where investment agreements are alleged to restrict the ability of States to fulfill their obligations in such a fundamental field. Empirical evidences recognized this problem but at the same time the recent trends show us a sort of reaction by governments and international organizations with the purpose to "balance" investor's interest with public needs and human rights.The Article points out that the increased number of State-Investor Agreements reflects a "diversification process" that involves both states and businesses. The former has become more and more "contracting parties" in order to attract capital, while enterprises became important regulatory agents able to create rules and to influence the evolution of national juridical regimes. Multinational enterprises become key regulatory actors able not only to choose the most favorable law but also to define the rules useful for their business. Codes of conduit or other corporate social responsibility tools could highlight this trend. But in this light we could also interpret the State-Investor Agreements, especially if they contain stabilization clauses. In other terms, we could identify multiple ways in which corporations influence laws and public policy and institutions to advance their private interests over the protection of human rights.

In the last Part, Giuseppe Casale and Mario Fasani offer a deep overview of the main ILO policies and tools in the organization of promotional activities for social rights. The global crisis has had significant negative repercussions for labor: financial instability, income inequality, unequal personal distribution of wages, deterioration of labor market and of social prospects. This highlights the necessity of inclusive growth, social justice and decent work, which are strongly promoted by the ILO, founded in 1919 which adopted 189 Conventions and 204 Recommendations covering all aspects of the world of work, and other important documents for the promotion of social rights on the world, as the 1998 Declaration on Fundamental Principles and Rights. This Declaration aimed to strengthen the application of the four principles and associated rights that are considered fundamental for social justice: (i) freedom of association and the effective recognition of the right to collective bargaining; (ii) the elimination of all forms of forced or compulsory labor; (iii) the effective abolition of child labor; (iv) the elimination of discrimination in respect of employment and occupation. After ten years, in 2008, the Declaration on Social Justice for a Fair Globalization institutionalizes the concept of decent work, which is addressed by four strategic ILO objectives: fundamental principles and rights at work and international labor standards; employment and income opportunities; social protection and social security; social dialogue and tripartismo. More recently, in 2015, decent work for all women and men, and the four pillars of the Decent Work Agenda become integral elements of the new 2030 Agenda for Sustainable Development, with seventeen Sustainable Development Goals (SDGs). In particular, SDG n. 8 calls for the promotion of sustained, inclusive and sustainable economic growth, full and productive employment and decent work, which is now widely recognized as a global goal. This Agenda is an opportunity for Members State to reinforce a fully integrated approach to decent work in the design and financing their sustainable development policies. Another promotional tool for a fair globalization is the Tripartite Declaration Concerning Multinational Enterprises and Social Policy (MNE Declaration) adopted in 1977 and constantly revised, which provides a sort of guidance to Multinationals on social policy and inclusive, responsible and sustainable workplace practices, as those actors are the principal drivers of globalization and they have a vital role in promoting economies and social progress.

Part I Sustainable Development and International Trade

CHAPTER 1
Sustainable Development, Global Trade and Social Rights: An Evolutionary Perspective

Adalberto Perulli

1 SUSTAINABLE DEVELOPMENT, GLOBAL TRADE AND SOCIAL RIGHTS: THE RENEWAL OF AN HISTORICAL LINK

Sustainable Development, Global Trade and Social Rights is a topic that presents several aspects and a lot of crucial theoretical issues not only for the analysis of international labor law, but also for political economy, international trade and, in general, it deals with the global governance problem induced by economic globalization. This historic link between fundamental social rights and market regulation has proved to be a major topic in the current context of economic globalization, whose trade expansion is a fundamental component along with renewed impetus towards economic regionalism and Free Trade Agreements (FTAs) that include labor provisions.

The purpose of this chapter is to outline the complexity of the topic and its numerous analytical dimension. Further, some evolutionary considerations will be introduced, with specific reference to the social clause and the linkage between global trade and social rights. We are dealing with evolutionary considerations which are based on a certain interpretation of phenomena; but, at the same time, they also lead to a thesis – to a way of looking at things – thus to a performative and prescriptive perspective.

The first point to notice is the evolutionary complexity related to the topic, which leads to the utilization of both economic and juridical knowledge. This complexity is due to the overlapping of different rationalities in the regulatory relationships of the market and the social sphere. There are two different, but converging underlying reasons that forge a linkage between promoting social rights and market regulation: one that seeks to act against distorted competition based on social dumping, which ultimately modifies the best allocation of resources on a global scale;[1] the other refers to the planning of an axiologically oriented global order, designed to redress the unwelcome social consequences of globalization.[2] The first reason stresses economic interest in balanced market expansion, based on the idea of fair trade. The safeguarding of basic social legislation in the framework of international trade is justified to the extent that this protection is liable to damage the economy of countries that respect an international level playing field. The notion of fair trade is thus a means to complete the interplay of free trade, assuring state and economic actors that all global players do not take advantage of unfair trade practices arising from the non-application of social legislation, whether national (following the North American Agreement on Labour Cooperation (NAALC) model, which imposes no minimum supranational limits)[3] or international (the International Labour Organisation (ILO) standards: the approach of European Union (EU) external relations, on which sections 4 and 5 below). Hence, social standards have permeated market regulation and competition law, as an instrument to implement the principles of fairness in international trade and the best way to limit the destructive phenomena of regulatory competition and social dumping.[4] One example, taken from the NAALC, can explain this kind of justification. In the logic of the agreement, the basis of the social clause is essentially economic: it deals with the *regulation of competition* and the preservation of comparative advantages at the same time. Indeed, the condition for the application of a sanction is the evidence of a competitive advantage deriving from the failed application of the internal labor legislation of a given party. The field of application of the sanctions is rigorously delimited: they apply only if the

---

1. See A. Lyon-Caen, *Pérennité d'une interrogation*, in *Dimension sociale de la mondialisation de l'économie*, Université Montesquieu-Bordeaux IV, 1996, pp. 13 et seq.; a theory of trade linkage has been developed by D.W. Leebron, *Linkages*, in AJIL 96 (202), 5; *see also* P. Alston, *Linking Trade and Human Rights*, in German YIL 23 (1980) 126, noting that the potential costs of linking trade and human rights may be considerable and calling for a careful weighing process; A. Perulli, *Globalisation and Social Rights*.
2. See T. Novitz, *Core Labour Standards Conditionalities: A Means by which to Achieve Sustainable Development?*, in J. Faundez, C. Tan (eds.), *International Economic Law, Globalization and Developing Countries*, Edward Elgar, 2010, pp. 234 et seq.
3. The list of labor standards referred to in the NAFTA side agreement (the North American Agreement on Labour Cooperation) is lengthier than that of ILO core labor standards in the 1998 ILO Declaration, but the norms are to be determined with reference to compliance with domestic labor law ("respect and effective application of their own labour laws", Art. 3 NAALC), rather than established international fundamental social rights recognized by international labor law.
4. *See* B. Bercusson, *Regulatory Competition in the EU System: Labour*, in D.C. Esty and D. Geradin, *Regulatory Competition and Economic Integration. Comparative Perspectives*, Oxford University Press, 2001, pp. 241 et seq. On the dual value of social legislation, as an instrument to regulate the market and the moral dimension, *see* B. Hepple, *Labour Laws and Global Trade*, Oxford, Hart Publishing, 2005.

violation of the agreement proves to be "trade related" and "covered by mutually recognized labour law" (NAALC, Article 49).

It is well-known that this logic was accused of masked protectionism. Indeed, if we face this topic from a point of view related to standard economic analysis concerning international trade, the question about social conditionality would be denied consideration on the basis of the neo-liberalistic theory of the market, which, basically, sees in the social (and environmental) conditionality a barrier to free trade. Developing countries, free-trade economists and many private enterprises in developed countries are the primary opponents to the linkage between international trade and social rights. These opponents argue that conditioning free trade on social rights is detrimental to the promotion of welfare-enhancing free trade. In this perspective the social clause has been, especially by developing countries, accused of being a form of masked protectionism. As a matter of fact, the history of American protectionism has been characterized by arguments in favor of a concept of equity within trade and level playing field, in order to avoid the negative effects of free trade, which are essentially the inequality of conditions of competitions among countries and the international competition on salaries. It's not for nothing that, since its inception, the World Trade Organization (WTO) which shares a free-trade philosophy, has excluded from its agenda the compliance with social rights as a criterion of conditionality on trade exchanges, and it has confirmed the developing countries' right to use social differentials as a legitimate comparative advantage, basically applying to our topic the comparative advantages economic theory, which dates back to David Ricardo.

But economic theory can also offer a *justification* to the linkage perspective.

The first perspective is offered by the neo-classic competition theory: according to the latter, if the forces within the market are unable to counter the dominating position of oligopolistic companies, public and structural measures must be carried out, in order to protect competition. In this perspective, dumping (also *social* dumping) activities, subsidies and so on are unfair, because they generate a war on prices, with the aim to exclude less powerful parties, or to prevent new subjects entering the market. Based on the idea of *fair* trade, the safeguarding of basic social legislation in the framework of international trade is justified to the extent that this protection is liable to damage the economy of countries that respect an international level playing field. The notion of fair trade became thus a means to complete the interplay of free trade, assuring state and economic actors that all global players do not take advantage of unfair trade practices arising from the non-application of social legislation, whether national (following the NAALC model, which imposes no minimum supranational limits)[5] or international (the ILO standards: the approach of EU external relations). Hence, social standards have permeated market regulation and

---

5. The list of labor standards referred to in the NAFTA side agreement (the North American Agreement on Labour Cooperation) is lengthier than that of ILO core labor standards in the 1998 ILO Declaration, but the norms are to be determined with reference to compliance

competition law, as an instrument to implement the principles of fairness in international trade and the best way to limit the destructive phenomena of regulatory competition and social dumping[6].

Once again we find the concept of level playing field, the abandoning of the principle of comparative advantages as the basis of trade policies, of trade based on low salary costs and so on. This is the background which led the United States of America (USA) to mark, in its internal legislation, as "unfair" and unreasonable the trade practices of foreign partners based on devaluing labor rights, and to sanction with trade measures these practices. The accusation of masked protectionism is thus overturned: in fact, the compliance with common standards would prevent States from restricting trade on the basis of domestic standards, so that a linkage would eliminate one of the main justifications for trade restrictions.

The second perspective is about Sustainable Development, which is, indeed, an economic theory as well as being juridical and ethical. Development is often understood as a synonym for economic development or economic growth. Sustainable Development builds and modifies the international approach to development which needs to be understood more broadly. In the international community development in the past half-century includes at least four related concepts: peace and security, economic development, social development and national governance that secures peace and development. Each concept is reflected in major multilateral treaties that provide a common framework for relations among nations as well as a shared set of national purposes. In particular, the idea stressed is that social and economic development are closely related, not only conceptually, but also in the practices of social and economic relationships. Countries that have emphasized education, health and related aspects of social development tend to have the best economic performance. Therefore, the link between the economic and social spheres is not an unnatural invention and is not related to utopia or ideology. It is not for nothing that a fundamental treaty on human rights, The International Covenant on Economic, Social and Cultural rights contains in itself the idea of integration between economic and social spheres.

Nowadays, the United Nation (UN), with its 2030 agenda for Sustainable Development pursues an integrated vision with economic, social, environmental aspects; and a specific feature of this vision (Number 8) is related to employment and decent work. This provides an inducement for the promotion of sustained, inclusive and sustainable economic growth; full, productive employment; and

---

with domestic labor law ("respect and effective application of their own labour laws", Art. 3 NAALC), rather than established international fundamental social rights recognized by international labor law.

6. See B. Bercusson, *Regulatory Competition in the EU System: Labour*, in D.C. Esty and D. Geradin, *Regulatory Competition and Economic Integration. Comparative Perspectives*, Oxford University Press, 2001, pp. 241 et seq. On the dual value of social legislation, as an instrument to regulate the market and the moral dimension, *see* B. Hepple, *Labour Laws and Global Trade*, Oxford, Hart Publishing, 2005.

decent work for all. In particular point 8.8 of the agenda concerns the protection of labor rights and the promotion of safe and secure working environments for all workers, including migrant workers and those in precarious employment. So, labor standards are fully present in the conceptual framework and in the political agenda of Sustainable Development, and can constitute a new important element of theoretical and practical justification for the legal systems at national, international and supranational level.[7] At the same time, labor law is undoubtedly an element of that paradigm, capable of providing a response to coordination failures and imperfections which are inherent in the labor market and contribute to economic development and growth.[8]

It is evident that, inside the Sustainable Development paradigm, the economic concern coincides with the political-institutional, juridical and ethical concerns. Basically, through the paradigm of Sustainable Development, some values coming from afar are reconsidered and are today re-discovered by a non-standard development in economic thought. Moral concepts such as prudence, social justice, equity are thus revitalized and a particular emphasis is placed on the use of fundamental social rights in achieving Sustainable Development.[9] The most accomplished example of this trend is offered by the European Model of Sustainable Development, from the Amsterdam Treaty of the EU that declared that one of the objectives of the EU is to promote economic and social progress and to achieve balanced and Sustainable Development, through to the Lisbon Declaration in 2000, where the European Council set for the Union the strategic ambitious goal of becoming the most competitive and dynamic knowledge-based economy in the world capable of sustainable economic growth with more and better jobs and greater social cohesion. Another important innovation introduced by the Treaty that can be interpreted in this spirit, regards the goal of achieving relations *"with the wider world", according to which the EU upholds and promotes its values and among other things "contributes [...] to the sustainable development of the Earth, solidarity and [...] free and fair trade" as well as to the "eradication of poverty and the protection of human rights"* (Article 3 TUE). In order to comply with a strategy of sustainable economic growth, when the EU re-planned the regulations on GSP (the generalized system of preferences which allows favorable conditions to least developed countries in trade matters) in the field of its external relations, has titled this chapter "Sustainable and Good Governance." In the same perspective, within the Transatlantic Trade and Investment Partnership (TTIP) negotiations between EU and USA, they are discussing the social clause within a chapter of the Treaty

---

7. See T. Novitz, *The Paradigm of Sustainability in a European Social Context: Collective Participation in Protection of Future Interests?*, IJCLLIR, 2015, 243; T. Treu, *Labour Law and Sustainable Development*, WP CSDLE "Massimo D'Antona".INT-130/2016.
8. See S. Deakin, *The Contribution of Labour Law to Economic Development and Growth*, Centre for Business Research, University of Cambridge, Working Paper No. 478, March 2016.
9. See R. Zahn & D. Mangan, *Labour Standards and Sustainable Development: Unpicking the EU's Approach*, IJCLLIR, 2015, 233.

dealing with Sustainable Development.[10] Generally, it can be safely stated that, thanks to this paradigm, the promotion of the international labor rights has become part of a wider framework on *Trade and Sustainable Development*, assuming the status of an "unobjectionable norm" in EU trade agreements.[11]

Inside this complex framework, there is an important evolutionary perspective to be attentively considered. Up to now, it was for the social dimension to "push" on the trade dimension in order to find acknowledgment. Today, the situation is far more balanced and it is up to the "trade sphere" to be interested in internalizing the social concerns coming from society, as there would otherwise be a failure to achieve any sort of growth without taking social issues into consideration. This is demonstrated by the substantial failure of the policies – dating back to the 1980s – of the International Monetary Fund (IMF), World Bank (WB) and WTO. As a matter of fact, the countries which actually followed their prescriptions did not achieve any economic development or democracy.[12] In almost all countries involved in such policies, the effect has been a massive increase of debts versus foreign creditors, and heavy cuts of public funds to the welfare, education, health system infrastructures. Considering this, the current challenge is not to liberalize the trade regime, nor go back to anti-historic nationalisms, but to make the existing openness of trade sustainable and compatible with wider social aims.

2 THE EVOLUTIONARY PERSPECTIVE OF THE LINKAGE

It is common knowledge that the main instrument of social conditionality within the regulation of trade is represented by the "social clause." With "social clause"

---

10. See A. Perulli, *Sustainability, Social Rights and International Trade: The TTIP*, IJCLLIR, 2015, 473.
11. *See* L. Van Den Putte & J. Orbie, *EU Bilateral Trade Agreements and the Surprising Rise of Labour Provisions*, IJCLLIR, 2015, 263. The approach of the EU to social issues in the sphere of external action consists of two main perspectives. On the one hand, it has a highly developed practice in including human rights clauses in its international agreements (including regional trade agreements) which allow for the suspension of the agreement in the event that one of the parties violates human rights or democratic principles. On the other, it deals with social matters, including labor standards, by way of cooperation, entailing where necessary financial and technical assistance. For instance, concerning the agreement which contains a type of human/social rights clause on the model of EU agreements, we can make reference to the EU-Algeria Association Agreement, the EU-Jordan Agreement, the EU Chile Agreement and the EU-Syria Agreement, in which the term "fundamental social rights" is used for the purpose of "giving priority to such rights" or to "recognize the responsibility to guarantee basic social rights". In the Cotonou Agreement the parties have incorporated legally binding standards "reaffirming their commitment to the internationally recognized core labour standards, as defined by the relevant International Labour Organisation (ILO) Conventions"; see A. Perulli, *Fundamental Social Rights, Market Regulation and EU External Action*, IJCLLIR, 2014, 41.
12. See S. Sassen, *Expulsion: Brutality and Complexity in the Global Economy*, Cambridge, Mass., Harvard University Press, 2014.

we refer to particular norms concerning internationally acknowledged social rights, which countries and firms must comply with in order to use the benefits induced by the liberalization of trade, thereby avoiding actual sanctions. Let's consider, for example, the hypothesis of temporary suspension for all or some products, relative to the special regime of EU Sustainable Development and Fair Administration provided by the EU regulation; or the possible adoption of restrictive measures for importations in compliance with Article XX of the General Agreement on Tariffs and Trade (GATT). Of course, the instrument of a social clause does not rule out other tools such as softer mechanisms like codes of conduct and Corporate Social Responsibility (CSR). From my perspective, there should not be an alternation among these instruments, because they act together. Further, as it will be pointed out later, these instruments are more and more inter-linked among themselves, under the sphere of the social clause. It is a co-regulation perspective, in which hard-law instruments are used within soft instruments and *vice versa*. A classic example is the FTA and Cambodia in the textile industry. The implementation of this hybridization between hard regulation (social clause) and soft regulation (technical assistance, ILO cooperation) has promoted the improvement of working condition and productivity increases.[13]

In the same practices of international trade relationships, especially on a bilateral level, the social clause is having a progressive likewise quantitative expansion. Developments are promising and it is worth highlighting the evolutionary aspects of this trend.

3 INTERNORMATIVITY AND GLOBALIZATION: AN EVOLUTIONARY PERSPECTIVE

The first is a theoretical profile of the social clause in its evolutionary aspects. The social clause is an inter-normative tool, based on the inter-dependency of global phenomena such as trade, environment, labor, so that the regulation of a certain sphere (e.g., trade relationship, or market regulation) involves another sphere (for instance social, or environmental) and the latter is as a result regulated by the first.[14] This inter-dependency not only encourages constructing a common space of regulation able to limit the negative effects of the regulatory competition, but also promotes the integration of the sectorial disciplinary strategies and the objectives of regulation. This internormativity lies on the functional connection one can observe between the different topics or the different phenomena affected by such internormative regulation. So, the social

---

13. *See* John A. Hall, *The ILO's Better Factories Cambodia Program: A Viable Blueprint for Promoting International Labour Rights?*, Stan. L. & Policy Rev., Vol. 21, No. 3, 2010; ILO, Better Factories Cambodia, Programmes and Projects, http://www.ilo.org/asia/projects/WCMS_099340/lang--en/index.htm.
14. On the concept of internormativity *see* M. Delmas-Marty, *Les forces imaginantes du droit, III, La refondations des pouvoirs*, Edition Seuil, Paris, 2007.

clause may be reconsidered in the wake of the theory of the horizontal connections among different *connecting regimes*, used in the perspective of the global juridical order as an answer to the inconveniences of the high sectionalism of the regulation and of the lack of principles and general rules.[15] Moreover, *connecting regimes* does not necessarily induce regulations according to general inter- or supra-national principles, because they can also refer to the interconnection between the *national* dimension of labor law and the *international* regulation of economy and exchanges. This happens within the North American Free Trade Agreement (NAFTA)-NAALC model, in which the parties promote the "compliance and the actual application of their *own laws* in matter of labor, through appropriate actions of government" (Article 3), not tending to harmonization or, even more, to standardization of the levels of protection within social issues. The linkage between firms and human rights, or between international trade and non-trade issues, allows a focus of regulation on related and interdependent domains, which produce more relevant results thanks to a no longer differentiated and fragmented global vision of economical and social processes.

A way of achieving such internormativity is contemplated by USA domestic regulation on trade law (1974 Trade Act), that deems unfair the domestic practices of USA's trade partners, which it labels "unjustifiable," "discriminatory," and "unreasonable." This last concept of unreasonability includes the violation of internationally recognized workers' rights. Of course, it raises the question of knowing the legal nature and the identification of these rights, and we can say that probably the intention of American legislators was deliberately kept vague: they didn't refer to ILO Conventions, using an eclectic methodology inspired by the human rights principles and the general principles of international law (e.g., the prohibition of degrading and inhuman treatment).

Apart from this issue, to which we will return in the next paragraph, what is important to stress in our perspective is the internormativity contained in such provisions, which employ a concept – unreasonability – related to incorrect labor law practices adopted by companies (and by the States that accept or tolerate such behaviors). This concept belongs to trade law but it interferes with labor law, and this interference is normatively structured in order to create a connection between regulatory regimes.

Another example: when the EU introduced the General Systems of Preferences GSP+ (Article 9 of the current 2012 Regulation) as a special incentive arrangement to promote Sustainable Development and Good Governance,[16] it created a linkage between two different but interrelated issues: a non-trade issue (the promotion of sustainability in governance, meaning the respect of human rights) and a trade issue (the special arrangement in favor of developing countries).

---

15. *See* S. Cassese, *Il diritto globale*, Einaudi, Torino, 2009, p. 25.
16. *See* M. Weiss paper, in this Volume.

But we can also go back to the very origin of such idea of internormativity, that is contained in the Preamble of the ILO Constitution: "the failure of any nation to adopt human conditions of labor is an obstacle in the way of other nations which desire to improve the conditions in their own countries." This outlines two important elements for our analysis: (1) first, the recognition that, under the burden of international competition, the social progress of one state depends on the behavior of others; (2) second, it also means that labor law norms have had by nature an impact on competition. And this is precisely the dimension of reciprocity in international labor law enforcement and competition law that needs to be valued in a future evolutionary perspective.

Indeed, the evolutionary perspective which is stressed here is the following: although internormativity was already existing at the first stages of the idea of social clause, as a matter of fact, the complex process called "Globalization" has increased in a significant way the interrelation between phenomena, social/economic/political/environmental phenomena, and these interrelationships make the co-regulation of a complex situation not only a real possibility, but a necessity.[17]

It should be pointed out that such internormative technique does not necessarily induce regulations according to international or supranational principles and rights. Internormativity can also refer to the interconnection between the national dimension of labor law and the international regulation of trade. This happens within the NAFTA-NAALC model, in which the parties promote the "compliance and the actual application of their own laws in matter of labor, through appropriate actions of government" (Article 3). Here we don't have an attitude tending to harmonization or to standardization of the levels of labor protection, but a mutual obligation to comply with the respective national labor law norms.

4 SOCIAL RIGHTS, CONTENT AND REGULATORY VALUE OF THE SOCIAL CLAUSE IN AN EVOLUTIONARY PERSPECTIVE

The second evolutionary aspect concerns the sources of international law and the content of the trade-labor linkage. It also allows tracing an evolutionary framework in the contents of social clauses. The starting point consists in the identification of a nucleus of unconditioned social rights: that is to say, they are not to be inflected according to different economic and cultural situations. These rights were originally included in the Universal Declaration of Human Rights and in the two 1966 UN Covenants on Civil, Political, Economic, Social and Cultural Rights. As a matter of fact, they are acknowledged to be "fundamental" by the Copenhagen Declaration on social development and eventually legitimized by

---

17. *See, inter alia,* P. Singer, *One World. The Ethics of Globalization,* Yale University Press, 2004; U. Beck, Macht und Gegenmacht im globalen Zeitalter – Neue weltpolitische Ökonomie, Suhrkamp Verlag, 2002; Joseph E. Stiglitz *Globalization and Its Discontents,* W.W. Norton & Company, New York London, 2003.

the Declaration of the ILO 1998 international Conference of Labour and fundamental rights. This set of core labor standards must be considered universally applicable. The main FTAs have by now acknowledged the value of these fundamental social rights, by adopting them in their social clauses. In the position paper in the field of TTIP, the EU has expressively declared its interest for the protection and the promotion of social rights, referring to both, 1998 ILO Declaration and 2008 Declaration on "Social Justice for a Fair Globalization:" the core labor standards are defined "an essential element to be integrated in the context of the trade agreement," and should act as "to complete other standards and related ILO conventions, and as a means to promote the decent-work agenda." This position has been confirmed in the round of negotiation in July 2015 whereby it is stated that the "Discussions to date have allowed for a detailed exchange of views on the possible scope of Trade and Sustainable Development provisions, covering both substantive Environment and Labour issues, with a view to preparing the ground for an exchange of textual proposals. Key issues discussed include the prevention of a race-to-the-bottom on labour and environment, adherence to core labour standards, the protection of natural resources (wildlife, timber, fisheries) and the promotion of cooperation on trade-related sustainable development issues both bilaterally and at global level."

However, it is true that some criticalities and ambiguities persist. In particular, on the distinction between the principle of freedom of association in the 1998 ILO Declaration and the guarantee of freedom as expressed in Convention n. 87; as well as on the possibility to implicitly consider as re-integrated the right to strike in the Convention n. 87. Of course, in Europe, these ambiguities do not exist, also thanks to the work of Strasbourg and Luxembourg Courts,[18] but they exist in the USA and in other countries in the world.[19]

Three evolutionary elements are discussed below:

(1) The first one concerns the *normative value* of the labor provisions, which are reflected in a stronger commitment of parties within FTAs agreements to effectively respect the fundamental ILO conventions in a more strict and transparent network of obligations set by the social clause. In order to guarantee the typical aims of the social clause, the trade agreement tends to use a more transparent and committing language than in the past, where we could find rather vague and weakly binding expressions. For example, in the EU FTA the social chapter has

---

18. See K. Lörcher, *The New Social Dimension in the Jurisprudence of the European Court of Human Rights (ECtHT): The Demir and Baykara Judgment, its Methodology and Follow-up*, in F. Dorssemont, K. Lörcher and Isabelle Schöman (eds.) *The European Convention on Human Rights and The Employment Relation*, Hart, Oxford and Portland, Oregon, 2013, 3; J. M. Servais, *The Right to Take Industrial Action and the ILO Supervisory Mechanism Future*, in Comp. Lab. L. & Policy J., Vol. 38, No. 3, 2017, 375.
19. See J. Bellace, *Back to the Future: Freedom of Association, the Right to Strike and National Law*, King's L. J. (U.K.), Vol. 27, No. 1, April 24–45, 2016.

now strengthened the language of social clauses in the sense that labor provisions are formulated in a more constraining way.

(2) The second evolutionary aspect concerns the protection of these social standards from possible attacks in terms of guarantee about investments of multinational companies. In the case of TTIP, a guarantee related to the prerogatives of the investors – particularly within the risk of provisions of Investment-State Dispute Settlement (ISDS) which risk an anti-social function – is offered by the same Directives of Negotiation. They provide that the protection of the investments and the provision of ISDS must not compromise the right of the EU and Member States to "adopt and apply, in conformity to the respective competences, the necessary measures to not discriminatorily pursue legitimate interests of public policy in social, environmental, national security, financial system stability, public health and safety fields."

(3) The third concerns the broadening of the sphere of rights to be taken into consideration within these treaties. The ambition to go beyond the ILO agenda, including far wider issues in the field of collective and individual labor relationships, is the major evolutionary factor to be considered. In the author's opinion, this perspective is also to be promoted from a theoretical point of view, considering labor law as juridical pillar of Sustainability (equal to environmental Law). It's no coincidence that, according to what it is stated in the Final Report of the High Level Working Group on Job and growth, the TTIP negotiations should take place with the aim to dedicate a chapter on Sustainable Development and Trade (TSD Chapter), which should not be conceived as foreign body in the trade agreement, but, on the contrary, it should condition all parts of the agreement. The aims of Sustainable Development are reaffirmed in the Directives of negotiations on the Transatlantic Partnership for exchanges and investments between the EU and the USA, dated June 17, 2013. According to the Directives, the TTIP foreword will have to state that "the partnership with the USA is based on principles and common values that are coherent with the principles and the aims of the external action of the EU," and will have to contain *inter alia*: (1) The shared values like human rights, fundamental freedoms, democracy and Rule of Law; (2) The commitment of the parties in favor of Sustainable Development and the contribution of international trade to Sustainable Development concerning its economical, social, environmental aspects, as well as economic development, full and productive employment and decent work for everybody and the conservation of environment and natural resources: (3) The right of the parties to undertake the necessary measures to realize legitimate objectives of public policies on the basis of the level of safeguard of health, of safety of workers, of consumers, of environment and of the promotion of diversities of cultural expression.

Set in these terms and placed within the theoretical coordinates of Sustainable Development, the social clause overcomes, content-wise, the narrow boundaries of core labor standards and spreads to a wider and evolutionary range of action. It is obvious that this evolutionary vision of social clause can be supported if partners operate in comparable social-economic and institutional contexts. For example, in the TTIP negotiations between the EU and the USA, the issues about health and safety may leverage on the USA's tradition about the "duty to safeguard lives and the well-being of employees," which, in its turn, may be connected to the "duty of care," a very well-known concept in all the area of application of common law. Similarly, the promotion of guarantees of rights of collective matrix should refer not only to the national dimension, but also to the transnational front of industrial relations, through the promotion and the diffusion of the transnational company level agreements. Moreover, it should guarantee further spaces for reciprocity, like in the case of the fruition of rights of information and consultation provided by the European Directive on multinational companies with headquarters in Europe but operating in the USA. Further guarantees may refer to the protection of social rights, specifically facing the widespread use of ISDS clauses, relative to the arbitral resolution of litigations between countries and foreign investors while applying the treaties, with possible negative consequences on the level of the legislation. In the EU position paper it is provided that the TSD chapter of TTIP should reflect a vision of investments which might be respectful of fundamental rights, in the sense that "the respective domestic authorities will not fail to enforce, and will not relax, domestic labour or environmental domestic law as an encouragement of trade and investment." The same orientation is expressed in the Directives of negotiation of the Council, whereby it is provided that "the agreement must acknowledge that the parties will not promote exchanges or foreign direct investments, thus making the legislation and the national norms in the matter of environment, labour, health and safety on the working place less strict. Furthermore, also the policies and the fundamental labour norms or the legislative regulations aimed at the protection and at the promotion of cultural diversity must not be weakened" (point 8).

5 SOCIAL CLAUSE AND INDUSTRIAL RELATIONS

The third evolutionary aspect concerns the linkage between social clause and industrial relations at international level. In fact the social clause can become the means to spread practices of transnational collective bargaining at a regional but also at global level. The linkage between Regional Trade Agreements and Global Labour and Trade Framework Agreement (GLTFA) represents a new perspective in the international practices of industrial relationships. As a matter of fact, the social clause is being put forward as a framework not only to promote – in a traditional perspective – the principles of international labor law as instrument of domestic regulation, but also to widen in an eminently dynamic perspective the currently existing experiences of social international dialogue; as well as in order to institutionalize the method of good praxis and the solutions being negotiated by the labor-management disputes.[20] Adopting these kind of practices of social dialogue as a "continuation" of Regional Trade Agreements (RTAs) and Regional Labour and Trade Framework agreement (RLTFA) can represent a theoretical framework of reference in the field of TTIP negotiations, for which they have proposed a "dynamic cross-reference" to sector framework agreements (ATS) that have autonomous enforceability/lawfulness at a national level.[21] The dynamic cross-reference from the social clause to the social transnational dialogue would allow, to some extent, to renew a proposal for what has been the ultimate paradigm of labor law on a domestic scale: law (in this case represented by the social clause) as a minimum standard, collective bargaining (International Framework Agreements (IFAs), RLTFA, etc.) as an adaptation and extension of protections, thanks to the mobilization and the assumption of responsibility of the social parties at a global/supranational level.

6 ECONOMIC AND SOCIAL RATIONALITIES: THE POSITIVE EFFECTS OF RESPECT FOR SOCIAL RIGHTS

The fourth evolutionary point concerns the evolution of a positive relationship between economic and social rationalities, in the field of international trade. This trend is confirmed by empirical evidence. The positive effects of social clauses both in terms of economic efficiency and protection of fundamental social rights represent a mostly confirmed result in the scientific literature of economic matrix. Analyzing the data relative to the linkage between social rights and development of trade exchanges in India in the period 2005–2014, we can see that the growth of salaries does not reduce exports, but it rather facilitates internal spending and promotes exports, contradicting the traditional objections on the negative effects induced by social conditionality, as well as proving wrong the competition concerns legitimating social dumping.[22] Even China, which is promoting a strong FTAs policy, has developed an openness in the sectors of cooperation on labor and employment, without anyway recurring to international standards (like in China-Switzerland FTA) or providing for the protection of domestic labor force (like in China-Costa, China-Singapore, China-New Zealand FTAs). The references contained in the trade agreements have stimulated the protections of social rights, as showed by the total cancellation of practices of reeducation against ILO Convention n. 105. Effective measures in the matter of discrimination assumed by the Chinese Government show its potentialities to implement social clauses relative to condition of labor at a

---

20. *See* K. Addo, *Core Labour Standards and International Trade*, Springer, 2014.
21. *See* M. Faioli, *Global Trade and Workers' Protection. Why and if the TTIP can Promote a (New) Labour Law Vision*, Riv. Giur. Lav. 2015, 781.
22. *See* H. Chen, *Social Clause in Trade Agreements and China's Experience*, in Beijing Law Review, 2015, 6, p. 1 s.

domestic level, with particular reference to principles of equal retribution, equality of treatment between man and woman in remuneration matters and nondiscrimination (think about the efforts made in order to overcome the "Hukou" system, despite the number of migrant farmers that keep on being discriminated in the access to labor).[23] Other researches have recently surveyed, on the basis of the Global Preferential Trade Agreements Database (GPTAD), the quantitative effects of social clauses in countries with medium-low Gross domestic product (GDP).[24] The confrontation between systems that have adopted the social clause and those who haven't show a strong and positive impact on conditionality on the ratification of the ILO conventions, especially the fundamental ones, with an average of + 27%. Better Factories Cambodia is as well an excellent example of the benefits derived from a proper implementation of labor standards. Originally known as the ILO Garment Sector Project, subsequently has changed the name in Better Factories Cambodia to better reflect the ILO's aim of continuous improvements in working conditions.[25]

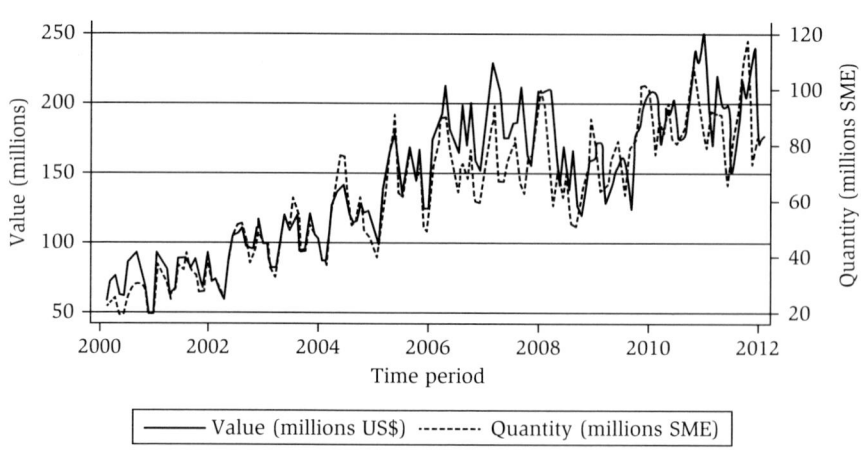

Figure 1.1   U.S. Apparel Imports from Cambodia

Source: Interwoven. How the better work program improves jobs and life quality in the Apparel Sector, 2015 International Bank for Reconstruction and Development / The World Bank.

---

23. H. Chen, *supra.*, p. 7.
24. R. Baziller & A.T. Rana, *Social Clauses in Free-Trade Agreements: An Efficient Tool to Improve Labor Standard?*, 4th Conference on the Regulating Decent Work Network, July 9, 2015.
25. John A. Hall, "*The ILO's Better Factories Cambodia Program: A Viable Blueprint for Promoting International Labor Rights?*," 2010.

Since its establishment in 2001, the program evolved also with the help of the trade agreement between Cambodia and the United States.[26] Figure 1.1 shows how exports increased over the years, with exception to the biennium 2008–2009 when trade performance decreased due to the financial crisis.

This positive impact at a macroeconomic level explains the beneficial outcomes also at a microeconomic level. Brown, Dehejia and Robertson (2016) evidence the relationship between the factory-level compliance and factory survival.[27] The analysis confirms that factories that increase compliance with labor standards are more likely to survive compared to factories that do not. Indeed, the probability of survival grew as firms conformed with the wage standards. Productivity and profitability increase as well when working conditions are improved.

7 IMPACT ASSESSMENT AND IMPLEMENTATION MECHANISMS

The last evolutionary point is about the impact assessment and implementation mechanisms. In this evolutionary perspective, the social chapters of trade treaties should contemplate a clause requiring the evaluation of the impact of a social clause in order to facilitate monitoring the effectiveness of the linkage strategy. In the field of the Strategy 2020, the EU has provided for the activation of evaluations of economic, social and environmental impact for all the initiatives, with "particular attention to wide consultations and to the involvement of civil society in the evaluations of impact on sustainability which we will carry out during the trade negotiations."[28] The Article 9 of TFUE, on one hand, supplies a renovated juridical basis to the social impact assessment. In this perspective, the EU Commission has adopted an ambitious mechanism of social impact assessment with 2009 guidelines in the following areas: labor market, standards and rights connected to quality of labor, social inclusion, equality of treatment and nondiscrimination, access and effects of social protection, health and education system, public health and safety. So, the impact assessment can undoubtedly be part of the contents of social clauses, contributing in a massive way to re-equilibrate the confrontation between social rights and economical freedom. The TTIP Directives of negotiations are to be seen in this perspective, with a provision relative to a "sustainability impact assessment (SIA)" with the aim to verify the impact at economical, social and environmental level of the treaty during the phase of negotiations, to which all the components of the civil

---

26. ILO, Better Factories Cambodia. http://www.ilo.org/asia/projects/WCMS_099340/lang--en/index.htm.
27. D. Brown, R. Dehejia and R. Robertson, "Laws, Costs, Norms, and Learning: Improving Working Conditions in Developing Countries," IZA Discussion Paper No. 10025, June 2016.
28. Communication of the Commission to the EU Parliament, Council, Social and Economical Committee and Regions Committee: "Trade, growth and world business. The trade policy as an essential component of 2020 EU Strategy", COM (2010) 612 def.

society involved in the agreement may participate (point 33). Moreover, the evaluation of the social repercussions should disregard the terms of finalization of the agreement and represent a permanent mechanism, able to supply not only ex ante, but also ex post indications on the effect of the chapter on Sustainable Development, with procedures of follow-up able to indicate the measures to be adopted in order to guarantee the expected results.[29] In the case of TTIP, the monitoring on the impact should involve the social parties, the Non-governmental Organizations NGOs and the Social and Economical European Committee, which has adopted several opinions in matter of trade and sustainability, providing for an assessment mechanism that may involve the civil society: thus re-evaluating at established intervals, the risks and opportunities individuated in the initial impact assessment.[30] This activity of monitoring and assessment of the impact should connect with further follow-up and review mechanisms to be provided in the agreement, relative to the reciprocal learning and to the circulation of good praxis to be adopted on the basis of shared guidelines. This is being provided for by the EU in order to coordinate the labor policies of Member States, in the field of an open mechanism of coordination.[31]

The social clause should also contemplate an adequate mechanism of implementation of conditionality intended to monitor its effectiveness and the compliance with the obligations deriving from it; particularly, referring to the provisions of compliance with international obligations, notably deriving from joining ILO and from the consequent obligation to guarantee the compliance with the Declaration on fundamental social rights. In this perspective the social clause should provide for the constitution of an independent committee of experts, with a member of ILO as a consultant, with the following functions: (a) publishing of periodical reports on the state of effectiveness of social standards, taking into account the information given by governments and other parties; (b) gathering and evaluating the claims and publishing recommendations, promoting consultative forums to exchange information among governments, social parties and other stakeholders (on the model of NAALC); (c) with reference to the latter, they should activate institutionalized deliberation procedures through the creation of a Forum for Trade, Investments and Sustainable Development, as the place for public discussion about social issues linked to the treaty. It is necessary to point out that an interest in monitoring, aimed at promoting profiles of effectiveness of the commitments undersigned in the field of trade, is the basis of foreign policies of the USA in matter of Trade and Investments. The Central America Free Trade Agreement (CATFA) provides for enhancing as much as

---

29. Also according to K. Lukas e A. Steinkellner, *Social Standards in Sustainability Chapters of Bilateral Free Trade Agreements*, p. 11, "A continuous repeated review of the impact of the agreements is also required".
30. *See* Opinion of SEEC on "Trade and political Sustainability assessment impact." (2011/C 218/03).
31. In this sense, cfr. T. Treu, *Labor and Industrial Relations in the Transatlantic Free Trade Agreements Guidelines*, Italian Cultural Institute, New York, November 21, 2013.

possible the cooperation and the exchange among the countries involved, so as to monitor the implementation of the agreement and the possible problematic points that may arise in the phase of implementation. In this perspective, that is why the Labour Affairs Council (LAC) has been established, with tasks of periodical verification of the state of implementation of the agreement, but also of consultation and coordination among the parties in the agreement. On the same level, the provision for the Capacity Building Mechanism has the role of promoting and strengthening the cooperation, improving the labor standards and favoring the consultations and the moments of encounter among the parties. In the case of TTIP, we could opt for the constitution of an equal controlling organ between the EU and the USA, involving the ILO in the monitoring activity, on the basis of what has already happened in the field of the program of international cooperation between USA and Cambodia. If it were so, the model anticipated in the Article 7 of the Havana Charter would be effective, after so many years. It contemplated an institutional connection between the International Trade Organization and the ILO, aiming at monitoring the compliance with the fair labor standards on part of Member States of the Organization.

To conclude, in the author's opinion, all the elements that have been mentioned are part of a concept of Sustainable Development as a conceptual framework to achieve economic growth that may be socially equitable and that could represent a useful response to the current challenge for a fair and social globalization.

CHAPTER 2
Sustainable Development, Social Rights and International Trade

Antoine Lyon-Caen

1 INTRODUCTIVE PROPOSAL

The reasonable field of the introductive proposals cannot be but limited. Such proposals have the ambition to bring about some clarification on the notions that will be utilized and on the perspectives of analysis and reflection that might be chosen.

1.1 Notions

The conditions of international competition have changed. In order to point out such changes, two notions are nowadays utilized. The first, resulting as essential, is regulatory competition. With this expression, we highlight the importance of levels of regulation within international competition.

Surely, the existence and most of all the measure of the differences of regulation levels raise a debate, in particular about what a level of regulation is matter-of-factly about. Of course, it is not enough to examine the enunciations, that are synonyms of norms, in order to determine the level of regulation in the Country or in the space whereby the enunciations act as a reference point.

One text in itself does not set a level. In fact, the actual idea of level implies a confrontation and, in order to found and explain a comparison, we need to have a measure that is external with regards to the terms that are compared.

The level of regulation should no longer have the chance to be appreciated relatively to simple opinions, whether they come from experts. As a matter of fact, opinions actually drive enterprises managers, since they are sensitive to the relative level of regulation of one given Country, in order to take a decision connected to the localization of an activity.

Enterprises are, matter-of-factly, actors of this resolutory competition. Since, if this competition exists among Countries in the exercise of their normative competences – the latter might be tempted to modulate the content of their norms in order to ensure economic attractiveness of their territories – the competition is fuelled by enterprises. It is enterprises that actually utilize the different levels of regulation.

This plurality of actors must not be forgotten when the attention is shifted to the ways in order to preserve or to promote sustainable development.

A second notion deserves to be introduced in order to characterize the new outlook on international competition: we are talking about its *intensity*. We must point out that competition must not be considered as a space of confirmation. It must be considered for its extent, that is to say in the variety of relationship spheres involved.

Nowadays, we can in fact state that the general conditions of population, the working conditions, the utilization of natural resources (only to mention some examples) have become elements of international competition. If we should translate this mutation into the traditional language of international trade, we should say that the restrictions to freedom, the conditions of health and security of people and the excessive exploitation of natural resources are to be considered as comparative advantages. Therefore, we should, at the same time, evaluate whether such advantages are unjustified, so as the lack of normative framework or the weakness of regulation should be considered, in many cases, as an unjustified competitive advantage.

Even though largely popular, the expression 'sustainable development' has not been accepted by the totality of people.

The genesis helps in perceiving that this notion is associated to a project, whose heart is the research of a new balance between economic growth, social progress and the protection of environment. In the linkage among these three elements we can measure the needs of sustainable development. The disrespectful action of such needs must therefore keep an eye on the linkages among the three elements and, most of all, on the fact that it may comply with certain qualities, as the following schematic presentation suggests.

Within the interaction between economic growth and social progress, it is necessary to pay attention to the equity of the action. This happens, in particular, in the subdivision of the outcomes of growth. Within the interaction between social progress and environment protection, we need to make sure that the development is livable. Finally, within the interaction between growth and environment protection, it is necessary that the development may be implemented. The qualification given to each interface does not resolve all things but it shows the main orientations of the project.

What we need to highlight are the incidences of such a project on the juridical system. Some are substantial and, among these, we need a vision of the time, in its double chronological and chronometric dimension. In order for the development to be equal and sustainable, we need to take into consideration long-term policies, in order to, for example, make sure that the long-term effects of decisions or, again, the incidences on the relationship among generations are integrated. Further, a different vision of pertinent space must be adopted in order to benefit from the outcomes of decisions (or of merits), in particular the outcomes of enterprises' decisions, not only within the workplace, but also in the local territory and on the totality of the value chain.

Other incidences of needs of sustainable development have a more procedural dimension. The decisional processes must in fact be re-considered since the different rights and interests affected by the action to which the abovementioned needs are imposed may find expression. For the moment, it is useful to try to identify the evolutions occurred, like the sources of resistance observed by the changes required.

Through the clarifications so far taken into consideration, both on the current dimensions of international competition, and on the project to promote sustainable development, it is possible to identify the problem on whose resolution everybody is summoned to reflect: how to have the needs for sustainable development to be taken into consideration in the field of international trade? In other words, how may we subordinate international trade to the conditions required by sustainable development?

This reflection entails the knowledge and the analysis of the past and current experiences. Among these, it is possible to distinguish the ones pertaining to the State as an epicentre and the ones that operate a displacement towards the enterprise.

1.2 State or Inter-State Perspectives

How may we get to a limitation and to a control of the regulatory competition that States make large use of? This is a historical question, since, without having the meaning that nowadays it bears, it has been present since the inception, in 1919, of the International Labour Organization (ILO), that has allowed to establish a multilateral framework of international norms on labour.

The author will not analyse here the work done by the ILO. What is important to highlight is the reason why the adoption and the implementation of the international norms on labour are not enough to fully respond to the needs of sustainable development, considered here in its social dimension in international trade.

At least two factors indicate these differences.

First of all, after the creation of the ILO, and most of all in the last five decades, the framework of international trade has considerably evolved, most of all under the effect of global negotiations tending to the suppression or at least to the reduction of the obstacles to the circulation of commodities, services and capitals. Such evolution has raised very soon and strongly risen again – around the hypothetical International Trade Organization – the matter of the linkage among trade rules and social rules, in particular the matter of the articulation of places and ways of elaboration of the actual rules. Moreover, the international scene is not limited to States. Multinational enterprises take advantage of the movements of liberalization of exchanges and have fully become actors of regulatory competition, not only because they play on the differences among social rights, but because this game constitutes a powerful invitation addressed to States, that are sensitive to economic attractiveness of their territories, in view of the adoption of their social rights.

Therefore, the promulgation of international labour norms is not enough. We need possibly international mechanisms of monitoring, in order to avoid or to limit social rights to be set into competition.
It is with this ambition that the idea of social clauses has taken root, whose first formulation elaborated seems to be present in the Constitutional Charter of the International Trade Organization, which, as we know, was never active as an actual organism.

In general, a social clause requires the states that have signed a trade agreement – through control and sanction procedures – to monitor the compliance with their own labour norms, so as the international norms on labour. By extension, this *liaison* established between the facilitated access to one or more markets and the compliance with the social and environmental norms may be unilaterally constituted by one or more States, and this entails that such State or the group of States involved has a certain power, within international exchanges.

This concise presentation must not hide the existing variety of social clauses. This variety is shown in the conception of norms, whose compliance is thus promoted and controlled. Are they seen as norms subject to giving rise to the enunciation of normative minimums or as norms instituting rights? Are such rights nominated or only mentioned in a concise formula? Is it necessary to distinguish between the rights that condition social progress and the rights that express it?

This variety is also shown in the linkage that we may create between facilitated access to market(s) and social and environmental norms. Should we focus on the products and relative dangers, promising a better protection of environment and health, or should we focus on the conditions of production, allowing to better monitoring on the conditions of workers? As we can see, there are different ways to conceive a policy of social and environmental conditionality.

The results of such policy have given rise to several researches. An inter-institutional cooperation – not without negative side effects – has appeared: ILO, World Trade Organization, World Bank and Organization for Economic Cooperation and Development (OECD) have been consulting each other and finally edited consensual recommendations. It is no doubt the sign of one of the greatest awareness raising towards a framework for globalization.

1.3 Perspectives Centred on Enterprises

Placing enterprises between exchanges liberalization and the needs of sustainable development means, in the version that illustrates the development of enterprises' social and environmental responsibility, to keep the States' intervention at a distance. We need to highlight that this balance should be achieved by the actual enterprises, or rather, to say that *lato sensu* social justice is to be found in the market or, again, social and environmental responsibility in its content is modelled by and on the market.

In these forms of coordination – called markets – enterprises meet consumers. It's in this interaction that enterprises think about choosing the extent of social and environmental responsibility, which falls on them and which they must actually assume. Such responsibility has therefore a domain, an extent and an autonomous regime, if we are allowed to define as autonomous what is regulated by the actual addressees of the norms. Nevertheless, this autonomy does not exclude that States and International Organizations play a certain role. But this role can be inferred from the registers of information, from awareness raising and from suggestion and from the diffusion of good practices.

We may shift our attention to enterprises, without postulating or admitting their complete autonomy in the determination of their social and environmental responsibilities. The complex debate on the constitutionalization of private powers created by multinational enterprises lies within this perspective.

Indicating the coordinates of this debate imposes an obligation of simplification. However, it has no doubt great importance, since the constitutionalization of private powers offers a framework of analysis in order to understand the evolutions of juridical systems.

First, we face again the need to know who is responsible and in the name of whom (or what?). This first question gives an answer to the ambition to establish a responsibility for parent companies or for those who give orders, which is spread along the whole value production chain. Such large-entity responsibility has a strong pertinence because it finds support on the expression of power itself that takes place in the relationship with subsidiaries and sub-contractors.

Second, getting to know to whom a broad responsibility is actually acknowledged is deeply relevant and deserves attention. We need to determine the intensity of the responsibility that might have different degrees. On the first grade, we find the obligation to inform and to warn about the risks to be prevented in the name of the needs of sustainable development and the initiatives to be taken. On the second grade, we have an obligation to rectify, whose consistency depends on the damages to sustainable development, that is the conception of rectifiable damages, whether they are related to environment or damages caused to workers. On the third grade, grounded into a demanding philosophy of sustainable development that is sensitive to future damages, we have the prevention and possibly the precaution, which become actual object of an obligation.

Third, we may not ignore the matter related to getting to know before whom the report of responsibility connected to the prevention and to the rectification of social and environmental damages may take place. It is to this very degree that we may face an interruption with the conception of an environmental and social responsibility that is delimited to the market alone.

As a matter of fact, the reflections on the constitutionalization of private powers show the importance of external forces before which the responsibilities may be object of discussion and end up in actual sanctions. On the other hand, it is not forbidden to imagine a diversity and a dispersion of external forces, since – differently from the constitutionalization that public powers have come across for some centuries – the ones related to private powers do not get and will not get (within a reasonable scenario) to unite with the birth and the development of the State and of an international organization.

The Constitutional framework of globalization self-discovers by self-inventing, without an apparent plan. This makes it exciting to be studied.

PART II International Trade Agreements: The Linkage Between Trade and Social Rights

CHAPTER 3
The MERCOSUR (Southern Common Market): Argentina, Brazil, Paraguay, Uruguay and Venezuela

Adrián Goldin

1 SUSTAINABLE DEVELOPMENT AND DECENT WORK

Far from the idea that work protection impairs well-functioning markets, today, it seems evident that sustainable development is not an obstacle but it is, on the contrary, a requirement for economic growth.

Actually, sustainable development is strongly linked to the concept of Decent Work, as developed by International Labour Organization (ILO), which has been defined as *productive work offered in conditions characterised by freedom, equality, security and dignity.*

Among such typical features, I would like to highlight *security*, which was introduced when the generous and progressive concept of *human security* proposed by United Nations Development Programme (UNDP) in its Human Development Report 1994 became widespread and has gained strength since then; thus, virtually replacing the concept of State Security prevailing at the time. Indeed, sustainable development depends mainly on the creation of *safe livelihood* through freely chosen productive employment. From this perspective, such a significant concept as *security* entails and enriches the dogmatic and finalistic concept of Labour Law, enables an alternative taxonomy of its principles[1] and

---

1. I have attempted a description of such classification in 'La seguridad del trabajador; otra taxonomía del Derecho del Trabajo a partir del concepto universal de seguridad humana' ['Workers' Security, Another Taxonomy of Labour Law Based on the Universal Concept of Human Security'] published in Trabajo y Derecho (Madrid) No. 9, September 2015, pp. 16–34.

allows the creation of new legal concepts and protection instances within the legal order, while it sheds light from the point of view of the law, on both the concept of *decent work* and, as a consequence, sustainable development.

In addition, sustainable development, a renewed factor for the legitimacy of social rights, involves, *inter alia,* the purpose of preserving the workforce, and at the same time, coexisting with the global economic order, and companies' productive needs. In other words, work protection institutions must simultaneously be capable of realizing workers' security and meeting companies' requirements. Such a complex capability requires a legal conception serving a profound social commitment (precisely, such commitment involved in the concept of *decent work)* but also a beneficial link to the performance of the productive system.

2 ON THE MERCOSUR

2.1 Institutional Development

In a few words, it should be reminded that the process for the creation of the MERCOSUR began at the inception of the integration process between Brazil and Argentina in 1985 (Foz de Iguazú Agreement[2]), followed by the Argentine-Brazil Integration Agreement signed a few months later (July 1986). The birth of the MERCOSUR is evidenced by the Treaty of Asunción (1991) whereby the MERCOSUR was created as a free-trade zone. Said initial document was amended a few years later (1994) by the Ouro Preto Protocol, whereby the MERCOSUR became a customs union, actually an irregular customs union with numerous exceptions applicable to foreign trade. The Ouro Preto Protocol also created the government bodies of the MERCOSUR. Under said Protocol, the organization is an intergovernmental body whose decisions are adopted by consensus and, therefore, it features no traces of supranationality.

In 1998, the States Parties executed the Democratic Commitment (Ushuaia 2005) which prescribes that any State Party failing to comply with democracy rules will be excluded from the MERCOSUR. In 2007, the institutional organization process was completed by the inauguration of the MERCOSUR Parliament (PARLASUR), whose creation had been decided in 2004.

Argentina, Brazil, Paraguay and Uruguay are the founding members of the MERCOSUR. In 2006, the incorporation of Venezuela was approved, though such decision was not made effective until 2012 as the Paraguayan Congress delayed the ratification of the Protocol of Adherence of Venezuela.[3] Moreover, in 2015 it ratified the Protocol of Adherence of Bolivia, whose ratification by the

---

2. Signed on 30 November 1985 by the Argentine President (Raúl Alfonsín) and the Brazilian President (José Sarney).
3. Venezuela is currently suspended as it is accused of breaching the Democratic Commitment.

legislative powers of the remaining States Parties is still pending. Chile, Ecuador, Peru, Colombia, Guyana and Surinam are currently Associate States.

The territory of the MERCOSUR is about 13 million square kilometres and its population amounts to 293 million inhabitants (7 out of 10 South Americans live within the MERCOSUR). The region accounts for over 80% of the South American Gross domestic product (GDP).

The trade performance of the MERCOSUR has been somewhat weak, as its common customs duties have been subjected to numerous exceptions and the elimination of interregional trade restrictions has been impaired by the restrictions on exports imposed by Argentina and, to a slightly more limited extent, by Brazil. There is great asymmetry in the subregion: Brazil and Argentina, whose territories are much larger than those of Uruguay and Paraguay, have tended to privilege their now mutually dependent bilateral relations.

Yet, the MERCOSUR has managed to accomplish some institutional achievements, such as the Work and Residence Agreement, signed by the States Parties of the MERCOSUR, Chile and Bolivia), the citizenship status, the Social and Labour Declaration, the reciprocal acknowledgment of Social Security systems and of primary and secondary school degrees, which will include university degrees in 2021. The region is characterized by a satisfactory climate of relations conducted in a peaceful and harmonic atmosphere,[4] where regional integration has intensified in the social, cultural and political field.

2.2 Labour Rights

2.2.1 *Influences and Common Traits*

Far from asserting that there is some sort of Labour Law of the MERCOSUR, but with the aim of avoiding an abstract approach to the subject matter under analysis, there are some common traits of labour rights in the subregion. It is true that it may not be asserted that the MERCOSUR has exerted any significant influence to date in the development of said legal orders as, on the contrary, is the case in the European Union.

One of the distinctive features of labour rights in the MERCOSUR as compared to such rights in developing countries is that they are *influenced rights* which, roughly speaking, evidence the legal tradition inherited from continental Europe, rather than *transplanted rights*. All nations comprising the MERCOSUR gained their independence in the first decades of the nineteenth century; that is to say, before the development of the industrialization process and, consequently, the installation of a true labour law system in said former colonies.

As stated above, it is worth mentioning that labour rights in Latin America have a common origin, namely the continental legal system. From this point of

---

4. As it is publicly known, Venezuela is currently an exception to such widespread subregional climate.

view, their 'particular ideas'[5] of Labour Law are clearly different from others arising from other legal systems (such as those of the *common law*), and allows to analyse the hypothesis that *much of what the legal systems within the region have in common is the influences from external countries and; therefore, what they share with the latter.* Thus, the legal orders of the countries comprising the MERCOSUR recognize the law as their first legal experience,[6] and are grounded on the *standard* of social public order, active state intervention, prevalence of imperative rule and a source system which is a mixture – in different dosages in every nation – of laws and collective conventions that, as a whole, constitute a complex system of techniques for the restriction of the autonomy of will.

Certainly, belonging to the continental system does not necessarily mean that those countries of the MERCOSUR replicate in any way the so-called European social model. Due to various historical, cultural, and political factors influencing the social experience of the countries in the region, this essay holds the hypothesis that the social rights in the region express, in a different degree, *a weak sense of belonging to such European social model.* This circumstance has made them more sensitive to the neo-liberal compulsions prevailing in the 1990s, and therefore to their abrupt and often disproportionate impact, the ensuing introduction of biased and inconsistent reforms, the ineptitude to start out a more rigorous process to react to the challenges aforementioned and even the tendency to subsequent restorations, anachronistic or deviated in some cases, produced in some countries as from the first years of the new millennium.

Within this framework, it must be taken into account that ILO's Conventions and recommendations have had a remarkable influence (still present) on the legal systems of the MERCOSUR, where the role of such international rules has been '… to boost and clearly inspire the new legal systems they started to establish in societies that were predominantly industrial, rather than to harmonise existing legislation, as is case of some industrialised countries.'[7] In 1941, expert David Blelloch[8] claimed that the majority of Latin American labour legislation was inspired in ILO's conventions and recommendations; particularly, in relation to working hours maximum, the prohibition of night work for women, maternity protection, the minimum age for industrial employment, occupational accidents and diseases. Needless to say that such documents are

---

5. The author thoroughly explained the basic idea of Labour Law and the 'particular ideas', (2011), in 'Global Conceptualization and Local Constructions of the Idea of Labour Law' in Davidov G., Langille B. (eds.) The Idea of Labour Law, Oxford University Press, Oxford pp. 69–87.
6. L Diez Picaso, Experiencias jurídicas y teoria del derecho ['Legal Experiences and the Theory of Law'] (Ariel, 1973).
7. Conf. Hernández Álvarez, transcription by the author of his participation at the round table in the 18th World Congress on Labour Law and Social Security (Paris, 5–8 September 2006), Report on the topic 'What future for statutory regulation in the field of labour law?'
8. Cited by von Potobsky, Geraldo in 'Evolución de la legislación laboral en América Latina: influencias y tendencias' ['Evolution of Labour Legislation in Latin America: Influences and Trends'], Derecho del Trabajo (Buenos Aires) Ed. La Ley, pp. 773–797

the expression and result of the earliest European legal experience, which, this way, would also influence the new continent and, particularly, the subregion.

We should not disregard, finally, the reciprocal influences among Latin American orders, constantly present from their inception; particularly, the 1924 Chilean legislation and the Chilean and Mexican Labour Codes enacted in 1931, which were the initial steps of a codification process which – whether due to emulation or prestige (even by authoritarian governments) – have achieved a surprising implementation level.[9] The resulting codes have influenced each other; hence, they tend to feature a similar structure.[10]

Another characteristic trait of said legal orders is the broad gap between law and reality[11] or, as Deveali calls it[12] the *authenticity crisis*, and the ensuing lack of effectiveness[13] (in different degrees) of such legal orders, clearly distinguishable at two levels: the generalized presence of informal work[14] and a certain tendency to establish rules that exceed the regional contexts or practices and that, therefore, are not applied or, at least, not always or not fully applied.

Finally, and from a different perspective, in conjunction with the ensuing process triggered in the countries of the European Union, in the countries of the MERCOSUR there has also been a growing trend towards highlighting the fundamental rights of people, including such rights established in the eight fundamental ILO Conventions and any other rights to which every human being

---

9. Chile and México in 1931, then Venezuela in 1936, Bolivia in 1939 (still effective), Ecuador in 1938, Panama in 1941 and 1947, Brazil and Costa Rica in 1943, Nicaragua in 1944, Guatemala in 1947, Colombia in 1959 and Honduras in 1959, the Dominican Republic in 1951, Paraguay in 1961 and El Salvador in 1963.
10. *See* von Potobsky (*supra* in note 8, p. 778) for a detailed explanation of reciprocal influences between Latin American codes and legislation.
11. *See* O Ermida Uriarte, 'Las relaciones de trabajo en América latina' ['Labour Relations in Latin America'] (1990) Revista Andaluza de Trabajo y Bienestar Social; Temas Laborales, No 18.
12. M Deveali, El derecho del trabajo en su aplicación y sus tendencias ['Labour Law, Application and Trends'] (selected texts by JI Brito Peret, AO Goldin, and R Izquierdo) (Astrea, 1983).
13. Such lack of effectiveness, probably, does not result from a single cause: in conjunction with an extended culture of anomie (regarding Argentina, the essay on anomie of the renowned legal scholar Carlos Nino is worth mentioning ('Un país al margen de la ley' ['A Country Outside the Law'], Ariel 2005); there is the lack of control resources (or a lack of interest in providing them), the incorporation of rules or influences disregarding the social and productive reality, the disinterest in the strengthening of structures and application procedures (labour justice and inspection) (*see* Bensusan, Graciela (2006), 'La distancia entre normas y hechos: instituciones laborales en América Latina' ['The Gap Between Rules and Facts: Labour Institutions in Latin America], Revista de Trabajo' (Buenos Aires) (year 2, No. 2 (nueva época), defective legal structures, dominant incitements to law infringement.
14. Informality alternatively attributed to excessive legislative intervention and rigidity, or the insufficient presence of the State, or unemployment and the drop in actual salaries (*see* Ermida Uriarte, Oscar, 1990 'Las relaciones de trabajo en América latina' (['Labour Relations in Latin America'], Revista Andaluza de Trabajo y Bienestar Social; Temas Laborales, (Albolote, España), (1990) No. 18, p. 84).

is entitled, in this case, regarding the exercise of such rights in the work environment.

2.2.2 The Authoritarian Factor

The link between labour legislation and the authoritarian regimes repeatedly prevailing within the region[15] does not seem to have altered the protective nature of social rights, at least in the field of individual labour relations. Either populistic or paternalistic, authoritarian regimes shared that nature by virtue of which the authoritarian State presented itself also as a protective State.[16]

As proved below, the authoritarian influence was, undoubtedly, more characteristic in the field of Collective Labour Law. The reason for this is that collective relations regulations seem to be a response to a quite more autochthonous conception. This conception is mostly based on the Latin American legislator's original distrust of trade unions, their politicization, their rebellious attitude and their ensuing conflictive nature. Preventive measures have been implemented by most nations in the region in the form of an intensive restrictive regulatory framework, namely: the creation of a trade union registry, structural and functional limitations, strict conditions to become a union leader, control of election processes, excessive procedural requirements for strikes and means of conflict resolution, limitation on the duration, purpose and entitlement to industrial action, etcetera.[17]

Such regulatory treatment has led in many countries of the region to the *imposition* of a trade union structure confined to the company level (thus often preventing workers from unionizing due to the reduced size of productive units) and even subject to restrictions on the formation of federations and confederations. Needless to say that such a strategy was aimed at preventing the accumulation of power which might lead to certain forms of concentration and centralization of trade unions.

In other countries of the region – particularly, Argentina and Brazil – the control strategy was analogous, considering its ensuing regulatory extent, *but quite different in terms of the structure imposed*: the European corporative experience in the 1930s and early 1940s has influenced the imposition of highly

---

15. Arturo Bronstein (1997) 'Reforma laboral en América Latina: entre garantismo y flexibilidad' ('Labour Reform in Latin America: between Protective Legislation and Flexibility'), Revista Internacional del Trabajo (Geneva), vol. 116-1, pp. 5–27. particularly, p. 8) stresses the existence of 'a very noteworthy correlation between dictatorships and protective legislation' and mentions the Labour Codes of Nicaragua (Somoza in 1944), Dominican Republic (Trujillo in 1951), Haiti (signed by Duvalier, after whom it was named), and Paraguay (Stroessner in 1961), as well as the Peruvian legislation of the 1970s or the 1971 Labour Code of Panama, the latter two resulting from populistic military regimes.
16. Except for, indeed, Chile during the Pinochet administration and, to a lesser extent in this regard, the Argentine military dictatorship which took in office in 1976.
17. *See* Ermida Uriarte, *supra* in note 14, p. 67, and von Potobsky, *supra* in note 8, p. 779).

centralized regimes in such countries,[18] both in terms of its functional and territorial implementation (even in the form of a representative monopoly), as well as its governance structure, markedly pyramidal; all of which would enable political control 'from the top and the outside' of such pyramid.[19]

It should be mentioned, however, that in many cases such orders have gone through several encouraging changes over the last three decades – which were induced by the subsequent democratic rationale – leading towards a *convergence point* (without achieving it completely) marked by ILO's Convention of Freedom of Association and the Protection of the Right to Organise, 1948 (No. 87) and the Right to Organise and Collective Bargaining Convention, 1949 (No. 98).

It should be highlighted, finally, that in the MERCOSUR the most remarkable centralizing trends converge, as precisely Brazil and Argentina are expressions of the *imposed centralization* described above; also, Uruguay, though it may not be described as such, has centralized union and collective bargaining structures.[20]

3 SUSTAINABLE DEVELOPMENT IN THE MERCOSUR

The social dimension of sustainable development involves fostering social integration, building stable, safe and fair societies and is based on the promotion and protection of human rights, as well as non-discrimination, tolerance, respect for diversity, equal opportunities, security and everyone's participation, including all members of neglected groups and vulnerable sectors of society.

---

18. Within the framework, respectively, of the political regime of the then Coronel Perón (the first union regulation in effect issued by such administration can be traced back to 1945), and the self-styled Estado novo [New State] of President Getulio Vargas, who had been in office since the 1930s.
19. In this regard, *see* Goldin A., La centralisation imposée de la représentation par les syndicats en Argentine et au Brésil, published in La représentation collective des travailleurs, Marie- Ange Moreau (ed.), Dalloz, 2012).
20. It should be mentioned that Uruguay is also familiar with a centralized union structure, which is the result of a centralizing intervention, namely the call to Salary Councils to establish a framework for collective bargaining with state intervention, which would give rise to a correlatively centralized union structure. In the Uruguayan experience, however, there have been no signs of a controlling intent or authoritarian domination nor may such centralization be attributed to a certain legal framework for labour organization, as it was inexistent in Uruguay. Until the recently enacted Law No. 17.940 for the protection of labour organization, there were no applicable regulations other than ILO's Convention on Freedom of Association and the Protection of the Right to Organise, 1948 (No. 87). Therefore, if in Argentina and Brazil it was the imposed union centralization which determined collective bargaining centralization (*see supra* in note 19), in Uruguay, it was the centralization of collective bargaining which resulted in a centralized union system.

3.1 Analysis of Certain Social Indicators

Below, the author mentions some indicators which will allow us to assess how far the MERCOSUR is from achieving the sustainable development goals. For such purpose, first a few quantitative indicators will be considered, as stated in the table below, before proceeding to the regulatory analysis.

	Salaried Employ.	Inform-ality	Unemploy-ment Rate	Employ Rate	Participa-tion Rate	Union Density	Collective Bargaining Coverage
Argent	73.3%	34%	6.5%	53.9%	57.7%	42%	60%
Brazil	73.8%	27%	6.8%	51.9%	55.7%	28%	60%
Parag	65.1%	65%	6.8%	60.4%	64.8%	18%	10%
Urug	74.2%	20%	7.8%	59%	64%	35%	90%

The rate of salaried employment is the ratio between salaried employees and the aggregate number of people employed, and shows us the weight or influence of salaried employment as against total employment. In the countries of the MERCOSUR, the highest rates of salaried workers constitute an indication of social development, as in such countries where this ratio is lower it has been determined that such lower rates are usually the result of the predomination of autonomous means of support, low productivity, and reduced income. Argentina, Brazil and Uruguay have quite similar rates to those recorded in more developed countries, whilst Paraguay's rates are a bit lower.

Moreover, the general informality affecting the countries of MERCOSUR (and most Latin American countries as well), constitutes a cause for serious limitations to the exercise of such rights.

In connection with employment, participation and unemployment rates, it should be mentioned that following years of strong growth (particularly between 2004 and 2011, excluding 2009), the unemployment rate did not grow significantly, due to mainly a drop in the participation and employment rates.

In the field of industrial relations, union density rates are relatively high, whilst collective bargaining coverage rates are among the highest in Latin America. In both cases – union density and collective bargaining coverage – this noteworthy performance in the field of collective labour relations *is most definitely connected with the high union centralization prevailing in Brazil, Argentina and Uruguay*, which is not the case of Paraguay.

3.2 Regulatory Level

The belief that competitiveness should be based on values, human rights and international labour regulations, particularly such regulations governing freedom of association, collective bargaining, the abolishment of child labour, forced labour and other forms of discrimination, is a distinctive feature of the societies that have successfully been part of social sustainability through decent work.

Thus, some data on the ratification of ILO's conventions on labour rights have been analysed; thus, verifying that the countries in the region have ratified fundamental labour conventions almost in their entirety, a large part of priority conventions and a significant number of technical conventions.

	Ratification of ILO Conventions	Fundamental Conventions	Priority Conventions	Technical Conv	Conventions Still in Force
Argentina	80 convs. 1 protocol	8/8	3/4	69	61 – 18 reported
Brazil	96 convs	7/8	3/4	86	80 – 14 reported
Uruguay	109 convs 1 protocol	8/8	4/4	97	81 – 27 reported
Paraguay	39 convs	8/8	2/4	29	77 – 2 reported
Venezuela	54 convs	8/8	3/4	43	50 – 4 reported

Indeed, the foregoing chart shows that the countries comprising the MERCOSUR have ratified all fundamental labour conventions, other than Brazil, which has ratified all but one of them – namely, Convention No. 87 – as their Constitution prescribes the principle of a sole trade union organization, which is inconsistent with this Convention. The countries comprising the MERCOSUR have ratified also the majority of the so-called priority Conventions ('governance' conventions),[21] to wit: Uruguay has ratified all four of them; whereas, Brazil and Argentina have ratified three out of such four and said three countries maintain a high number of technical conventions in effect. Paraguay has ratified only two of said four priority conventions and has a significantly lower number of technical conventions in force.

---

21. To wit: Labour Inspection Convention (1947), No. 81; Employment Policy Convention (1964 No. 122; Labour Inspection (Agriculture) Convention (1969) No. 129 and Tripartite Consultation (International Labour Standards) Convention (1976), No. 144.

It should be added, nonetheless, that Latin America is the region with the highest number of complaints for infringement of fundamental conventions in connection with freedom of association (87 and 98). The total number of claims in such regard by regions amounts to 393 in Africa, 1760 in America, 352 in the Arab States and 652 in Europe. The number of claims in the countries of the MERCOSUR totals 431, out of which 185 claims have been recorded in Argentina, 64 in Brazil, 55 in Uruguay and 53 in Paraguay.[22]

In the region a thorough child labour database has been created, and within this framework, workers and employers together with the civil society and the media have allied against such a scourge. Under the IPEC (International Programme on the Elimination of Child Labour), the Regional Plan for the Prevention and Eradication of Child Labour was implemented. Its legal framework comprises the International Convention on the Rights of the Child, the Convention concerning Minimum Age for Admission to Employment (138), the Worst Forms of Child Labour Convention (182), the Social and Labour Declaration of the MERCOSUR (to which a few lines below are dedicated) and both declarations made by the presidents on child labour in the MERCOSUR (2002 and 2012); where they agreed to strengthen national plans for the prevention and elimination of child labour, in addition to the Project for supporting the Regional Plan for the Prevention and Eradication of Child Labour founded by the Brazil/ILO Alliance.[23]

Within said regulatory framework, in Brazil between 1992 and 2009 *the number of employed children aged between 15 and 17 decreased from 19.55 % to 9.8%*. In Argentina in 2004, 6.5% of children aged between 5 and 14 were employed as well as 20.1% of teenagers ranging from 14 to 17 years of age. In Uruguay, in 2000 still 6.5% of children aged between 5 and 17 years were employed. The most critical situation was recorded in Paraguay, where yet more than 50.5% of children aged from 5 to 17 years were employed (24.8% of children aged between 5 and 9 years, 67.2% of 10–14 year-old children, and 78.4% of 15–17 year-old youngsters were employed).

3.3 Specific Regulatory Instruments of the MERCOSUR

Finally, a special focus will be done on any regulatory instruments in labour and social matters as approved by the States Parties within the framework of the institutions of the MERCOSUR, particularly, on two of them: the Social and Labour Declaration of the MERCOSUR and the Multilateral Agreement on Social

---

22. Argentina has 8 cases open, 10 cases on follow-up and 167 cases closed (in total 185); Brazil has 2 cases on follow-up, 62 cases closed (in total, 64); Uruguay has 1 open case, 1 on follow-up, 53 cases closed (in total 55) and Paraguay has 6 open cases, 4 on follow-up and 43 cases closed (53 in total).
23. These actions include regulatory harmonization with ILO Conventions No. 138 y 182 and permanent action to combat child labour, including monitoring, inspection and assessment of impact and results.

Security, both closely related with the realization of the sustainable development principle in the region.[24]

3.3.1 *The Social and Labour Declaration of the MERCOSUR*

Obviously, at this regulatory level the Social and Labour Declaration of the MERCOSUR, as approved in 1998 and amended in 2015, is of utmost significance.

3.3.1.1 Its Approval and Amendment

As was the case of the European Union, the preamble of the Treaty of Asunción only stated in reference to social matters that the MERCOSUR had been created in order to accelerate the processes of *economic development with social justice* of its States Parties. It was not until 1998 that the presidents of the four founding members signed the Social and Labour Declaration of the MERCOSUR, though the States Parties had begun considering labour issues in 1991 (at a meeting of labour ministers) so that the integration process would be accompanied by an actual improvement on working conditions in the countries within the subregion. It was then that a proposal was made for conducting the studies required for the execution of an instrument which would consider labour and social issues.

The Common Market Group – an executive body of the MERCOSUR – opted for a non-binding document which, therefore, would not be subject to the dispute resolution mechanisms existing in the MERCOSUR. Said choice was attributed to – as it was claimed – the inconvenience of linking social and labour issues to instruments of commercial policy. For this reason, in December 1998, in Rio de Janeiro the presidents of the States Parties did not sign a protocol but a Declaration, which had been prepared by a working group especially created for such purpose.

The Declaration was revised in 2015 by its own supervisory body – the Social and Labour Commission of the MERCOSUR[25] – and, as a result, it was approved, as amended, in Brasilia in June, 2015.[26]

The Declaration incorporates the major conventions and declarations on human rights which are part of the regulatory heritage of humankind; thus, it has been argued that it is part of the so-called *jus cogens* and is therefore a

---

24. As stated below, the 2015 amendment to the Declaration expressly ascribes it to such sustainable development goal.
25. It is a tripartite body created in the original declaration.
26. While the amended text was approved, the OAS had approved the Social Charter of the Americas (2012) and the Inter-American Convention against Racism, Racial Discrimination and Related Forms of Intolerance and the Inter-American Convention against All Forms of Discrimination and Intolerance (both in 2013), as well as the Inter-American Convention on Protecting the Human Rights of Older Persons, in 2015.

binding rule which may be cited by the citizens of the States Parties in their competent courts. Supporters of the interpretation that deems the Declaration as a treaty add that such is the interpretation which best complies with the *favor tractatus* rule.[27] Others believe, however, that as the Declaration was not approved by the organs of the MERCOSUR responsible for passing regulations of this sort, the Declaration is not binding. In any case, it is clear that all individuals and legal entities intending to take part in projects financed by the MERCOSUR are to abide by the principles and rights established by the Declaration.

3.3.1.2 The Principles

The Declaration states and recognizes several principles, among them, particularly the *promotion of sustainable development and sustainable enterprises*, to wit:

(1) Economic development must be subordinated to mankind and society.
(2) The Declaration is an open text and constitutes the minimum ground rules; hence, it does not conflict with the minimum standards already established by the State Parties. The parties to the declaration also agree to prevent any form of unfair competition in interregional trade by way of any deregulation involving any form of social *dumping.*
(3) The parties undertake to ratify and implement ILO's fundamental conventions and to follow ILO's recommendations in terms of job quality, healthy working conditions, workers' welfare and social dialogue.
(4) The Declaration further sets forth the parties' commitment to the international public order, comprising a set of basic recognized human rights, which are part of the legal heritage of humanity.
(5) The parties also express their commitment to decent work; and
(6) the *promotion of sustainable development;* and
(7) *sustainable enterprises,* under ILO's 2007 resolution;
(8) Labour laws should not be used for the purpose of trade protectionism.

3.3.1.3 Regulation Contents: Rights

Among other regulations, the Declaration addresses non-discrimination, equal opportunities and treatment between men and women and disabled workers,

---

27. There are precedents issued by lower courts which applied the Declaration, mostly in Argentina, though also in Paraguay, Uruguay and Brazil.

and the necessary effectiveness of the principle of equal pay for work of equal value.[28]

The Declaration also addresses the issue of migrant and border workers, already incorporated in the original Declaration, whose scope was extended by the 2015 amendment to include workers from both Bolivia and Chile. The amendment also ratifies the provisions regarding the elimination of forced labour and includes regulations on the prevention and elimination of child labour and the protection of young workers, as well as any individual rights which had not been previously considered, such as provisions governing the length of a working day,[29] leave and holidays, and the right to a minimum wage according to the national laws, which wage must be sufficient to meet the worker's needs and those of his/her family. It also includes provisions on protection against dismissal.[30] Furthermore, the Declaration *acknowledges the right of employers to create, organize and run the company economically and technically.*

In the field of collective labour relations, the Declaration ensures the right to collective bargaining, which currently extends to the public sector. It also prescribes the freedom of association of 'all employers and workers', as well as the right to strike, though such right is governed by the legislation of each State Party.[31] In terms of conflict resolution, the Declaration directs states to promote and coordinate the creation of self-resolution mechanisms for individual and collective work conflicts through independent, impartial and voluntary procedures. The States Parties undertake to foster social dialogue at a national and regional level, by establishing mechanisms of consultation between governments, employers and workers in order to create favourable conditions for *sustainable economic growth.*[32]

Under the heading 'Other Rights', the Declaration fosters public policies in terms of employment, work health and safety, Labour Inspection and Social Security. Following a provision on the *centrality of employment in public policies in order to reach the sustainable development of the region,* the Declaration

---

28. Consequently, gender equality and equal pay for work of equal value. The gender pay gap has narrowed over the last decades in the region, though not sufficiently, and is still an obstacle to overcome poverty and inequality. Such decrease of 12.1 percentage points in the gender pay gap recorded between 1990 and 2014 represents some progress made towards equality of pay within the region; nevertheless, women's pay amounts to only 84% of men's pay.
29. In this matter, the Declaration refers to the laws of each State Party, though it imposes in any case a daily limit of eight hours.
30. 'Every worker has the right to an adequate protection in case of dismissal, in accordance with the legislation in force in each State Party. States Parties shall ensure provisions in their legislation which take into account this right.'
31. Section 18 of the Declaration ensures the right to strike, though '… according to the national regulations currently in force in each State Party'.
32. Permanent consultation on the basis of tripartism as established in Convention 144 to encourage mutual understanding and good relations between authorities and organizations of employers and workers, and among the latter.

further addresses the protection of the unemployed, by requiring systems of protection against unemployment and easy access to relocation services and retraining as well as the implementation of public services of employment, employment offices and other relevant measures. Additionally, it establishes the right to professional training (both for employed and unemployed workers).

With regard to work health and safety, the Declaration includes the provisions of ILO's Conventions Nos 155, 161 and 187 and recommendations Nos 164, 171 and 197, namely, the involvement of workers and employers in order to prevent accidents and illnesses, the worker's right to refuse to carry out their work activities if there are serious and imminent risks, the need for information on risks and statistics on work accidents, adequate control of substances, processes and technologies, and competent work safety services.

The Declaration also provides for the obligation to establish and maintain labour inspection services and, in terms of Social Security, the right to social security for all workers under their applicable national legislation, in compliance with the provisions agreed upon by the States Parties in the Multilateral Agreement on Social Security of the MERCOSUR, which was already in force at the time the Declaration was amended.

3.3.1.4 Implementation and Follow-Up

The Declaration creates the Social and Labour Commission of the MERCOSUR, an auxiliary body of the executive organ. Said commission was established both at a regional and national level. Thus, there exists a tripartite commission in each State Party, and the members of said commissions, gathered as a whole, comprise the Regional Commission, consisting of twelve regular members plus an alternate member for each of them, out of which each State Party will have three members, who in turn must represent the government, the workers and employers. Each sector designates their regular and alternate members, and may replace them by giving notice forty-eight hours prior to each meeting.

The Social and Labour Commission of the MERCOSUR is an organ with controlling and promoting functions rather than punitive functions. It lacks jurisdiction, its resolutions are adopted by consensus, and are limited to formulating recommendations to community organs, particularly, the Common Market Group. Its function is to follow the legislative and administrative policies of the States Parties, thus completing the control mechanism that every State should conduct through labour inspection services.

It is clear that arbitral tribunals created to solve commercial disputes within the MERCOSUR have no jurisdiction over the application of the Declaration. However, said exclusion subjects the interpretation of the language of the Declaration to the controlling systems (both judicial and administrative) existing in each State Party, as section 20 of said Declaration ratifies the commitment of States Parties to the promotion of its implementation in accordance with national customs and laws. This provision would lack sense if the Declaration

Chapter 3: The MERCOSUR

failed to subject its application to the jurisdiction of national courts of the States Parties within the competence assigned to them pursuant to the relevant legislation.

3.3.2 *The Multilateral Agreement on Social Security*

The Multilateral Agreement on Social Security was signed in Montevideo in 1997, and became effective in 2005, after a delayed ratification process.

It consists in a system based on the mutual acknowledgement between the States Parties of the contributions to the Social Security systems made in each state by both national and foreign residents, in order for the benefits of social security to be granted by the State where the employee or beneficiary is residing and in accordance with the law of the country granting such benefit – pension or health coverage – though taking into account the contributions made in all States Parties.

CHAPTER 4
The Link Between Trade and Social Clauses

Janice R. Bellace

1 INTRODUCTION

After a decade of negotiations, the governments of twelve nations[1] signed the Trans-Pacific Partnership (TPP) a Free Trade Agreement (FTA) on February 4, 2016 with the requirement that it go through the internal ratification process of each country within two years.[2] In line with his public opposition to free trade agreements, United States (U.S.) President Donald Trump announced on January 23, 2017 that the U.S. would withdraw from the TPP.[3] Since the U.S. had been the strongest proponent of the TPP and has the largest GDP of any of the TPP countries, its withdrawal threw the future of the TPP into question. Other TPP Member States, particularly Australia and Japan, worked diligently to revive talks in an effort to preserve the gains negotiated over a number of years.[4] In November 2017, during the Asia-Pacific Economic Cooperation (APEC) summit,

---

1. The original twelve countries participating in the TPP were Australia, Brunei, Canada, Chile, Japan, Malaysia, Mexico, New Zealand, Peru, Singapore, the U.S. and Vietnam. After the U.S. withdrawal, the other eleven indicated willingness to move forward with the TPP.
2. The TPP can come into force if at least six of the original signatories who between them account for 85% of the group's GDP ratify the agreement.
3. "Withdrawal of the United States From the Trans-Pacific Partnership Negotiations and Agreement. Federal Register. January 25, 2017. https://www.federalregister.gov/documents/2017/01/25/2017-01845/withdrawal-of-the-united-states-from-the-trans--pacific-partnership-negotiations-and-agreement.
4. Anthony Fensom, "TPP Survives After Canadians 'Screwed Everybody'." The Diplomat. November 14, 2017. https://thediplomat.com/2017/11/tpp-survives-after-canadians-screwed-everybody/.

the other eleven members agreed to move forward with the "Comprehensive and Progressive Agreement for Trans-Pacific Partnership" or CPTPP.

Why this happened relates to the political situation in the U.S. regarding trade. The TPP generated much controversy in the U.S., particularly during 2016 presidential election year. The amount of controversy in some ways was surprising as the U.S. already had trade agreements with half of these countries.[5] In part, the criticism of the TPP reflected many Americans' growing frustration with the perceived impact of FTAs on jobs domestically. In part, it arose from the view that the TPP was a harbinger of the future. As the Obama administration had already observed, more countries in future may join the TPP, thus raising the likelihood that its importance will be even greater than the impact in the original signatory countries. The TPP may also serve as the template for future trade pacts because, as U.S. Trade Representative Michael Froman said, the TPP "will set the rules of the road."[6]

The TPP was also viewed as affecting negotiations on another FTA. At the same time, the U.S. has been negotiating an FTA with the European Union (EU), called the Transatlantic Trade and Investment Partnership (TTIP) although progress has been slow. The trade ties between the U.S. and EU Member States are extensive and in general, there are few disputes. Tariff barriers are already quite low (on average under 3%), such that the main attraction of the TTIP is the removal of non-tariff barriers. For the U.S., the TTIP is unusual in that the U.S. for the first time is negotiating with an entity as large, as advanced and as wealthy as it is. The negotiations have been difficult because powerful companies in a given industry in different countries may hold sharply different views on issues such as what are appropriate automobile vehicle safety regulations as opposed to unnecessary regulatory barriers. This difference in opinion on the two sides of the Atlantic arises in other areas. In the EU, unions are much stronger than in the U.S. andprolabor views are advanced by social democratic parties. This has generated another area of tension in the TTIP negotiations since the labor clause in the FTAs the EU has negotiated with other countries is stronger and more specific than the labor clause in American FTAs in that all EU FTAs expressly link worker rights to the ILO's eight core conventions. (Agusti-Panareda, 2015) EUs fear the loss of jobs, as more EU companies may source goods and services from the U.S., and in particular from certain states, where the rate of unionization is negligible and where wage costs and social benefits are much lower than in the EU.

Responding to critics, U.S. Trade Representative Michael Froman stated that the TPP "raises labour and environmental standards around the world to the highest level ever, and these are fully enforceable standards." (Council on Foreign Relations, 2016) Froman may be technically correct in saying that the

---

5. Canada, Mexico, Singapore, Australia, Peru and Chile.
6. This phrase was used consistently by the office of the U.S. Trade Representative during President Obama's presidency on its website. See, e.g., https://ustr.gov/sites/default/files/TPP-Strategic-Importance-of-TPP-Fact-Sheet.pdf [July 29, 2016].

TPP has the highest level labor standards ever in an American FTA, but that is quite different from its being a "high standard" clause. Moreover, the assertion that it is fully enforceable is highly dubious as crucial rights are not only not defined but the TPP expressly severs the link to international instruments defining these rights. It is difficult to argue that the TPP's labor clause has real meaning because it is impossible to identify definitions of these rights on which the twelve signatory nations agreed.

2 THE SPECTER OF NAFTA

In the U.S. the negotiations over the TPP were seen by many to be haunted by the ghost of the North American Free Trade Agreement (NAFTA). The 1993 NAFTA agreement opened a debate in the U.S. that has never ended; namely, whether that agreement benefitted the U.S. Supporters and opponents of NAFTA have very different answers to that question, which may result from the fact that they understand the question differently. Supporters of trade liberalization stress that NAFTA has benefitted both the American and the Mexican economies. Opponents emphasize that the U.S. lost jobs to Mexico, and that the loss of good-paying, middle-class manufacturing jobs has served as a significant restraint on overall wage rates, especially for the lower 40% of the labor force. In 1994, American presidential candidate Ross Perot coined an especially memorable phrase – "that giant sucking sound from the south" – to describe the job losses in the U.S. that would ensue if NAFTA were approved. In contrast, President Bill Clinton promised that NAFTA would create jobs in the U.S. NAFTA did create jobs, but overall the number of jobs lost outweighed the number of new jobs.[7] Most visible to average workers were jobs lost as American companies set up plants in Mexico.

2.1 The Impact on Jobs of Trade Liberalization

NAFTA has come to represent something much more than anFTA. Rather, it has become shorthand for the impact of international trade. (Scott, 2013) The reaction in some quarters against liberalizing international trade stems from the perception that average working people face job losses and gain little as gains accrue elsewhere. (Keller, 2016) Job losses are real although until recently not widely acknowledged. In looking at the impact of trade with China on the U.S. from 1990–2007, researchers at MIT found that "rising imports cause higher unemployment, lower labour force participation, and reduced wages in local labour markets that house import competing manufacturing industries." (Autor, 2013) This study found that import shocks triggered a decline in wages outside

---

7. Economists disagree as to the exact number, as it is very difficult to disentangle the fact of the free trade agreement from other factors that would have resulted in manufacturing moving to Mexico, such as the devaluation of the peso.

of the manufacturing sector, presumably due to the downward pressure on wages in other sectors from the job losses in manufacturing. The authors noted that reductions "in both employment and wage levels lead to a steep drop in the average earnings of households" and concluded that these changes "contributed to rising transfer payments through multiple federal and state programs, revealing an important margin of adjustment to trade that the literature has largely overlooked." (Autor, 2013: 2159)

The major difference between 1993 and 2015 is that today the public is aware that there are winners and losers from increasing international trade. Rather than confront that reality, many proponents of liberalizing trade often give reasons to explain job losses that are unpersuasive, most notably that technology is the reason for these job losses. Within any one country, new technology may result in job losses. But technology does not explain the entire decline in the number of manufacturing jobs. Moreover, it is not the reason for job losses in the higher wage country when a company opens up a production facility (using the same level of machinery and technology) in a lower wage country; for instance when shoe and garment manufacturers shifted production to low wage countries in Asia. The attraction was extremely low wages. If proponents of further liberalizing trade often refuse to confront the reality of job losses, opponents exhibit a similar blindness. FTAs per se are not the reason for job losses. The demise of the shoe and garment industries in the U.S., which occurred before 1990, was not due to an FTA as this offshoring occurred under the General Agreement on Tariffs and Trade (GATT) tariff regime.[8] Rather, it was simply that because it was so much cheaper to produce these labor-intensive products in low wage Asian countries, it made economic sense for companies to shift production abroad, even in the absence of an FTA and with tariff barriers still in effect.

3 THE RIGHTS IN LABOR CLAUSES

In the 1970s, the actions of foreign companies had prompted a spate of guidelines, such as the Organisation for Economic Co-operation and Development's (OECD) 1976 Guidelines for Multinational Companies, designed to bring corporate conduct within acceptable boundaries. For the most part, these guidelines were aimed at companies who directly owned and operated facilities in another country. But by the early 1990s, the inadequacy of this approach was evident. The problem was that the direct employer was a local company. The multinational company or brand was not the employer, was not covered by national labor laws, and often did not feel responsible for sub-standard or

---

8. The General Agreement on Tariffs and Trade. An example is Bangladesh. The Office of the U.S. Trade Representative reported that in 2013 Bangladesh imported USD 712 million in goods from the U.S. whereas it exported USD 5.4 billion in goods to the U.S. https://ustr.gov/countries-regions/south-central-asia/bangladesh The U.S. has no FTA with Bangladesh.

dangerous labor conditions at suppliers' factories. Then in 1992, when the U.S. and Canada moved to sign anFTA with Mexico, a controversy erupted. This was the first time that rich countries with high wages were aiming to drop tariff barriers with a low wage country. Companies and shareholders in the rich countries might benefit but the implications for workers in those countries were grim.

The furor during the negotiations over NAFTA about the potential for jobs to move to Mexico because of low labor standards produced an innovation. Decrying low wages and unsafe working conditions, opponents of NAFTA called for fair trade, not simply free trade. (Compa, 2001) Congress's political response was to include for the first time, a statement in the FTA whereby the three signatory nations agreed to uphold a set of labor standards. This was clearly an afterthought, for this commitment was not expressed in the main body of the agreement. Formally named the North American Agreement on Labor Cooperation (NAALC), it is often (and accurately) labeled the NAFTA "side agreement." The idea of inserting a clause relating to labor in an FTA led logically to the question of what standards or principles should be included. In 1993, there was no obviously correct answer. One could argue in favor of listing general principles, or of referring to specific ILO conventions, or listing standards with reference to national law and practice (but that would then have led to the question of which country's law and practice should govern). Within five years, a ready answer became available.

The device of tying trade privileges to adherence to labor standards failed when proposed in December 1996 at the first World Trade Organization (WTO) Ministerial meeting in Singapore. The position taken by the WTO ministers was that there was a specialized United Nations (UN) body that handled such matters, the International Labour Organization (ILO), and as a result the WTO should not consider them.[9]

Despite this setback, the adoption in 1998 at the International Labour Conference of the ILO Declaration on Fundamental Principles and Rights at Work proved over time a to be the vehicle for linking trade to workers' rights. In a sense, the winning formula had emerged. The 1998 ILO Declaration contained a succinct statement of four fundamental principles which had been agreed to and received overwhelming tripartite acceptance at the June 1998 International Labour Conference. The 1998 Declaration set out four rights, "the principles concerning the fundamental rights which are the subject of those Conventions," namely:

(a) freedom of association and the effective recognition of the right to collective bargaining;
(b) the elimination of all forms of forced or compulsory labor;
(c) the effective abolition of child labor; and

---

9. Singapore Ministerial Declaration Adopted on December, 131996 WT/MIN(96)/DEC, available at: https://www.wto.org/english/thewto_e/minist_e/min96_e/wtodec_e.htm.

(d) the elimination of discrimination in respect of employment and occupation.

Ever since the adoption of the 1998 Declaration, those drafting an FTA and needing language for a labor clause have turned to the principles set out in the 1998 ILO Declaration. Other UN bodies have also utilized this language. For instance, the "Labour" section of the June 2000 UN Global Compact lists four principles and repeats word-for-word the language of the 1998 ILO Declaration. Drafters of labor clauses in FTAs quickly seized upon the noncontroversial four fundamental principles found in the 1998 ILO Declaration. All U.S. FTAs after 1998 have utilized them.

More recently the four fundamental principles in the 1998 ILO Declaration have been cast in another light, arguably elevated to another plane. In June 2011, the UN Human Rights Council unanimously endorsed the Guiding Principles for the Implementation of the UN" Protect, Respect and Remedy" Framework. This clarifies the meaning of the corporate responsibility to respect human rights. To do so, there had to be clarification of what rights businesses are supposed to respect. The Guiding Principles states that this obligation "refers to internationally recognized human rights" and lists the International Bill of Human Rights and the ILO's 1998 Declaration, and in the commentary expressly states these "coupled with the principles concerning fundamental rights in the eight ILO core conventions as set out in the Declaration of Fundamental Principles and Rights at Work" set the benchmarks for assessing human rights impacts. From this, it seems evident that the UN Human Rights Council viewed the meaning of the ILO Declaration's four fundamental principles as incorporating the principles flowing from the eight core conventions. (Bellace, 2014: 184)

3.1 Meaning of the ILO Fundamental Principles

The 1998 Declaration expressly links eight core conventions to the four fundamental principles, two for each principle:

- Convention No. 87, Freedom of Association and Protection of the Right to Organise (1948) and Convention No. 98, Right to Organise and Collective Bargaining (1948).
- Convention No. 29, Forced Labour (1930) and Convention No. 105 Abolition of Forced Labour (1957).
- Convention No. 138, Minimum Age (1973) and Convention No. 182, Worst Forms of Child Labour (1999).
- Convention No. 100, Equal Remuneration (1951) and Convention No. 111, Discrimination (Employment and Occupation) (1958).

This linkage however is expressed in an elliptical fashion. Since most, but not all ILO Member States, had ratified these eight core conventions, the International Labour Conference in 1998 considered the obligations of the non-ratifying states, such as the U.S. The Declaration in section 2 states that "all Members, even if they have not ratified the Conventions in question, have an obligation arising from the very fact of membership" in the ILO "to promote and to realize ...the principles concerning the fundamental rights which are the subject of those Conventions."

This direction given to the Member States is so elliptical as to raise questions. Regardless of whether they have ratified the core conventions, the Member States are to promote and realize principles concerning rights expressed in the core conventions with each linked to one of the four principles. The question that logically arises is whether there is some difference in content or in specific obligations between a principle and the linked core conventions, and if so, what difference. There is no answer to that question. But the fact that the U.S. has refrained from linking the core conventions to the ILO principles in U.S. FTAs, whereas the EU has not, indicates that there is an open question on this issue and opinions vary as to the answer. (Bellace, 2016).

Equally curious is the slight variation on the articulation of these four principles in the TPP[10] (Chapter 19.3) where it states:

> Each Party shall adopt and maintain in its statutes and regulations, and practices thereunder, the following rights as stated in the ILO Declaration: (a) freedom of association and the effective recognition of the right to collective bargaining; (b) the elimination of all forms of forced or compulsory labour; (c) the effective abolition of child labour and, for the purposes of this Agreement, a prohibition on the worst forms of child labour; and (d) the elimination of discrimination in respect of employment and occupation.

It is curious that the recital of the four principles is almost word-for-word the same as the recital in the Declaration itself, but with regard to (c) – child labor – it adds that there is a prohibition on the worst forms of child labor. Yet in 1999 upon the adoption of ILO Convention No. 182, Worst Forms of Child Labour, the ILO immediately linked that convention to the principle regarding abolition of child labor in the 1998 Declaration. (Bellace, 2014: 179) For those familiar with the ILO's four fundamental principles, it was clear that the meaning of child labor is set forth in ILO Conventions Nos. 138 and 182. Why then was there a reason to insert the title of Convention No. 182 into the TPP's labor clause? One wonders if this implies that the detailed minimum age convention which is applicable to ordinary factory work, Convention No. 138, Minimum Age for Entry into Employment, for the purpose of the TPP does not govern the notion of what is child labor. That some country apparently felt a need to specify a particular convention as a way of explaining what one of the four worker rights meant might indicate that some of the signatories did not think that these four rights have specific meanings. It may also indicate that the U.S. was willing to be bound by a meaning of "child labour" that accords with

---

10. https://ustr.gov/trade-agreements/free-trade-agreements/trans-pacific-partnership/tpp-full-text. [July 29, 2016].

the positions it has taken; namely, the U.S. has ratified Convention No. 182 but it has not ratified Convention No. 138.

In light of the position taken by the 2011 UN Human Rights Council in its Guidelines on business and human rights, that the four fundamental principles are dependent on the eight core conventions for meaning, the question arises of how the twelve signatory nations view the four worker rights listed in Chapter 19, the labor clause of the TPP, and in particular, whether they are simply general concepts or whether they are phrases with specific legal meaning.

3.2 The Meaning of the Rights in Labor Clauses

This use of ILO principles in FTA labor clauses at first glance indicates governments' acceptance of these principles. Thus this link between FTA labor clauses and the 1998 ILO Declaration, which expressly refers to eight core conventions, implies a common understanding of what these principles mean. But, as has been noted, "in application, this link runs the risk of implementing inconsistent practices, namely, if the States or bodies established by trade agreements use the ILO instruments, as incorporated in their provisions, under a normative or legal meaning that deviates from that previously provided by the ILO supervisory bodies." (Agusti, 2014: 6)

A specific real-life example highlights this grey area. Recent events in Cambodia illustrate that this risk is not merely theoretical. In 2001 the U.S. and Cambodia signed a Bilateral Textile Agreement which set quotas for textile imports into the U.S. In extending this agreement in 2002, the U.S. Trade Representative's office stated: "The nine percent increase for 2002 reflects Cambodia's progress towards ensuring that working conditions in its garment sector are in substantial compliance with internationally recognized labour standards and provisions of Cambodia's labour law" and noted that the ILO and the U.S. had projects underway "assisting Cambodia with the implementation of its labour law."[11] Cambodia has ratified all eight of the ILO's core conventions. Yet in February 2014, at a time of violent labor confrontations in the garment industry, the Cambodian Federation of Employers and Business Associations (CAMFEBA) and the Garment Manufacturers Association in Cambodia (GMAC) ran large advertisements in local media saying the public had been misled over the right to strike. The ads stated: "The right to strike is not provided for in … [the ILO's Convention 87 on Freedom of Association] and was not intended to be…. Is the right to strike therefore a fundamental right? NO. The right to strike is NOT a fundamental right."[12] Called upon to respond, Tim de Meyer, a senior

---

11. January 7, 2002 press release available at: http://fordschool.umich.edu/rsie/acit/LaborStandards/LaborInUSCambodiaTextile.pdf.
12. Shane Worrell, *Groups Tell ILO to Retract 'Right to Strike' Claim*. The Phnom Phenh Post, February 6, 2014. http://www.phnompenhpost.com/national/groups-tell-ilo-retract-%E2%80%98right-strike%E2%80%99-claim.

ILO official in Asia stated: "The claims that the right to strike is not a fundamental right and that C. 87 does not establish a right to strike are not consistent with the position taken by the ILO and its tripartite constituency as a whole (i.e. governments, employers and workers) over a period of at least the last 60 + years."[13] Although this statement is factually correct, the CAMFEBA (employers' federation) vice president, Sandra D'Amico, demanded that the ILO retract the statement since the "remarks in *The Phnom Penh Post* do not reflect global developments, tripartite consensus or interpretation of right to strike and convention 87."[14] This pressure from employers in a country dependent on exports (Kolben, 2014) led the government to propose curbing workers' freedom of association. In April 2016, the legislature passed a Law on Trade Unions which not only sets numerous conditions on the formation of unions, but also severely constrains workers' ability to strike, for instance by requiring that workers who want to stage a protest receive permission from the factory owner to do so or face arrest. (Cheang, 2016) Even more striking, this new law completely undermines the belief that underlies ILO Convention No. 87; namely that employers' associations and workers' associations each have freedom of association, and that the two therefore engage in collective bargaining independent of each other.[15] If one party is dependent on the other party even to exercise a right, the right is meaningless.

As FTAs increase, this question of the meaning of the labor clauses in FTAs is likely to become more troubling if there is not acceptance of the ILO statements on the meaning of the right. For instance, the TPP includes Vietnam, a country which does not permit free trade unions (although because of this glaring inconsistency with the principle of freedom of association, the TPP stipulates a "consistency" plan for Vietnam).

4 MONITORING AND ENFORCEMENT

Without precise, agreed upon definitions of what the standards in the labor clause mean, it is difficult to monitor compliance. Egregious violations will be noted, such as the murder of union officials or the deaths of workers in a factory fire where the fire escapes were locked. But even in these instances, enforcement may prove problematic as the experience of the U.S. itself demonstrates. Since 1993, no country that has signed an FTA with the U.S. has ever been fined or had its trade privileges revoked, even when severe infringements of freedom of association have occurred. The complaints procedure is designed to make

---

13. *Ibid.*
14. *Ibid.*
15. *See* ILO, Observation of the Committee of Experts on the Application of Conventions and Recommendations, adopted 2016, published 106th International Labour Conference (2017), regarding Freedom of Association and Protection of the Right to Organise Convention, 1948 (No. 87). Accessible at http://ilo.org/dyn/normlex/en/f?p=1000:13100:0::NO:13100:P13100_COMMENT_ID3298863:NO.

enforcement difficult. Aggrieved workers must find another government that is willing to put forward their complaint (as their own government is extremely unlikely to do so). For labor complaints, there is nothing equivalent to the Investor-State Dispute Resolution process in the TPP or any FTA. Even if a complaint is filed, it languishes for years as discussions occur.

Only one case has even reached the arbitration stage, that of Guatemala,[16] where a complaint was filed in 2008 and a decision did not come until 2017. Moreover, the rationale for the decision indicates that it would be very difficult for workers' complaints to be upheld. Under CAFTA, complaining parties must demonstrate that labor violations occur "in a manner affecting trade." In addition, the complaining party must show sustained and recurring violations and must prove that the trading partner country did not take sufficient action. The burden of proof can become an insurmountable hurdle when one considers that low paid workers, who are being threatened and harassed for seeking union assistance to remedy labor law violations, must document with specificity what has happened and that years later, a trading partner must be able to prove the violations of labor standards and that the other country did not take sufficient action.

5 THE UNDERCUTTING OF ANY MEANING OF THE LABOR STANDARDS IN THE TPP

In light of this controversy over the critical question of what ILO fundamental rights mean, it is startling to find buried in the TPP's labor clause, in footnote 3 of Chapter 19, the statement that "The obligations set out in Article 19.3 (Labour Rights), as they relate to the ILO, refer only to the ILO Declaration." Only international labor lawyers would recognize that this means the four principles found in the ILO's 1998 Declaration have been severed from the eight core conventions and would understand what this means. Without being moored to specific meanings, terms such as "freedom of association" mean what any signatory nation thinks it means. This then reveals the hidden agenda in the curious re-phrasing of the four rights in TPP's labor clause, Chapter 19. As noted above, in the recital of child labor, there was added the phrase that the worst forms of child labor are not permitted. Since the prohibition on "child labour" in Chapter 19 is now de-linked from the core conventions mentioned in the 1998 Declaration, we only know that children under 18 should not be permitted to engage in work dangerous to their physical or moral being. We do not know at what age they are permitted to work in a factory (which is stipulated in ILO Convention No. 138).

---

16. In the Matter of Guatemala – Issues Relating to the Obligations Under Article 16.2.1(a) of the CAFTA-DR. June 14, 2017. Pages 50–63. For the final report, *see* https://www.trade.gov/industry/tas/Guatemala%20%20%E2%80%93%20Obligations%20Under%20Article%2016-2-1(a)%20of%20the%20CAFTA-DR%20%20June%2014%202017.pdf.

The future of the TPP (as the "Comprehensive and Progressive Agreement for Trans-Pacific Partnership" or CPTPP) is not clear. It appears that there will be little or no modification to the text of the final statement of the TPP. As of January 1, 2018, no mention has been made of any proposed change to the labor chapter of the TPP. One aspect of the TPP, however, that must be confronted before the CPTPP is finalized are the Consistency Plans with Brunei, Malaysia and Vietnam. These plans detail changes that are to be made in the labor laws and institutions of each country so that they come into conformity with the labor standards of the TPP (Cimino-Isaacs, 271–274). Drafted in response to concerns that the labor record of these three countries was so poor that they should be part of the TPP, the Consistency Plans were written as bilateral instruments in accordance with Chapter 19 of the TPP between the U.S. and the individual country. The Consistency Plans were in effect improvement plans whereby the individualcountry agreed to improve labor standards, inspections and overall enforcement with U.S. collaboration and monitoring. Now that the U.S. is no longer part of the TPP, it remains to be seen whether another member, such as Canada or Japan, will be willing to assume the U.S. role in these bilateral Consistency Plans.

6 NEXT GENERATION LABOR CLAUSES

A truly "high standard" labor clause would specify that signatories are bound to observe, apply and enforce internationally recognized labor standards, and in particular the four fundamental principles set forth in the 1998 ILO Declaration *and* the linked eight core conventions. To avoid confusing and/or conflicting interpretations, such a clause would expressly state that "these rights should be understood in a manner consistent with that expressed by the ILO's supervisory system." Such a statement included in an FTA would lay the basis for a justiciable claim. But more is needed.

Dispute Resolution. Rather than the tortuously slow process for complaints arising under the labor clause of existing FTAs, what is needed is a form of dispute resolution with a long history in American labor relations; namely, arbitration. A speedy dispute resolution process needs to be designed. FTAs already include Investor-State Dispute Resolution Mechanisms for nonlabor matters which permit foreign corporations to sue governments for what a company sees as unfair treatment. Rather than going to court, investors can compel governments to litigate the matter in a private arbitration system. This mechanism could be adapted to apply to labor matters.

Whether such provisions would actually result in arbitration hearings is not clear, but the distinct possibility of going to arbitration would most likely have a beneficial effect in moving the offending state to take action. (Banks, 2011: 95) These provisions would persuade parties to observe labor standards that comport with the meaning generally accorded them in international law, and would likely compel parties to resolve violations promptly thus realizing workers' rights. The TPP as it currently stands is unlikely to produce that result, especially as it includes no language that would remedy the weaknesses of the arbitration enforcement procedure that became apparent in the *Guatemala* case.

References

Agusti-Panareda, Jordi, Franz Christian Ebert and Desirée LeClerq, 2015. "ILO Labor Standards and Trade Agreements: A Case for Consistency," *Comparative Labor Law & Policy Journal*, vol. 36, no. 3 (Spring 2015), pp. 347–380.

Agusti-Panareda, Jordi, Franz Christian Ebert and Desirée LeClerq, 2014. *Labour Provisions in Free Trade Agreements: Fostering Their Consistency with the ILO Standards System.* International Labour Office, March 2014. http://www.ilo.org/wcmsp5/groups/public/---dgreports/---inst/documents/genericdocument/wcms_237940.pdf [July 29, 2016].

Autor, David H., David Dorn, and Gordon H. Hanson, 2013. "The China Syndrome: Local Labor Market Effects of Import Competition in the United States," *American Economic Review*, vol. 103, no. 6 (October 2013), pp. 2121–2168.

Banks, Kevin, 2011. "Trade, Labor and International Governance: An Inquiry into the Potential Effectiveness of the New International Labor Law,"*Berkeley Journal of Employment & Labor Law*, vol. 32, pp. 45–142. http://scholarshi;.law/berkeley.edu/bjell/vol32/iss1/2 [July 29, 2016].

Bellace, Janice R., 2016. "Back to the Future: Freedom of Association, the Right to Strike and National Law," *King's Law Journal*, vol. 27, no. 1 pp. 24–45.

Bellace, Janice R., 2014. "Human Rights at Work: The Need for Definitional Coherence in the Global Governance System," *International Journal of Comparative Labour Law and Industrial Relations*, vol. 30, no. 2, pp. 175–198.

Callahan, David and Christina Vasile, 2009. *A Voice for Workers: Expanding U.S. Capacity to Promote International Labor Standards and Enforce Trade Agreements*, New York, Demos. http://www.demos.org/publication/voice-workers-expanding-us-capacity-promote-international-labor-standards-and-enforce-tr [July 29, 2016].

Cheang, Sopheng. 2016. "Cambodia Lawmakers Pass Proposed Law Making Rules for Unions," *The Seattle Times,* April 4, 2016. http://www.seattletimes.com/business/cambodian-parliament-passes-disputed-trade-union-law/ [July 29, 2016].

Cimino-Issacs, Cathleen. 2016, "Labor Standards in the TPP," in Cathleen Cimino-Isaacs and Jeffrey J. Schott, eds. *Trans-Pacific Partnership: An Assessment.* Washington D.C. Peterson Institute for International Economics. July 2016. pp. 261–297.

Compa, Lance A. 2001. "Free Trade, Fair Trade, and the Battle for Labor Rights," in Lowell Turner, Harry Katz & Ronald Hurd eds., *Rekindling the Movement: Labor's Quest for Relevance in the 21st Century,* Ithaca, NY 314–338. ILR Press, pp. 314–338.

Compa, Lance A. 2016. "How to Make the Trans-Pacific Partnership Work for Workers and Communities," *The Nation*, January 14, 2016. https://www.thenation.com/article/how-to-make-the-trans-pacific-partnership-work-for-workers-and-communities/ [July 29, 2016].

Council on Foreign Relations, 2016. *"The Future of U.S. Trade and the Trans-Pacific Partnership: A Conversation with Michael Froman: TPP and American Leadership in the Pacific."* June 20, 2016. http://www.cfr.org/trade/future-us-trade-trans-pacific-partnership-conversation-michael-froman/p37973[July 29, 2016].

Keller, Wolfgang and Hâle Utar, 2016. *International Trade and Job Polarization: Evidence at the Worker-Level*, National Bureau of Economic Research, Working Paper 22315. http://www.nber.org/papers/w22315 [July 29, 2016].

Kolben, Kevin, 2014. "Trade, Monitoring and the ILO: Working to Improve Conditions in Cambodia's Garment Factories." *Yale Human Rights and Development Journal*, vol. 7, no. 1 (2014) pp. 79–107. http://digitalcommons.law.yale.edu/cgi/viewcontent.cgi?article=1043&context=yhrdlj [July 29, 2016].

Kolben, Kevin, 2007. "Integrative Linkage: Combining Public and Private Regulatory Approaches in the Design of Trade and Labor Regimes," *Harvard International Law Journal*, vol. 48, no. 1 (Winter 2007) pp. 203–256. [July 29, 2016].

Scott, Robert E., 2013. *NAFTA's Legacy: Growing U.S. Trade Deficits Cost 682,900 Jobs*, Economic Policy Institute (December 17, 2013). http://www.epi.org/publication/nafta-legacy-growing-us-trade-deficits-cost-682900-jobs/ [July 29. 2016].

U.S. Government Accountability Office (GAO). *Free Trade Agreements: U.S. Partners Are Addressing Labor Commitments, But More Monitoring and Enforcement Are Needed*. GAO-15-160, November 2014. http://www.gao.gov/assets/670/666787.pdf [July 29, 2016].

U.S. Trade Representative, 2016. *The Trans-Pacific Partnership*. https://ustr.gov/trade-agreements/free-trade-agreements/trans-pacific-partnership/tpp-full-text [July 29, 2016].

CHAPTER 5
Atlantic Transitions for Law and Labor: CETA First and TTIP Second?

Michele Faioli

> It is not matter that generates thought,
> but thought that generates matter.
>
> Giordano Bruno

This essay is based on an ongoing legal analysis of the investment-labor linkage in the forthcoming transatlantic investment mega-treaties (in particular, the Comprehensive Economic and Trade Agreement, CETA). Should there be a form of EU-wide screening for foreign investment? Theories and practice are observed in order to create a possible template proposal for the forthcoming mega-treaties' labor chapter involving the EU (paragraph 5). From this viewpoint, it will be pulled out from the impact of labor rights on the investment law the meaning that labor rights can have in the transatlantic relations, also in view of the Investor-State Dispute Settlement (ISDS)/labor law conflict (i.e. Can the EU conclude investment treaties on its own, or only together with the Member States? Can the EU's proposed investment court system be implemented? (paragraphs 1, 2, and 3). This allows the detection of the rationale of labor provisions in the CETA (paragraph 4). In paragraph 2, in particular, it will be described the method he is using in his current investigations to comparatively evaluate quasi-similarities in the application/implementation of labor protections in the involved domestic labor systems.

1 INTRODUCTION: REGULATORY DISTORTIONS

Since 2009 the EU has concluded trade and investment agreements. One of the most recent is the CETA – with Canada[1]. It is a special mega-treaty, based on bilateral negotiations, given the European single market, on one side, and the Canadian single market, on the other. The EU is also negotiating an agreement with China and the TTIP agreement with the USA. In connection with those negotiations, the European Union (EU) has also prompted a reexamination of policies regarding promotion and protection of foreign direct investments, and the use of ISDS.

As to the geographical free trade agreement (FTA) and labor approach, the transnational labor/industrial relations should be analyzed nowadays at least in view of the following trade negotiations: (i) EU/USA – the first round of the *TTIP* talks took place in Washington, D.C. *in July 2013*; (ii) *EU/Canada* – the 2014 developments are related to the CETA;[2] (iii) EU/Asia – *the EU and China* are two of the biggest traders in the world. At the 15th EU-China Summit held in September 2012, both sides agreed to launch negotiations on a bilateral investment agreement as soon as possible; the parties had a meeting in July 2017; (iv) *the EU and India* hope to increase their trade in both goods and services, as well as investment through the FTA negotiations launched in 2007. Following the EU-India Summit in February 2012 negotiations entered an intense phase; at the EU-India Summit of October 6, 2017 the leaders "expressed their shared commitment to strengthening the Economic Partnership between India and the EU and noted the ongoing efforts of both sides to re-engage actively towards timely re-launching negotiations for a comprehensive and mutually beneficial FTA";

---

1. On July 6, 2017, the EU and Japan reached an agreement on the main elements of an Economic Partnership Agreement at the EU-Japan summit.*See also* the EU Global Trade developments in http://trade.ec.europa.eu/doclib/docs/2006/december/tradoc_118238.pdf.
2. The European Parliament voted in favor of the CETA on February 15, 2017. The CETA is considered a mega-treaty based on mixed competencies. Although the CETA is already effective, at least for the sections related to the exclusive EU competencies, the national parliaments must approve the CETA before it can take full effect (*see* Article 207 of the Treaty on the Functioning of the European Union – TFEU).*See also* the recent opinion 2/15 of the Court of Justice of the European Union of May 16, 2017 "The Free Trade Agreement between the European Union and the Republic of Singapore falls within the exclusive competence of the European Union, with the exception of the following provisions, which fall within a competence shared between the European Union and the Member States: (i) the provisions of Section A (Investment Protection) of Chapter 9 (Investment) of that agreement, in so far as they relate to non-direct investment between the European Union and the Republic of Singapore; (ii) the provisions of Section B (Investor-State Dispute Settlement) of Chapter 9; and (iii) the provisions of Chapters 1 (Objectives and General Definitions), 14 (Transparency), 15 (Dispute Settlement between the Parties), 16 (Mediation Mechanism) and 17 (Institutional, General and Final Provisions) of that agreement, in so far as those provisions relate to the provisions of Chapter 9 and to the extent that the latter fall within a competence shared between the European Union and the Member States".

(v) the *EU/Latin America* – the EU is currently negotiating a trade agreement with Mercosur as part of the overall negotiation for a bi-regional association agreement that also covers a political and a cooperation pillar. At *the EU-Mercosur* trade ministerial meeting held in Santiago in January 2013, the EU and Mercosur agreed to exchange offers on customs duties and quotas no later than in the last quarter of 2013. These negotiations with Mercosur were officially launched at the EU-Mercosur summit in Madrid in May 2010. The next round had taken place in the first week of December 2017.

Such mega-treaties also deal with labor and industrial relations.[3] Labor relations choices, impacting on the globalizing world, have significant moral and economic consequences (Katz, 2015). Mega-treaties are instruments to foster globalization and, to some extent, they may become an important occasion to advance better work conditions, too.

Starting around 1970, the Western economies began to be knocked by three global changes: (i) the technological revolution (computers, internet, mobile telephony); (ii) the rise of Asia within the world economy; and (iii) the emerging ecological crises (Sachs, 2011). Such changes determined ongoing shifts of incomes, jobs, and investments all over the world. Between 2003 and 2011, GDP in current prices grew by a cumulative 35% in the USA, and by 32%, 36%, and 49% in the United Kingdom, Japan, and Germany, respectively, all measured in U.S. dollars. In the same period, nominal GDP soared by 348% in Brazil, 346% in China, 331% in Russia, and 203% in India. Even Kazakhstan's output expanded by more than 500%, while Indonesia, Nigeria, Ethiopia, Rwanda, Ukraine, Chile, Colombia, Romania, and Vietnam grew by more than 200% each (Hausmann, 2013).

According to the Atlas of Economic Complexity (http://www.atlas.cid.harvard.edu/), these economies began to produce and trade more and more products/services. In this view, mega-treaties are instruments of inter-state cooperation for the promotion of economic growth. As such, mega-treaties were aimed at creating the conditions to foster an exchange between the flow of capital, technology, and human resources into the economy of the host State, on the one hand, and a basic treatment guarantee for foreign investors, on the other (e.g., the right to be treated in a nondiscriminatory, fair, and equitable manner, and to be compensated in case of expropriation). Such an exchange was mainly based on the assumption that a proper treatment of investors could determine the flow of capital/technology and, to a certain extent, the development of the host State. There is an exchange between economic objectives and noneconomic

---

3. For the specific purpose of this research, "mega-treaty" means any international investment agreement (IIA), and in particular the essay refers also to the bilateral investment treaties (BITs), the multilateral investment agreements, FTAs, and the economic partnership agreements (EPAs) that contain investment chapters and, in some way, labor/social clauses. The TTIP and CETA are here considered the most significant mega-treaties in course of negotiation. *See also*, for a recent analysis of the complex mega-treaties systems, Johnson and Sachs (2014).

objectives. It appears like an equation where the latter were subordinated to the economic ones in order to increase investments and create a positive growth spillover effect. Economic objectives and emphasis on the high level of protection for investments influenced the construction of terms of mega-treaties. Noneconomic objectives, and thus labor and industrial relations protection, do not influence the construction of mega-treaties.

But, in this context, we are wondering where the labor problem is with mega-treaties. The forms of protection they guarantee are broadly formulated standards (e.g., decency at work, fairness, equality, etc.), not directly enforceable under the domestic law, and therefore it depends on how these standards are applied by tribunals in the circumstances of each case (*see* the debate, Alston, 2004 and 2005; Langillle, 2005. *See also* Compa, 2002 and 2014; Perulli, 2015; Treu, 2016).[4] Understanding why, what, and how to compare labor/industrial relations systems, also by means of an interdisciplinary approach, is a starting point to detect the impact of such broad standards on the domestic labor laws. In order to investigate these items, two important trends in world labor markets of these last decades should be stressed (Ansley, 1998). The mobility of industrial capital from North to South, from West to East, and vice versa, on the one side, and the mobility of immigrant workers from South to North, from West to East, and vice versa, on the other, are opposite sides of a single global phenomenon. As trade has caused markets of goods and services to interpenetrate among countries, labor markets have intertwined simultaneously through movement of work between countries and through movement, lawfully or unlawfully, of workers. But such a double approach is no longer suitable to the current investigations. We need to observe the lead protagonist of globalization, that is the multinational company, with operations located in more than one country. U.S. multinational giants often have half (or more) of their global workforce outside the USA (e.g., in 2010, General Electric – GE – employed 133,000 workers in the USA, 154,000 overseas, with more than half of its revenue earned outside the USA – *see* the GE website for details). This is to emphasize the erosion of nation-state control over other actors like multinational corporations and the debate about the meaning of labor law (i.e., whether domestic, European, or international, and the extent to which private actors can or should be able to create something labeled "law" without state or prior

---

4. According to Alston (2005), "it is precisely the role of the scholar to evaluate the policies put forward by the officials of the ILO against the normative framework agreed to by the Member States and to call them to account when their choices are clearly found wanting. The bottom line is that the ILO's traditional system of promoting respect for labour rights is in crisis". However, although obligations under the 1998 ILO Declaration on Fundamental Principles and Rights at Work are broadly formulated, they should be interpreted according to the *Djibouti v. France* case, i.e., the ICJ (International Court of Justice) stated that it is possible to refer to the provisions of another treaty, even where the latter were "formulated in a broad and general manner, having an aspirational character."– *Certain Questions of Mutual Assistance in Criminal Matters (Djibouti v. France)*, I.C.J. Reports 2008, judgment (June 4, 2008), paragraph 113.

governmental delegation of authority and without subsequent legislative enactment). There is a challenge to central State power from local/district levels, even firm level, seeking more autonomy beyond borders, and in particular beyond geographical and legal borders of a nation-state labor/industrial relations system (*see also* Treu, 2016. As to the U.S. experiences, *see* Estlund, 2005).

The most general trade frame is based on the facts that by 2009 China's exports to the USA had soared to USD 296.4 billion, i.e., 2.1% of U.S. GDP – 19% of the value added of the U.S. manufacturing. The involved sectors are computers, telecommunications, television sets, textiles, apparel, and toys. Although the USA lost around 2 million jobs in those sectors between 1998 and 2009 (U.S. Bureau of Labor Statistics), the exports significantly increased in the same period.[5] According to the 2012 National Intelligence Council, it is likely that China and/or India will overtake the USA/Europe within the next two decades. This will change not only trade but labor/industrial relations systems as well. The integration of China, Brazil, India, and other emerging economies is causing shifts in income, employment, investment, and trade.[6]

From this viewpoint, mega-treaties may create labor regulatory distortions. Regulatory distortions delineate the host State's right to regulate, vis-à-vis other States, situations in which standards are explicitly lowered in order to attract investments. There can be a form of jurisdictional competition between States to attract investments and this may lead to derogations from labor standards that would not have occurred absent the investments and the movement of capitals. States could decide to lower standards to attract mega-treaties related investments. Regulatory distortions can be analyzed within an: (i) '*ex post*'vision – i.e., evaluating the derogations from labor standards once the mega-treaties are implemented and effective, and an (ii) '*ex ante*'vision – i.e., creating legal frames to avoid the derogations from labor standards (Faioli, 2015; Prislan and Zandvliet, 2014).

Ex post investigations should be carried out on a case-by-case basis in respect of the States that, by means of their already existing low labor standards,

---

5. Therefore, in this research, changes in geopolitics are significant if they have played a key role in the emergence of globalization. We take into consideration that, starting in the 1960s, several developing economies in Asia joined the global trading system, welcoming foreign investments from the USA, Europe, and Japan. This created hosting export-oriented production facilities in special areas. In 1978 the People's Republic of China opened its economy to global trade and foreign investments; in 1991 India followed this model. Virtually the entire world is connected by trade finance and production: goods and services that were produced in Europe or in the USA are now produced in developing countries and then exported to high-income countries. This determines effects on employment and incomes in the USA and/or Europe: employment and income are subjected to a tremendous upheaval (Sachs, 2011).
6. The law itself in this area is in constant development as the pressure of changing trends reshapes labor and industrial relations systems. Questions arise such as what is a transnational labor and industrial relations system, whether it may exists, what such a changing trend underlies. The dynamics labor academics note worldwide are: (i) flexibilization, (ii) globalization, and (iii) privatization (Stone, 2007).

are effectively more attractive for foreign investments (i.e., multinationals and corporations exploit the opportunities in regulations and legal systems) or, in order to remain attractive, decide to further deteriorate existing labor standards. There is no alternative to such case by case analysis. The risk to carry out an ideological analysis is high. The case by case analysis should detect whether the law is subject to modifications in line with the aim to make more attractive domestic labor regime, or the enforcement of such labor standards is weakened on the basis of a specific intent to attract foreign investments (e.g., by decreasing public enforcement or investigations). The labor law approach can only evaluate, case by case, the effects of labor standards on inward investments and the effects of competition for inward investments on labor standards. Such an evaluation of the effects of labor standards could be more easily carried out when the economies are not peer (developing country versus developed country). The evaluation can be not easy, almost impossible, when we face with *peer-to-peer economies* (developed country versus developed country – CETA and TTIP) and there is "quasi-similarity" between the two legal labor systems (exp., EU versus Canada)

The *'ex ante' vision* of regulatory distortion phenomena is strictly related to the capacity of the mega-treaty to vest direct rights and to subject them to obligations. While there may still be disagreement as to whether the substantive rights in the mega-treaties are owed to the contracting party itself or directly to its nationals,[7] for sure the investors have been vested with the right to enforce the provisions of the investment treaty.[8] On one side, this means that the ISDS mechanisms are part of such a legal frame in which foreign investors can exercise rights against States (Faioli, 2015). On the other side, there are also (increasing) obligations under investment treaties to ensure compliance with labor rights by corporations (mega-treaties' labor chapters). However, such labor obligations, in case of violations, are generally without effective and applicable sanctions against corporations (Compa, 2010 and 2014; Vogt, 2014; Treu, 2016). The effect would be creating obligations under international law to ensure labor rights compliance directly by corporations.[9] Given that, the *ex ante*

---

7. Both views have been upheld in the jurisprudence of investment tribunals; *see*, e.g.: *Archer Daniels Midland Company and Tate & Lyle Ingredients Americas, Inc. v. The United Mexican States*, ICSID Case No. ARB (AF)/04/05, award (November 21, 2007), paragraphs 161–180; and *Corn Products International, Inc. v. United Mexican States*, ICSID Case No. ARB (AF)/04/01, award (January 15, 2008), paragraphs 161–179.
8. This is a point that has been acknowledged by the ICJ already in its judgment in *Barcelona Traction, Light and Power Company, Limited (Belgium v. Spain)*, I.C.J. Reports 1970, second phase, judgment (February 5, 1970), paragraph 90.
9. *See also* the Guiding Principles on Business and Human Rights (2011), developed by J. Ruggie, UN Special Representative. The UN Guiding Principle stressed the importance for States to clearly set out the expectation that corporations domiciled in their jurisdiction respect human rights. In the same line, *see also* the recommendations of the Human Rights Committee under the ICCPR (International Covenant on Civil and Political Rights).

vision is the field that in the future will open more chances to labor law researches concerning policies to implement and, likely, case law to study.

2 FOR DELINEATING AN EX POST INVESTIGATION METHOD: CONVERGENCE AND QUASI-SIMILARITIES

Varieties of liberalization may mean varieties of labor laws (Thelen, 2014). National borders are becoming more and more permeable, also in favor of labor regulations spreading "by other means" (Arthurs, 2010; Stone, 2007). At least three contradictory views can be pointed out. First viewpoint: unionists feared that globalization can mean the demise of workplace rights in the Western world. Second viewpoint:, labor economists have found that generally companies are moving low-skilled jobs to low-wage, low-union density countries. Third viewpoint: many labor lawyers have found that globalization undermines the strength of domestic labor organizations and laws. The Western labor legal regimes fashioned a stronger link between labor rights and trade, creating a sort of global common law in the field of labor and industrial relations. Such a global common labor law arises from precedents under applications, interpretations, and international protocols.

As labor law and industrial relations researchers, also in relation to the TTIP and CETA, we are requested to be comparative, transnational, and local (Stone, 2007).[10] In order to focus the specific problem statement, we assume that *all workplaces can generate their own law* (Arthurs, 2010).[11]

---

10. Being comparative can mean that we should understand how work practices are in relation to the established collective labor relations. Being transnational can mean imagining the possibilities of cross-border unionism and employers' organizations. This is to some extent a form of transnational labor regulation. This is to go beyond the labor protections offered by the ILO, the EU, and NAFTA (North American Free Trade Agreement). The challenge of globalization forces us to think transnational and protect labor rights across borders. Being local can mean understanding how strategies are working in the localized context.
11. According to Arthurs, 2010, the law of the workplace "comprises not only state labor law but also formal contractual understandings, workplace customs, low-visibility behavioral, daily routines, and workplace cultures. The law of the workplace, given the unwillingness or incapacity of states to regulate the labor practices of transnational corporations, is relatively free to develop their own normative regimes. The law of the workplace is therefore not unduly influenced by national legal systems, though for their own reasons corporations may choose whether and to what extent they will comply with the local law of the countries in which they operate. Labor is not a discrete domain of law and policy. Trade and taxation, homeland security and health insurance, insolvency, immigration laws and policies (to name but a few) have profound effects on labor markets in general, and therefore on particular economic sectors, enterprises, and workplaces. The result is that in many advanced economies, industrial relations, labor and policy become an incidental by-product, an externality, of other political preoccupations. The bargaining power of unions, the enforcement of labor standards legislation, and the provision of employment opportunities for excluded minorities are often determined in a practical

The questions the ongoing investigations are trying to answer are the following:

(i) what kind of new labor and industrial relations systems can be developed in the USA and the EU in the context of the TTIP and CETA? Will the TTIP or CETA affect labor and industrial relations at domestic and transnational levels? Does economic dependency change the nature of rights as human or labor rights, or is their status independent of their environment?

(ii) are guidelines and/or soft laws and/or indications provided by the International Labour Organization (ILO), the EU, OECD (Organisation for Economic Co-operation and Development) (and/or further institutions) or contained in FTAs an avenue for unions and employers' organizations to guarantee labor rights and the improvement of working conditions in the USA, in Canada and the EU? If so, why and how?

(iii) Do extraterritorial effects of foreign labor law have an effect on the domestic labor laws and practice in the TTIP or in the CETA frame? If yes, when and how? To what extent does the TTIP or CETA impact on profits of corporations versus wages of workers? How are the configurations of the labor and industrial institutions changing in the TTIP or the CETA frames?

(iv) Will we improve our understanding on who controls the global workplaces within the TTIP or the CETA frames? And who will be the global counterpart? Will it be worth supporting actions in disseminating transnational framework agreements in connection with the TTIP or CETA? How will the TTIP or CETA influence the current practice in investors-to-state dispute clauses and their relation with labor/industrial relations systems?

The method could be perceived as a field of nearly theoretical interest with some practical approaches (Aaron, 1977). Therefore the investigation is based on three schemes of legal comparison: (i) *comparing standards*,[12] (ii) *comparing implementation and enforcement*[13] of standards and regulations, and (iii) *comparing firm-level regulations*. The normative sources of labor/industrial relations

---

sense by public policies whose primary purpose is to encourage or discourage consumption, pacify or punish particular political constituencies, or realign relations with foreign trading partners."

12. Comparing standards. This analysis is performed knowing that the difficulty increases in direct proportion to the economic, political, cultural, and legal language, translation of legal concepts, and legal culture distance between any of the labor/industrial relations systems being compared. These include labor law, industrial relations, labor market, economic factors, legal procedural differences, differences in institutional enforcement, judicial capabilities, and remedies.

13. Comparing enforcement. The domestic law and the surrounding legal and institutional regime in which labor/industrial relations are embedded must be compared to the provisions and requirements of international instruments. In case of a clause such as those

may be found at the micro-level of the workplace, and this workplace is more global and permeable than whatever national or global macro-level.[14]

To this purpose, this essay will analyze: (i) the economic background, such as GDP, employment, unemployment, female employment, productivity, inflation, labor costs, gross annual earnings, and minimum wages; (ii) industrial relations characteristics, such as collective bargaining coverage, organization density, industrial action, collectively agreed pay, collectively agreed working hours, and actual working hours; (iii) the economic and legal context, as well as the main industrial relations trends; and (iv) the main developments, such as labor market issues, policies, workplace representation, and tripartite dialogue. The comparative method is conceptualized as a vertical line (international law versus domestic law), in the sense that a common body of public international law applies to all nation-states (all those accepting treaties or international instruments[15]), as well as being based on a horizontal line (domestic law – nation-state versus nation-state). This is more specifically the case. In particular, this research is dealing with comparative law that examines the similar bodies of law, such as dismissal, collective bargaining, equal treatment, etc. between nation-states.

The domestic labor and industrial relations items are categorized, focusing on the body of domestic labor/industrial relations in terms of strengths and weaknesses (i.e., the substantive labor and industrial relations provisions; the procedures necessary to be protected against violations; the availability and effectiveness of any publicly provided prosecutorial enforcement agency or other institutional support to take the burden of enforcement off the workers' shoulders; the deterrent effect of any remedy provided as well as of the litigation process itself; the compensatory effect of any remedy in terms of making the victim whole; the ability of the remedy to encourage workers to step forward).

---

contained in the ILO or UN frames or in regional agreements that include labor rights provisions obligating countries to enforce their domestic labor laws, a further comparative and international law analysis is required. The comparative method is aimed at taking into account the interaction effects of all types of domestic and international law. This will allow for the possibility of tracing out the chain of causation, and of showing how different the regimes are, the power of state and non-state actors, the labor market and its regulation, and collective bargaining at national and firm level.

14. They may be secreted in the interstices of corporate organization, encoded in systems of production and distribution, embedded in shop-floor customs and usages, or imbricated in patterns of quotidian relations between and amongst workers and managers. To some extent, of course, global workplaces are regulated by labor laws enacted by home and host States; but to a considerable extent, workplace actors are the primary authors of the visible and invisible rules that govern employment relations on a daily basis (Arthurs, 2010).
15. These international obligations appear directly within the party States' domestic system through automatic incorporation or are transformed into domestic law by adopting statutory provisions. I will observe when and how international instruments, if any, are being developed, and our comparative analysis will take place in relation to the potential impact of those instruments on domestic law.

Labor/industrial relations comprise all normative influences, of whatever provenance, that deeply conform to labor markets. These influences are not strictly related to geographical borders. They originate in a certain political economy, in its demography or culture, in its social structures or relations, or in its system or legal culture that is beyond the borders we assume being at stake. In fact, in the current context, it is important to note that they may also originate in the global political economy, in the institutions governing labor rights within the economy, or in relations amongst transnational actors.

At the end of the investigation process, it will be feasible to formulate a classification of the elements found in most substantive labor/industrial relations systems that may lead to check out to what extent the U.S., Canadian, and EU legal labor orders can be considered in a *pathway of quasi-similarity*.[16]

The main outcomes of this ongoing comparative investigation will be related to three scopes: (i) *firm-level bargaining, (ii) contingent work, and (iii) dismissal regime.*

3 FOR TESTING AN EX ANTE INVESTIGATION METHOD: THE EU MODEL VERSUS THE ISDS MECHANISMS

Foreign investors may activate the ISDS regime to challenge labor law introduced by host States for the specific purpose of improving labor rights (Faioli, 2015). Given the competition at local level, foreign investors are interested that the host State does not introduce labor standards, which could be considered as excessive, with more burdensome obligations and cost.[17] The most critical point

---

16. The concept of "similarity" in the comparative labor law is developed in theories and practices (*see*, in particular, Stone, 2007). The concept of "quasi-similarity", that is a matter of interpretation, is specifically based on the legal frame that this comparative research selected (i.e.,de facto application of EU, Canada and U.S. labor laws) and what here it is called the de facto implementation of labor law at domestic levels. De facto implementation means that the analysis should focus on what in the reality occurs in relation to labor law application.
17. There are cases, already well known in the labor law academic community and unionists, referring to *Centerra v. Kyrgyz Republic* and *Veolia Propreté v. Egypt*. Those cases are quite limited in precedential value and are not useful for examination related to the possible use of the ISDS in the TTIP. This is because the investment treaties such cases are related to cannot be considered properly applicable to the theoretical scheme here we are looking for. The facts and the argumentation could be explained in this way. In particular, taking into consideration that arbitration official documents are not available, *Centerra v. Kyrgyz Republic* is referred to an arbitration that Centerra commenced against the Kyrgyz Republic. The facts are based on a labor reform that the Kyrgyz Republic implemented in order to improve the salary of workers operating at high altitude. Centerra, a multinational operating in the gold mines, alleged that, given the implementation of such a reform, its labor costs in the Kyrgyz Republic would have significantly increased (approximately USD 6 million per year), and at the bargaining stage of the mega-treaty, the salary conditions were not expected to change. The arbitration was settled in 2009. As to the *Veolia Propreté v. Egypt* case (the official documents are not available), it should be noted that Veolia is a French multinational corporation that in 2012, using the ISDS, filed a petition against

Chapter 5: Atlantic Transitions for Law and Labor

of the ISDS clauses is generally related to the stabilization clause the mega-treaties fixed (i.e., the clauses that the parties bargained in order to "freeze" the law of the host State in respect of the life cycle of the investments). The ISDS is a procedural instrument that the parties used to litigate on the stabilization clause effects (Faioli, 2015). The ISDS is a system of enforceability of corporations' interests over the right of States to govern their own affairs. It is a sort of private self-regulation of sanctions for violations of mega-treaties' rules on trade, between corporations and States, with possible prevalence of corporations' interests on States'/citizens' interests.[18] Such prevalence is decided by means of arbitrations; significant pecuniary sanction may be applied.

By means of the ISDS, the arbitration may decide on matters indirectly related to labor items: if the ISDS concerns the direct or indirect action of foreign investors to use arbitration proceedings against States for labor items, mega-treaties could represent the legal ground/means to allow foreign investors to go further and probably obtain to not reform domestic labor law, or to freeze domestic labor law reform, or lowering domestic labor standards.[19] The violations toISDS awards and/or, more in general, ISDS regime means financial responsibility for the State that is not in line with mega-treaty's obligations. Should be this the case, also in labor matters, the ISDS application would be referred to the following legal items: (i) allocation of costs (i.e., how much will the case cost and how will it be paid for?) (ii) remedies and enforcement (i.e., what happens if the investor prevails in the case?); (iii) forum shopping (i.e., who is going to decide the case and subject to what rules?); and (iv) predictability (i.e., what are the chances of success?). These four items can be summarized

---

Egypt, asking for damage compensation amounting to approximately USD 110 million. The ISDS is related to the France-Egypt BIT. The main violation that Veolia alleged concerned the fact that Egypt wrongfully terminated a fifteen-year contract for waste management in Alexandria. One of the secondary claims was related to labor items. In particular, Veolia argued that Egypt's labor laws aimed at increasing minimum wages indirectly impacted the company's investments, creating damages. Veolia considers this as a breach of the contract and of the France-Egypt BIT. The case is pending.

18. *See* the recent research of Van Hurten and Malysheuski, 2016. They collected "data on the size and wealth of the foreign investors that have brought claims and received compensation due to ISDS. [...] main findings are that the beneficiaries of ISDS, in the aggregate, have overwhelmingly been companies with more than USD 1 billion in annual revenue – especially extra-large companies with more than USD 10 billion – and individuals with more than USD 100 million in net wealth. ISDS has produced monetary benefits primarily for those companies or individuals at the expense of respondent states. Incidentally, we also found that extra-large companies' success rates in ISDS, especially at the merits stage, exceeded by a large margin the success rates of other claimants. It was evident that ISDS has also delivered substantial monetary benefits for the ISDS legal industry."
19. For the sake of completeness, we could also refer to further, not marginal three cases: *Caratube International Oil Company LLP v. The Republic of Kazakhstan*, Claimant's Memorial (May 14, 2009); *Sergei Paushok, CJSC Golden East Company and CJSC Vostokneftegaz Company v. The Government of Mongolia*, UNCITRAL, award on jurisdiction and liability (April 28, 2011); and *Piero Foresti, Laurade Carli & Others v. Republic of South Africa*, ICSID Case No. ARB(AF)/07/01, award (August 4, 2012).

into the legal concept of "financial responsibility" of institutions negotiating and applying the ISDS.

In the EU system, the matter is stated by Regulation (EU) No. 912/2014 of July 23, 2014, establishing a framework for managing financial responsibility linked to ISDS tribunals established by international agreements to which the EU is party.[20] The regulation sets that international responsibility for treatment subject to dispute settlement follows the division of competence between the EU and Member States.[21] As a matter of fact, in light of the regulation, the EU mega-treaties have to afford foreign investors the same high level of protection as that offered to investors from within the Union by EU law and the general principles common to the laws of the Member States, but not a higher level of protection (Faioli, 2015; Kleinheisterkamp, 2013).[22] The European Parliament stated a negative cap on forthcoming mega-treaties, expressing the principle according to which mega-treaties: (i) shall not provide more protection to foreign investors than that European investors are granted by EU law, and (ii) they shall include the rules on liability as elaborated by the Court of Justice of the European Union (CJEU).[23] The latter is also defined as "the no greater rights for

---

20. Financial responsibility is an "obligation to pay a sum of money awarded by an arbitration tribunal or agreed as part of a settlement and including the costs arising from the arbitration" and to the ISDS as a "mechanism provided for by an agreement by which a claimant may initiate claims against the Union or a Member State". The ISDS can result in awards for monetary compensation. On the top, significant costs for arbitration will occur.
21. With the entry into force of the Lisbon Treaty, foreign direct investment is included in the list of matters falling under the common commercial policy. In accordance with Article 3(1)(e) of the TFEU, the Union has exclusive competence for the common commercial policy and may be party to international agreements covering provisions on foreign direct investment.
22. CJEU Case C-264/09 *European Commission v. Slovak Republic*, ATEL, 2011, stated that there is an international obligation assumed before Slovakia was part of the EU and that Slovakia cannot force SEPS (State-owned network operator in Slovakia) not to follow the terms of the contract without infringing its obligations under the investment protection agreement.
23. *See* CJEU 9 September 2008 in Joined Cases C-120/06 P and C-121/06 P, *FIAMM and Fedon v. Council and Commission*, 2008. *See also* the European Parliament 2013 report at: http://www.europarl.europa.eu/sides/getDoc.do?type=REPORT&reference=A7-2013-0124&language=EN. "(3a) Financial responsibility cannot be properly managed if the standards of protection afforded in investment agreements were to exceed significantly the limits of liability recognized in the Union and the majority of the Member States. Accordingly, future Union agreements should afford foreign investors the same high but no higher level of protection than Union law and the general principles common to the laws of the Member States grant to investors from within the Union. (3b) Delineation of the outer limits of financial responsibilities under this Regulation is also linked to the safeguarding of the Union's legislative powers exercised within the competences defined by the Treaties, and controlled for their legality by the Court of Justice, which cannot be unduly restrained by potential liability defined outside the balanced system established by the Treaties. Accordingly, the Court of Justice has clearly confirmed that the Union's liability for legislative acts, especially in the interaction with international law, must be framed narrowly and cannot be engaged without the clear establishment of fault. [...]

foreign investors in the EU principle." This creates a legal clash between the EU legal order and the ISDS (Faioli, 2015).

Such a legal clash can be partially found in the CETA. The Canada/EU mega-treaty fixes the right to regulate by means of the following: (i) better definition and narrowing of key concepts like "fair and equitable treatment" and "indirect expropriation," aimed at narrowing the scope for abuse; (ii) governments, not arbitrators, have ultimate control over the interpretation of rules (i.e., the EU and Canada can agree on making ineffective an arbitrator's determination); (iii) a code of conduct for arbitrators and transparency models; (iv) an appeal mechanism; and (v) rules on the mandatory dropping of cases in national courts if investors intend to pursue the ISDS.

There is maybe an alternative to such regime. Currently the European Commission's proposals are the following (*see* http://trade.ec.europa.eu/doclib/docs/2015/march/tradoc_153258.pdf): (i) including a full article in the TTIP text that "makes clear that governments are free to pursue public policy objectives and they can choose the level of protection that they deem appropriate;" (ii) "a clause that says that investment protection rules offer no guarantee for investors that the legal regime under which they have invested will stay the same;" (iii) appointing "a limited list of trustworthy arbitrators who would decide on all TTIP investment cases," but "this does not go the whole way to creating a permanent investment court, with permanent judges who would have no temptation to think about future business opportunities;" (iv) "the fact that ISDS tribunals don't have appeal mechanisms is one of the things that united business and NGO respondents to the consultation. [...] We will also be proposing an appeal mechanism to our other negotiating partners, including in Canada;" (v) as to the relationship between domestic legal systems and the ISDS, no second chance to overrule the decisions of national courts will be offered to investors (e.g., this by forcing investors to choose between national courts and the ISDS, or by obliging investors to abandon any proceedings they have started in national courts if they launch an ISDS case). However, although such EU alternative to the ISDS clause, the mentioned legal clash does not fully disappear. In fact, the EU proposal shaped such an international court as a commercial arbitral process. In fact, it is stated that "final awards issued pursuant to this Section shall be deemed to be arbitral awards and to relate to claims arising out of a commercial relationship or transaction." This is controversial because, on one side, it seems that the EU intends to move away from international arbitration as a means of resolving investment disputes (i.e., New York Convention model), also for the criticism and the possible legal clash with Regulation (EU) No. 912/2014 of July 23, 2014, and yet, on the other side, it seems that the EU intends to get back the advantage arising from the application of the international enforcement regime (Gaffney, 2016).

Future investment agreements to be concluded by the Union should respect these safeguards to the Union's legislative powers and should not establish stricter standards of liability allowing a circumvention of the standards defined by the Court of Justice."

4 THE CETA LABOR CHAPTER

The labor provisions in the mega-treaties have a great deal of diversity (Vogt, 2014). The large majority of labor provisions that are presently in mega-treaties try to get back to the distorting possible effects resulting from lowering labor rights protection as an incentive to attract foreign investment. Such labor provisions require the parties to refrain from lowering domestic labor rights protection. Their contents depend on the instrument they are associated with. For instance, labor matters in BITs are usually related to preambles or self-standing treaty clauses and they are not subject to detailed regulation. This is to stress that BITs are mainly limited to promotion and protection of investments. In FTAs, by contrast, labor matters are usually related to a more comprehensive chapter, specifically regulated (as in the case of U.S. FTAs) or side-agreements specifically devoted to labor issues (as in the case of some Canadian FTAs). If this is the theoretical frame, the practice is much more complex. My investigation determined a sort of scheme aimed at pulling out from the large majority of labor provisions a key idea. I discerned such labor provisions in relation to: (i) *language*, fixing the principle that we can have a high level of aspirational language (i.e., "should not waive or derogate" from the domestic labor standards) and a low level of aspirational language, given forms of obligations of conduct and obligations of result; and (ii) *commitments* for the States.

In particular, *first focusing on language*, this could be considered binding, under international law, if obligations of conduct (i.e., parties "shall strive to ensure") or obligations of result (i.e., parties "shall not or will not derogate" from their labor legislation) are fixed. On the contrary, under labor law, this language can be considered binding exclusively if obligations are created for States by the mega-treaties and, consequentially, individuals can vest/exercise rights in relation to such obligations, if sanctions are applied, and if labor judges/inspectorate can intervene. This does not occur in the cases we know. Let's observe, for instance, the obligation of conduct, not binding under labor law, given the aspirational language ("strive to ensure").[24]

---

24. We can pull out such aspirational language from a number of agreements: the Agreement between Japan and the Republic of the Philippines for an Economic Partnership (September 9, 2006), Article 103(1); the 2004 USA Model BIT, Article 13(1); the Treaty between the Government of the United States and the Government of the Republic of Rwanda concerning the Encouragement and Reciprocal Protection of Investment (February 19, 2008); the Agreement between the United States of America and the Hashemite Kingdom of Jordan on the Establishment of a Free Trade Area (October 24, 2000), Article 6(2); the USA-Singapore FTA (May 6, 2003), Article 17.2(2); the USA-Chile FTA (June, 6, 2003), Article 18.2(2); the USA-Australia FTA (May 18, 2004), Article 18.2(2); the USA-Bahrain FTA (September 14, 2004), Article 15.2(2); the Dominican Republic-Central America-United States FTA (August 4, 2004), Article 16.2(2); the USA-Morocco FTA (June 15, 2004), Article 16.2(2); and the Agreement between the Government of the United States of America and the Government of the Sultanate of Oman on the Establishment of a Free Trade Area (January 19, 2006), Article 16.2(2). The obligation of result determines similar effects in terms of legal labor binding provisions. We find aspirational language as well

Labor provisions could also be observed by means of the *commitments* the States assume. Also in this case, we cannot find labor provisions that allow individuals to vest rights. If we detect commitments, a variety of comprehensive duties are placed. First, some mega-treaties refer to derogations that can occur also as a result of omissions ["shall not fail to effectively enforce its labor laws [...] through a sustained or recurring course of action or inaction, in a manner affecting trade or investment between the Parties" – *see*: the USA-Colombia FTA, 2006, Article 17.3(1)(a); the 2012 USA Model BIT; the Canada-Peru Labor Cooperation Agreement (LCA), 2008, Article 3; the Peru-Korea FTA, 2010, Article 18.2(1); and the EFTA-Montenegro FTA, 2011, Article 34(1)]. In other cases, mega-treaties define only those derogations that are inconsistent with ILO norms. This means that the party that currently observes, in its domestic legislation, labor standards required by the ILO, can thus lower its standards without violating the labor clause. There are cases where a party cannot "defend failure to enforce its labor laws on the basis of resource limitations or decisions to prioritize other enforcement issues" [*see* the USA-Korea FTA, 2007, Article 19.3(1)(b)].

There is an ongoing set of international labor standards that can serve as benchmark for permissible derogations.[25] EU has evolved in its approach to the

---

where the form "shall not or will not derogate" is fixed [*see* labor chapters/side agreements of FTAs concluded by Canada, Korea, and the European Free Trade Association (EFTA): the Agreement on Labor Cooperation between Canada and the Republic of Peru (May 29, 2008), Article 2; the Agreement on Labor between the EFTA States and Hong Kong, China (June 21, 2011), Article 4; and the Peru-Korea FTA (November 14, 2010), Article 18.2(2)]. But, in this line of obligation of result, the worst aspirational language is related to "inappropriateness" (parties "recognize that it is inappropriate to encourage investment by weakening or reducing" labor protections). This is the worst case because it is not at all binding. You can find it, for instance, in the Agreement for the Promotion and Protection of Investment between the Government of the Republic of Austria and the Government of the Republic of Kosovo (signed on January 22, 2010). In this regard, two legal points should be stressed. First, all these labor provisions do not prohibit derogations from domestic labor law. This implies that if a State intends to abolish the right to unionize or strike, or to reduce the quality/quantity of social security schemes, also in order to attract investment, this would in any case not violate the terms of the mega-treaty's labor chapter and, should in theory a violation occur, no sanctions can be applied and no labor judges can intervene. Second, these labor provisions are mostly based on trade relations that are set up between developing States and developed States. In this context, we have to assume that developed States are subject to regulatory distortions (i.e., standards are lowered to attract investments) and developing States are more subject to regulatory chilling effects (States refrain from adopting new labor regulations). While, going back to the TTIP or CETA, it is important to stress again that we are facing with legal labor systems that feature a de facto application in a situation of quasi-similarity.

25. U.S. agreements have evolved since NAFTA's "enforce your own laws, they don't have to meet international standards" approach in its labor supplemental agreement, the NAALC (North American Agreement on Labor Cooperation). The latest U.S. agreements with Peru, Colombia, and Korea go farther. They require parties to "adopt and maintain" labor laws that comply with ILO core standards and provide "acceptable" wages, hours, and health and safety conditions and to effectively enforce such laws. The EU and Korea went

trade-labor linkage. In its 1990s trade agreements with Chile, Argentina, and Mexico, labor rights as such were absent. Instead, they were subsumed under a general human rights rubric and a mutual commitment in Article 1 that "Respect for democratic principles and fundamental human rights, proclaimed by the Universal Declaration of Human Rights, underpins the domestic and external policies of both Parties and constitutes an essential element of this Agreement." Recently the EU insisted on the democracy clause in all its trade agreements (Bartels, 2013). For instance, the *EU-Korea agreement (2010)* stressed language on labor rights and labor standards, starting with the objective "to promote foreign direct investment without lowering or reducing environmental, labor or occupational health and safety standards in the application and enforcement of environmental and labor laws of the Parties."[26]

In these lines, the *2017 CETA Labor Chapter* has slightly, but not marginally for the geopolitical scenario, advanced procedural/legal innovations concerning States' commitment. Unfortunately, the CETA did not significantly update the "classic" aspirational language we have already indicated above.

The *CETA* has a general purpose that is defined by means of a high-level commitment (the parties "recognise the contribution that international trade could make to full and productive employment and decent work for all and commit to consulting and cooperating as appropriate on trade-related labour and employment issues of mutual interest [...] and the importance of social dialogue on labour matters among workers and employers, and their respective organizations, and governments, and commit to the promotion of such dialogue" – Article 23.1 Context and objectives). As to the abovementioned aspirational language matters, the CETA states that each Party: (i) "shall seek to ensure those laws and policies provide for and encourage high levels of labour protection and shall strive to continue to improve such laws and policies with the goal of

---

further than the USA in their commitment to ratifying ILO conventions. The parties "reaffirm the commitment to effectively implementing the ILO Conventions that Korea and the Member States of the European Union have ratified respectively."

26. Chapter 13 of the EU-Korea agreement is titled "Trade and Sustainable Development". While they recognize that economic development and social development "are interdependent and mutually reinforcing components of sustainable development," the EU and Korea pointedly add that "it is not their intention in this Chapter to harmonize the labor or environment standards of the Parties" and "The Parties stress that environmental and labor standards should not be used for protectionist trade purposes. The Parties shall make their best efforts to accommodate advice or recommendations of the Panel of Experts on the implementation of this Chapter. The implementation of the recommendations of the Panel of Experts shall be monitored by the Committee on Trade and Sustainable Development. The report of the Panel of Experts shall be made available to the Domestic Advisory Group(s) of the Parties." In the EU-Colombia/Peru agreement it is stated that "the Parties agree to promote best business practices related to corporate social responsibility." It does not link labor to any dispute settlement mechanisms (EU-Colombia/Peru FTA (2012), Article 268). These EU agreements provide for consultation with civil society, but do not provide for a complaint mechanism allowing trade unions or NGOs to allege violations.

providing high levels of labour protection" (Article 23.2 Right to regulate and levels of protection); and (ii) shall ensure that its labor law and practices provide protection for the fundamental principles and rights at work.

Such principles are related to the ILO Declaration on Fundamental Principles and Rights at Work and its Follow-up of 1998 (freedom of association and the effective recognition of the right to collective bargaining; the elimination of all forms of forced or compulsory labor; the effective abolition of child labor; and the elimination of discrimination in respect of employment and occupation) plus the ILO Declaration on Social Justice for a Fair Globalization of 2008 (health and safety at work; establishment of acceptable minimum employment standards for wage earners, including those not covered by a collective agreement; and nondiscrimination in respect of working conditions, including for migrant workers).

In Article 23.4-5 the parties recognize that it is inappropriate to encourage trade or investment by weakening or reducing the levels of protection afforded in their domestic labor law. They state that they shall not waive or otherwise derogate from, or offer to waive or otherwise derogate from, their own domestic labor regime in order to encourage trade or the establishment, acquisition, expansion, or retention of an investment in their territory. Therefore, the parties shall promote compliance with and shall effectively enforce their labor law, including by labor inspection and not unnecessarily by complicated or prohibitively costly administrative and judicial proceedings.

In Article 23.7 the parties state that they will consider any views provided by "representatives of workers, employers, and civil society organisations when identifying areas of cooperation, and carrying out cooperative activities." Cooperative activities are mainly related to dialogue and information sharing on labor provisions.

Each Party will designate an office to serve as the contact point with the other Party for the implementation of the Labor Chapter (Article 23.8 Institutional mechanisms). In Article 23.10 it is stated that "a Party may, 90 days after the receipt of a request for consultations under Article 23.9.1, request that a Panel of Experts be convened to examine that matter, by delivering a written request to the contact point of the other Party." The Panel of Experts is composed of three panelists who have specialized knowledge in labor law or in the resolution of disputes arising under international agreements. They must be independent and must comply with the CETA Code of Conduct. The panelists are required to examine, in the light of the relevant provisions of the CETA Labor Chapter, the litigation matters and they can seek information from the ILO, including any pertinent available interpretative guidance, findings, or decisions. The Panel may request information to unions, too. This regime is regulated in accordance with the Rules of Procedure for Arbitration set out in Annex 29-A. The Panel of Experts has to draft and issue to the parties a report concerning facts, determinations, and recommendations. If such a report determines that a Party has not conformed with its obligations under the CETA Labor Chapter, the parties will "identify appropriate measures or, if appropriate, [...] decide upon a mutually satisfactory action plan." Article 23.11 fixes that obligations of the CETA Labor Chapter are "binding and enforceable through the procedures for the resolution of disputes provided in Article 23.10." This specifically means "meetings of the Committee on Trade and Sustainable Development, [...] policy developments in each Party, developments in international agreements, and views presented by stakeholders."

This CETA regime is, therefore, in line with experiences that have been already studied (Compa and Brooks, 2015). The effectiveness of the CETA provisions are mostly related to the political frame. For instance, we know that there are forty complaints under the NAALC/NAFTA and seven complaints related to the U.S. agreements.[27] Usually the National Contact Point, in case labor violations are proved, offers no fruitful solution (Compa and Brooks, 2015). The case related to the union rights violations in Guatemala can determine a possible new path, although it is based on severe labor violations and concerned a State of marginal importance for the USA.[28]

The real problem is still there, in spite of the slight innovations that the CETA introduced: there is no effective remedy to labor violations within mega-treaties legal frame (i.e., individuals cannot plead/complain in front of judges for obtaining protections) that can be compared to the ISDS legal scheme effects, where rights are vested by corporations and obligations are binding for States. There is, in other words, an unbalanced playfield under mega-treaties legal regimes: on one side, labor chapters are still ineffective, given that labor rights are not vested by individual and/or unions; on the other side, the ISDS are fully effective, as we already noticed, and the ISDS, directly or indirectly, may determine labor standards lowering or freezing.

This argumentation is merely aimed at basing, promoting and fostering (at least, at academic level) more in-depth investigations on a new generation of labor chapters for the forthcoming mega-treaties.

5 CONCLUSIONS: PROPOSAL

In light of the above, the following proposal is aimed at reducing the potential of normative conflicts between domestic labor laws and mega-treaty regimes. It is a theoretical proposal (already indicated in Faioli, 2015) for a labor chapter of new generation:

---

27. *See* http://www.dol.gov/ilab/trade/agreements/fta-subs.htm.
28. For the Guatemala case, *see also* Initial Written Submission of the United States, In the Matter of Guatemala – Issues Relating to the Obligations under Article 16.2.1(a) CAFTA-DR, November 3, 2014. This is the only case which is based on a dispute settlement mechanism activation. The process lasted more than six years. The dispute is related to serious breach of union/freedom of association rights in Guatemala.

1. The First Best
   1.1. The mega-treaty should fix that the right of establishment is connected to the mandatory application of the most favored domestic labor regime, beyond the application of the law where the worker performs his/her job activities (*lex loci laboris*) and/or the law of the place of origin of the worker (*lex loci domicilii*).

2. The Second Best
   2.1. The mega-treaty should fix that forms of stabilization clauses can never apply in labor matters (i.e., stabilization clauses are inserted in private contracts between investors and States, which either have the effect of "freezing" the law of the host State with respect to the investment project over its life cycle, or otherwise provide the investor with compensation for the cost of complying with new laws).
   2.2. The mega-treaty should empower international framework sectorial/industry agreements to add on top of the ILO/UN/OECD standards a list of labor rights, not yet included in the ILO/UN/OECD regime, but significantly linked to the sector they arise from, negotiated with unions/employers' organizations at transnational level, as well as in the same legal context (e.g., the right to strike,[29] protection of secondary or sympathetic action/strike, equal pay for women and men, prevention of occupational injuries and illnesses, compensation in cases of occupational injuries and illnesses, protection of migrant workers, maternity/paternity leave, etc.):
      2.2.1. Such mega-treaty related international framework sectorial agreements could be considered a new form of "nodal governance," given that they refer to temporary networks or alliances at transnational level.
      2.2.2. The mega-treaty international sectorial agreements will be empowered by a special extraterritorial effect, i.e., the workplace is not limited to the space of one nation and the mega-treaty international sectorial agreements will operate in any country that is a signatory of the mega-treaty.
      2.2.3. The mega-treaty should state enforceability mechanisms of the mentioned international frame sectorial agreements (please *see* point 1 above) and the listed labor rights (material scope), beyond the domestic labor judge. For the TTIP, a possible application of the section 301 unfair trade practice petition under the USA Trade Act, or an extension of the

---

29. Regarding the dispute at the ILO between employer and employee representatives regarding the unexpected question whether the right to freedom of association encompasses the right to strike, please *see*ILO, Provisional Record, 101st session, Geneva, May–June 2012, 19 (REV).

section 301 mechanism to international frame sectorial agreements can be studied.

2.3. The mega-treaty should define foreign investments for purposes of liberalization along the lines of the OECD/International Monetary Fund (IMF) as allowing for the definition of investor with the identification of ultimate beneficial ownership and control.

2.4. The mega-treaty should clearly define a legal instrument to connect labor rights law and investment arbitrations. This will be carried out in order to specifically integrate labor rights considerations into arbitral proceedings. This means that academics and think tanks should be formally appointed to periodically examine which labor rights issues may be implicated in investment disputes, and at the same time to provide an overview of labor rights norms and frameworks that are relevant to investors and governments and explore how parties might effectively raise labor rights norms and issues in the course of an arbitration. This material will be used as guidelines for the future:

2.4.1. The ISDS, affecting labor matters, should be related solely to non-regression clauses. Counterclaims, arising from States, should be allowed for labor matters, although connections to key matters of petition are not sure.

2.4.2. In any case, no second chance to overrule the decisions of national courts will be offered to investors by means of ISDS schemes.

2.5. The mega-treaty should impose a special section for migrant/posted workers. They have a special status and deserve, also in public procurement situations or supply of services, a special treatment. This will impact on the applicable labor law (*lex loci laboris v. lex loci domicilii*) and the applicable social security regime:

2.5.1. As a consequence, a new social security coordination regime for migrant workers, aimed at creating one and only one regulation, should be negotiated within and/or related to the mega-treaty. The principle of aggregation of contributions should be fixed in relation to old-age pension and for further social security schemes that can be compared. The contributions will be paid according to the *lex loci domicilii* (the place of origin) in case of secondment.

3. In Any Case

3.1. Also in light of the mega-treaties, the EU should adopt a common European unemployment scheme (Dullien, 2014; Faioli, 2014 and 2017) is key to coping with a mindful TTIP labor chapter. The EU should learn lessons from the common unemployment scheme in the USA, not only because such a scheme provides significant stabilization to U.S. business cycles, but also because the variety of unemployment schemes in Europe, although they are already coordinated under EU regulations, may be part of a possible unfair jurisdictional competition.

References

Adalberto Perulli, Diritti sociali fondamentali e regolazione del mercato nell'azione esterna dell'Unione europea, 2 Rivista giuridica del lavoro e della previdenza sociale, 321 (2013).
Adalberto Perulli, Sostenibilità, diritti sociali e commercio internazionale: la prospettiva del Transatlantic Trade and Investment Partnership (TTIP), WPCSDLEMASSIMO D'ANTONA.IT, 115, 2015.
Andrea K. Bjorklund (ed.), Yearbook on International Investment Law & Policy 2012–2013, Oxford University Press, 2013.
Anil Verma, Global Labor Standards: Can We Get from Here to There?, 19 International Journal of Comparative Labour Law and Industrial Relations, 4, 515 (2003).
Archon Fung, Dara O'Rourke and Charles Sabel, Ratcheting Labor Standards, Boston Review, February–March 2001, available at: http://bostonreview.net/BR26.1/fung.html.
Bob Hepple, Can Collective Labour Law Transplants Work? The South African Example, 20 Industrial Law Journal, 1 (1999).
Brian Bercusson, Globalizing Labor Law: Transnational Private Regulation and Countervailing Actors in European Labor Law, in Global Law Without a State, Gunther Teubner (ed.), 1997.
Brian Langille, Core Labour Rights – The True Story, 16 European Journal of Industrial Relations, 409 (2005).
Carolyn Penfold, Offshoring and Decent Work. Worlds' Apart?, 24 International Journal of Comparative Labour Law and Industrial Relations, 573 (2008).
Catherine Barnard, The Financial Crisis and the Euro Plus Pact: A Labour Lawyer's Perspective, 41 Industrial Law Journal, 98 (2012).
Charles-Emmanuel Côté, Toward Arbitration Between Subnational Units and Foreign Investors?, Columbia FDI Perspectives, 145, 2015.
Chris Howell and Rebecca Kolins Givan, Rethinking Institutions and Institutional Change in European Industrial Relations, 49 British Journal of Industrial Relations, 231 (2011).
Claire Kilpatrick, The ECJ and Labor Law: A 2008 Retrospective, 38 Industrial Law Journal, 180 (2009).
Clive Thompson, Borrowing and Bending. The Development of South Africa's Unfair Labor Practice Jurisprudence, in The Changing Face of Labor Law and Industrial Relations: Liber Amicorum for Clyde W. Summers, Roger Blanpain and Manfred Weiss (eds.), 1993.

Cynthia Estlund, Rebuilding the Law of the Workplace in an Era of Self-Regulation, 105 Columbia Law Review, 2, 319 (2005).

David Autor, The Polarization of the Job Opportunities in the US Labor Market: Implications for Employment and Earnings, Center for American Progress and the Hamilton Project, May 2010.

David J. Doorey, Who Made That?: Influencing Foreign Labor Practices Through Reflexive Domestic Disclosure Regulation, 43 Osgoode Hall Law Journal, 353, 384 (2005).

Don Wells, "Best Practice" in the Regulation of International Labor Standards: Lessons of the U.S.-Cambodia Textile Agreement, 27 Comparative Labor Law & Policy Journal, 357 (2006).

Donald H.J. Hemann and Yvonne S. Sor, Property Rights in One's Job: The case for Limiting Employment at Will, 24 Arizona Law Review, 763, 820 (1982).

Douglas Meyer, Building Union Power in the Global Economy: A Case Study of the Coordinated Bargaining Committee of General Electric Unions (CBC), 26 Labor Studies Journal, 60 (2001).

Edoardo Ales, Dal caso FIAT al caso Italia. Il diritto del lavoro di prossimità, le sue scaturigini e i suoi limiti costituzionali –FIAT and industrial relations in Italy, Diritto delle relazioni industriali, 4 (2011).

Enrico Moretti, The New Geography of Job, 2012.

Frank Borgers, Global Unionism – Beyond the Rhetoric: The CWA North Atlantic Alliance, 24 Labor Studies Journal, 107 (1999).

Frederick Meyers, Ownership of Jobs: A Comparative Study, 1964.

Gino Gorla, Il contratto; problemi fondamentali trattati con il metodo comparativo e casistico, 1954.

Gunther Teubner, Regulatory Law: Chronicle of a Death Foretold, 1 Social & Legal Studies, 451 (1992).

Gus Van Harten and Pavel Malysheuski, Who Has Benefited Financially from Investment Treaty Arbitration? An Evaluation of the Size and Wealth of Claimants, Osgoode Hall Law School – Legal Studies Research Paper Series, Research Paper, 14, 2016.

Harry Arthurs, Corporate Codes of Conduct: Profit, Power and Law in the Global Economy, in Ethics Codes, Corporations and the Challenges of Globalization, Wesley Cragged (ed.), 2005.

Harry Arthurs, Corporate Self-Regulation: Political Economy, State Regulation and Reflexive Labor Law, in Regulating Labor in the Wake of Globalization, Brian Bercusson and Cynthia Estlund (eds.), 2007.

Harry Arthurs, Extraterritoriality by Other Means: How Labor Law Sneaks Across Borders, Conquers Minds, and Controls Workplaces Abroad, Osgoode Hall Law School, Comparative Research in Law & Political Economy, Research Paper Series Research Paper No. 25/2010.

Harry Arthurs, The Administrative State Goes to Market (and Cries "Wee, Wee, Wee" All the Way Home), 55 University of Toronto Law Journal, 797 (2005).

Harry C. Katz, Thomas A. Kochan and Alexander J.S. Colvin, Labor Relations in a Globalizing World, 2015.

Henry J. Frundt, Trade and Cross-Border Labor Strategies in the Americas, 17 Economic and Industrial Democracy, 387, 405 (1996). http://www.nelmerito.com/index.php?option = com_content&task = view&id = 2060.

James Atleson, The Voyage of the Neptune Jade. The Perils and Promises of Transnational Labor Solidarity, 52 Buffalo Law Review, 85, 124 (2004).

Jan Kleinheisterkamp, Financial Responsibility in European International Investment Policy, 63 International and Comparative Law Quarterly, 2, 449 (2013).

Janice Bellace, Achieving Social Justice: The Nexus Between the ILO's Fundamental Rights and Decent Work, 15 Employee Rights and Responsibilities Journal, 1, 101 (2011).

Jeffrey D. Sachs, The Age of the Sustainable Development, 2015.

Jeffrey D. Sachs, The Price of Civilization. Reawakening American Virtue and Prosperity, 2011.

Jeffrey M. Hirsch, Employee Collective Action in a Global Economy, in Labor and Employment Law and Economics, Kenneth G. Dau-Schmidt et al. (eds.), 2008.

Jeffrey S. Vogt, Trade and Investment Arrangements and Labor Rights, in Corporate Responsibility for Human Rights Impacts, Lara Blecher, Nancy Kaymar Stafford and Gretchen C. Bellamy (eds.), 2014.

Jeffrey Vogt, The Evolution of Labor Rights and Trade – A Transatlantic Comparison and Lessons for the Transatlantic Trade and Investment Partnership, in 18 Journal of International Economic Law, 4, 844 (2015).

Joanna Howe, Poles Apart? The Contestation Between the Ideas of No Fault Dismissal and Unfair Dismissal for Protecting Job Security, 42 Industrial Law Journal, 122 (2013).

John Budd, The Thought of Work, 2011.

John Dunning, Bruce Kogut and Magnus Blomstrom, Globalization of Firms and the Competitiveness of Nations, 1991.

John Gaffney, The EU Proposal for an Investment Court System: What Lessons Can Be Learned from the Arab Investment Court?, Columbia FDI Perspective, 181, 2016.

John Russo, Strategic Campaigns and International Collective Bargaining: The Case of the IBT, FIET, and Royal Ahold NV, 24 Labor Studies Journal, 23 (1999).

Jonathan P. Doh and Terrence R. Guay, "Globalization and Corporate Social Responsibility." How Non-Governmental Organizations Influence Labor and Environmental Codes of Conduct, 44 Management International Review, 7 (2004).

Katheleen Thelen, Varieties of Liberalization and the New Politics of Social Solidarity, 2014.

Lance Compa and Tequila Brooks, NAFTA and the NAALC. Twenty Years of North American Trade-Labour Linkage, 2015.

Lance Compa, A Strange Case: Violations of Workers' Freedom of Association in the United States by European Multinational Corporations, Human Rights Watch report (2010).

Lance Compa, Labor Rights and Labor Standards in International Trade, 25 Law and Policy in International Business, 165 (1993).

Lance Compa, Labor Rights and Labor Standards in Transatlantic Trade and Investment Negotiations: An American Perspective, Transatlantic Stakeholder Forum Working Paper Series, J. Hopkins University, 2014.

Lance Compa, Pursuing International Labor Rights in U.S. Courts, 57 Industrial Relations, 48 (2002).

Lance Compa, The Wagner Model and International Freedom of Association Standards, in Autonomie Collective et Droit du Travail: Mélanges en l'Honneur du Professeur Pierre Verge, Dominic Roux (ed.), 2014.

Lance Compa, Trade Unions, NGOs, and Corporate Codes of Conduct, 14 Development in Practice, 210, 211 (2004).

Lise Johnson and Lisa Sachs, International Investment Agreements, 2011-2012: A Review of Trends and New Approaches, in Yearbook on International Investment Law & Policy 2012-2013, Andrea K. Bjorklund (ed.), 2014.

Lorand Bartels, Human Rights and Sustainable Development Obligations in the EU's Free Trade Agreements, 40 Legal Issues of Economic Integration, 297 (2013).

Lori M. Wallach, Investor-State Dispute Settlement in the Transatlantic Trade and Investment Partnership, Transatlantic Stakeholder Forum Working Paper Series, J. Hopkins University (2014).

Mario F. Bognanno and Jianfeng Lu, NAFTA's Labor Side Agreement. Withering as an Effective Labor Law Enforcement and MNC Compliance Strategy?, in Multinational Companies and Global Human Resource Strategies, William N. Cooke (ed.), 2003.

Michael Posner and Justine Nolan, Can Codes of Conduct Play a Role in Promoting Workers' Rights?, in International Labor Standards: Globalization, Trade and Public Policy, Robert J. Flanagan and William B. Gould IV (eds.), 2003.

Micheal Doherty, When You Ain't Got Nothin', You Got Nothin' to Lose.... Union Recognition Laws, Voluntarism and the Anglo Model, in 42 Industrial Law Journal, 369 (2013).

Michele Faioli, Adelheid Hege, Christian Dufour, Thomas Haipeter, Steffen Lehndorff, Contrattazione collettiva decentrata in Europa. Analisi comparata tra Francia, Germania e Italia, in 48 Economia&Lavoro, 1, 7 (2014).

Michele Faioli, Annamaria Simonazzi, Introduction, in Economia&Lavoro, 2, 7 (2015).

Michele Faioli, Decency at Work. Della tendenza del lavoro alla dignità, with the preface of Harry Arthurs, 2009.

Michele Faioli, Diritti al jobs compact europeo. Cosa può fare il diritto del lavoro a sostegno dell'Europa che cambia, www.nelmerito.it– (2014).

Michele Faioli, Effettività territoriale del diritto del lavoro e tutela del lavoro all'estero, in 8 Massimario di giurisprudenza del lavoro, 1 (2009).

Michele Faioli, The Quest for a New Generation of Labor Chapter in the TTIP, in Economia & Lavoro, 2, 103 (2015).

Michele Faioli, Libero scambio, tutele e sostenibilità. Su cosa il ttip interroga il (nuovo) diritto del lavoro, in Rivista Giuridica di diritto del lavoro e della previdenza sociale, 781, (2015).

Mick Blowfield, ETI: A Multi-Stakeholder Approach, in Corporate Responsibility and Labor Rights: Codes of Conduct in the Global Economy, Rhys Jenkins, Ruth Pearson and Gill Seyfang (eds.), 2002.

Mitchel Lasser, Judicial Transformations: The Rights Revolution in the Courts of Europe, 2009.

Natalino Irti, Norma e luoghi. Problemi di geo-diritto, 2006.

Nicholas Bloom, Mirko Draca and John Van Reneen, Trade Introduced Technical Change? The Impact of Chinese Imports on Innovation, Diffusion IT and Productivity, NBER Working Paper, 16717, National Bureau of Economic Research, 2011.

Nicola Countouris and Mark Freedland, Resocialising Europe in a Time of Crisis, 2013.

Niklas Bruun, Klaus Lörcher and Isabelle Schömann, The Economic and Financial Crisis and Collective Labour Law in Europe, 2014.

Orly Lobel, "The Renew Deal." The Fall of Regulation and the Rise of Governance in Contemporary Legal Thought, 89 Minnesota Law Review, 498 (2004).

Peer Zumbansen, Lochner disembedded: The Anxieties of Law in a Global Context, 20 Indiana Journal of Global Legal Studies, 1 (2013).

Phil J. White, Unfair Dismissal Legislation and Property Rights: Some Reflections, 16 Industrial Relations Journal, 98, 105.

Philip Alston, Core Labour Standards' and the Transformation of the International Labour Rights Regime, 15 European Journal of International Law, 457 (2004).

Philip Alston, Facing Up to the Complexities of the ILO's Core Labour Standards Agenda, 16 European Journal of International Law, 467 (2005).

Rainer Dombois, Erhard Hornberger and Jens Winter, Transnational Labor Regulation in the NAFTA – A Problem of Institutional Design? The Case of the North American Agreement on Labor Cooperation Between the USA, Mexico and Canada, 19 International Journal of Comparative Labour Law and Industrial Relations, 421 (2003).

Ricardo Hausmann, The End of the Emerging-Market Party, 2013, available at: http://www.project-syndicate.org/.

Robert W. Cox, Labor and Hegemony, 31 International Organization, 385, 394–400 (1977).

Robert W. Cox, Labor and Transnational Relations, 25 International Organization, 554 (1971).

Sebastian Dullien, A European Unemployment Benefit Scheme. How to Provide for More Stability in the Euro Zone, 2014.

Silvana Sciarra, The Evolution of Collective Bargaining. Observations on a Comparison in the Countries of the European Union, 29 Comparative Labor Law & Policy Journal, 1 (2007).

Silvana Sciarra, Uno sguardo oltre la Fiat. Aspetti nazionali e transnazionali nella contrattazione collettiva della crisi, Rivista italiana di diritto del lavoro, 2, 169 (2011).

Steffen Lehndorff, Before the Crisis, in the Crisis, and Beyond: The Upheaval of Collective Bargaining in Germany, in 17 Transfer: European Review of Labour and Research, 341 (2011).

Stephen B. Moldof, Union Responses to the Challenges of an Increasingly Globalized Economy, 5 Richmond Journal of Global Law and Business, 119 (2005).

Steven Hecker, US Unions, Trade and International Solidarity: Emerging Issues and Tactics, 14 Economics & Industrial Democracy, 3, 355, 362 (1993).

Tiziano Treu, Globalizzazione e diritti umani. Le clausole sociali dei trattati commerciali e negli scambi internazionali fra imprese, in WPCSDLE "Massimo D'Antona".INT – 133/2017 (2017).

Tiziano Treu, Le istituzioni del lavoro nell'Europa della crisi, Giornale di diritto del lavoro e di relazioni industriali, 140, 597 (2013).

Vera Glassner, Maarten Keune and Paul Marginson, Collective bargaining in a time of crisis: developments in the private sector in Europe, 17 Transfer: European Review of Labour and Research, 303 (2011).

Vid Prislan and Ruben Zandvliet, Labor Provisions in International Investment Agreements: Prospects for Sustainable Development, in Yearbook on International Investment Law & Policy 2012–2013, Andrea K. Bjorklund (ed.), 2014.

Wanjuru Njoya, Property in Work, 2007.

William B. Gould IV, Labor Law Beyond U.S. Borders: Does What Happens Abroad Stay Abroad?, 21 Stanford Law & Policy Review (2010).

Zoe Adams and Simon Deakin, Institutional Solutions to Precariousness and Inequality in Labour Market, 52 British Journal of Industrial Relations, 779 (2014).

PART III   The European Union Internal and External Action in the International Trade Relationships Context

CHAPTER 6

Globalization and Human Rights: Social Clauses in Trade Agreements and in International Exchanges among Companies

Tiziano Treu

1 ECONOMIC AND SOCIAL RATIONALE IN INTERNATIONAL TRADE

Globalization in its various aspects, international trade in the first place, has a major impact on all
aspects of personal and collective life. It puts in contact not only different economies but also national social and regulatory models, hence the varieties of capitalism.

This statement is far from irrelevant because it challenges the separation between the economic and sociopolitical spheres which has been a basic tenet underpinning most decisions of public institutions and even of the social parties.[1] The growing influence of global trade on the national systems may be a factor challenging this traditional separation between the two spheres because it alters the precarious balance by which national institutions have tried to conciliate the economic imperatives with social and personal interests.

The conflict between the commercial logic of trade and the socioeconomic interests of the various national constituencies has not been reduced by the positive economic performances of globalization.

On the contrary, it has increased in recent years, as shown by the popular protests in many countries and on the other side by the protectionist reactions of many European states traditionally open to international trade and lately of the U.S. government.

---

1. Ceruti; Treu, 2010, pp. 39 ff., 57 ff.

How these reactions will influence the future of international trade and of globalization is an open question. Equally uncertain is the impact of global trade and of its regulation on the social models of the trading countries.

The confrontation of the commercial logic of trade with social rights has been historically exorcised, as it is shown by the separation between the spheres of competence of the International Labour Organization (ILO) and of the World Trade Organization (WTO). Nevertheless, or due to this separation, the WTO has become the major object of the social protest against globalization. And the ILO has been left to elaborate its social norms in isolation, and without the advantages and the sanctions of commercial treaties.

1.1 The Diffusion of Social Clauses

The diffusion of social clauses has been gradual and promoted by the parties of the trade agreements, following the national circumstances and priorities.

The existing reviews of the agreements and of social clauses carried out mainly by American scholars[2] confirm the varieties of their content which depend on many variables: the economic characters of the periods (crisis-growth), the different economic and social conditions of the parties and their geopolitical position.

The coverage and the signatories of the trade agreements are also different. One can distinguish bilateral, multilateral agreements and mega treaties for macro regions, beginning with the pioneer North American Free Trade Agreement (NAFTA) and more recently Comprehensive Economic and Trade Agreement (CETA) and Trans-Pacific Partnership (TPP). Another difference relates to the contents of the agreements. Some are concerned with the promotion and regulation of investments (international investments agreements-IIAS) and bilateral investments agreements (BITs). Others regulate commerce (Free trade agreements) or economic partnership (economic partnership agreements).

The social clauses, or social chapters, have not only grown in number so as to become a common trait of these agreements but have acquired great substantive and procedural complexity.

Different systems and sources of social regulation. General system of preference (GSP), International organizations. Transnational collective agreements.

Social clauses on which this paper is concentrated, are not the only source of international social regulation.[3] Another important instrument to connect global trade with social rights is the so-called GSP by which a country recognizes preferential treatment, concerning tariffs or other benefits, to developing countries on the condition that they respect and apply certain social standards.[4] This

---

2. ILO 2013; Vogt 2014; Ebert Posthuma 2011; Compa 1993; 1998.
3. Bellace 2014, p. 177 and Compa 1993; 1998.
4. Perulli 2014; Pantano, Salomone 2008, Compa, Vogt 2000.

instrument which may be defined a milder approach to the social clause has been widely used also by the European Union which has repeatedly updated its regulation, lately with regulation, 732/2008. This regulation has introduced a mix of incentives and sanctions directed to promote in the countries concerned not only the respect of the standards but also a sustainable development and good systems of governance.Social principles of different contents have been introduced in international relations by a variety of international institutions. The ILO has a general competence in setting basic social standards to be respected by all member countries. The United Nations has approved the Human Rights council's Guiding principles on business and human rights, the United Nations Global Compact of shared values and principles (UNGC) approved in 2000 and with the Guiding principles on the responsibility of transnational corporations (Ruggie 2003, 2013).[5] The Organisation for Economic Co-operation and Development (OECD) has approved the Guidelines for multinational enterprises.[6] Social rights and standards have been sanctioned by the European Convention on Human Rights (ECHR) and by the European charter of fundamental rights.

In the last two decades many large enterprises have adopted voluntary codes of conduct and other practices inspired by the "corporate social responsibility". Finally, social rights of various contents have been included in transnational collective agreements, signed between multinational enterprises and workers representatives, mainly works councils. The relevance of these agreements for the social regulation of trade depends not only on the importance of the signing multinational enterprises but also on the fact that these firms often decentralize internationally their production and consequently their employment along the value chain.

The private nature of these latter sources of regulation has exempted them from any state legislation and control. Moreover these multinationals have usually paid little or no attention to the labor policy of their suppliers because they consider themselves buyers of products and not employers. In fact the public attention towards the violations of social standards committed by these enterprises or by their suppliers has been raised by the protest of civil and social organizations present in the countries of the suppliers and sometimes also of the headquarters of the multinational.

2 SOCIAL CLAUSES: ECONOMIC MOTIVATIONS AND SUSTAINABLE DEVELOPMENT

The variety of existing regulatory systems reflect different principles and motivations. The original motivation is strictly economic and follows the principle whereby fair trade does not allow comparative advantages based on the reduction of social standards, which are considered to distort fair competition.

---

5. Bellace 2014.
6. Blanpain 1979; 1983; 1985; Tegeist 2014.

This principle which still supports many trade and investments agreements has been considered inadequate to explain the complexity of factors influencing international trade and economic development. Comparative research indicates that competitive advantages depend on many variables, technological institutional, etc. beyond labor costs.[7] For this reason the ILO has always stressed the fact that the diffusion of labor standards cannot rest only on commercial sanctions but must be promoted by different instruments linked to the national contexts of the country concerned, namely technical assistance to apply the same standards and to labor market services, support to local development, support to better access to financial services, to contrast to informal and illegal economy. The national context must also be taken into account in order to identify and graduate the standards applicable, beyond those basic rights which must be respected unconditionally. The range of these unconditional rights is defined differently in the various clauses, e.g., it is uncertain whether the right of strike should be included.[8]

In this vision the promotion of basic social rights in international trade is an instrument not only to regulate competition but also to promote a more balanced and sustainable growth.[9] This approach has influenced to a different extent the contents of commercial agreements and contributed to insert the social clauses in the chapter on sustainable development next to the clauses on environment protection: see the Declaration on social justice for a fair globalization adopted by the ILO on June 10, 2008. Moreover the same approach is reflected in the terminology adopted in this respect which has changed from labor standards to human rights at work: a change which is not merely linguistic. In fact while labor standards sound rather technical and limited strictly to working conditions (wages, hours etc.) human rights implies broader values which pertain to the human being as such, to be recognized also when it is at work.(Bellace 2014). The implications and limits of a human rights-based approach to labor policy have been widely debated at the Capetown World Congress of the ISLSSL, in 2015.[10]

The influence of this approach in the actual contents and even more in the practice of global trade agreements has been rather limited, and indeed remained often only on paper. A wider conception of human rights at work is present in the European social model as illustrated in many official documents also concerned with international trade. A case in point are the directives to the TTIP European negotiators approved by the European Council in 2013 inspired

---

7. Onida 2009 The impact of labor regulations on competitiveness and growth has been widely debated. The position of international organizations such as the OECD and the World Bank has changed over the years: see for the recent balanced approach World Bank 2015, Treu 2016; D'Antona 2016.
8. Compa 1993.
9. Treu 2016; Perulli 2014; 2015; 2016; Prislan e Zandvliet 2014.
10. Blankett e Trebilcock 2015.

to the report of the High level working group on job and growth.[11] The actual impact of these directives on the negotiations is not known due to the scarce publicity given to the bargaining process.

2.1 The Reactions of the Public Opinions

The public opinions of the countries involved in trade negotiations have been seriously preoccupied of the possible negative impact on the working conditions and also on broader economic interests. Some reactions are supporting the return to protectionist policies as it is demonstrated by the opposition of the Trump administration to the TPP and to the continuation of the negotiations of the TTIP and by the European difficulties in ratifying the CETA. The reactions to globalization have indeed a much broader spectrum and impact since they are destabilizing the very political equilibrium of some nations.

The preoccupations of the public opinion are so deeply rooted that are not canceled by the formal assurances which have been given by the European governments on the specific contents of the TTIP.

In fact the directives to the negotiators clearly forbid the acceptance of any clause which could allow a reduction of the social and environmental standards adopted in the European countries. Indeed the Lange report is even more specific because it guarantees the safeguard not only of the European common standards but also of the labor standards of the individual Members States, which are indeed quite different also in Europe. The implementation of this guideline would be indeed rather problematic, but the issue will not be tested, at least for the time being, given the end of the negotiations.

The Lange report is even more ambitious because it commits the parties of the Treaty not only to defend the acquis communautaire but also to promote all the targets in the field of employment and social conditions set by the document Europe 2020, and more broadly to contribute to sustainable development.

Promotional clauses of this kind which are present in some other Treaties do not imply specific obligations of the negotiating parties but commit the Member States to be active in the pursuance of the agreed upon targets. However an observance of these commitments by the States would greatly contribute to reduce the preoccupations of the peoples for the possible negative consequences of global trade and to support the trust in the future of globalization.

3   DIFFERENT CATEGORIES OF SOCIAL CLAUSES

According to the ILO the presence of social clauses in international treaties has grown from four clauses in 1995 to twenty-one in 2005 and to fifty-eight in 2013.The Treaties where these clauses are present amount to over 5.5% of the total global trade; they are most common in Treaties between countries of the

---

11. Lange report of July 2015, P8_TA-PROV.(2015)0252.

North and of the South of the world but they are also growing in treaties among emerging countries particularly of Asia.

40% of the clauses are conditional, i.e., supported by sanctions for their violations, the others are promotional. Many combine the two types of content.[12]

The variety of regulatory techniques is a sign of vitality but implies heterogeneity and uncertainty of contents.

Conditional clauses provide different sanctions and procedures of enforcement (*see* below) Promotional clauses provide institutional forms of dialogue between the parties of the treaty for the respect of the social rights and for the monitoring of the relevant behaviors, short of specific sanctions.

Another type of categorization distinguish between post-ratification conditionality, when the clauses commit the parties to respect the terms of the treaty under some penalty, and pre-ratification conditionality when the respect of social standards is a precondition to the signing of the commercial treaty; these latter clauses are less common and their effectiveness is measured by their capacity to promote labor reforms prior to the agreement. This capacity may be strengthened if the benefits of the treaty are conditioned to the continued implementation of the reform bilaterally ascertained, as it is the case in the concession of some financial aids to the beneficiaries countries.

3.1 Different Contents and Languages

The difference of the language and content of the social clauses has implications on their legal and social impact.[13]

Many social clauses, particularly in the early treaties, are drafted in aspirational not binding language. They often express merely the will to respect the standards of the home country without any reference to the international standards. Other clauses stress with some ambivalence the right of each signing party to regulate in its own right the matters of public interest, among which are usually included the regulation of employment relations and of health and safety.

Recent agreements, particularly the CETA and TPP, have adopted a more assertive language in the definition of the commitments of the parties and better organized procedures to monitor their implementation, to solve the disputes and to establish the sanctions for the violations of the obligations.

A critical issue has to do with the types of rights which are included in the social clauses. The commitments vary from the respect of the "basic rights" or of the "internationally recognized labor rights," to the observance of the core labor standards of the ILO. This obligation usually refers (CETA, TPP) to the four fundamental principles sanctioned at the ILO conference of 1998, freedom of

---

12. *See* for these definitions ILO 2013, pp. 21 ff., 33 ff.; Vogt 2014 pp. 130 ff.; Compa 1993, pp. 187 ff.
13. Smit 2016.

association, right to bargaining, prohibition of forced and child labor, prohibition of all kinds of discrimination.

In other cases the commitment is wider and implies the observance of the eight core conventions of the ILO which specify the principles of 1998. The right to strike is usually not mentioned, apart from the CETA.

Some treaties contain broader commitments but stated in general terms, such as the will to guarantee acceptable working conditions (wages, hours, etc.) or the commitment to pursue the indications of the decent work agenda of the ILO. Similar commitments, which were advocated by the European Council, are present e.g., in the CETA and some investments agreements.[14]

Their effectiveness is totally dependent on the goodwill of the negotiating States.

4 PROCEDURES AND ENFORCEMENT

All commentators stress the decisive importance of the procedural aspects of the treaties. Procedures of enforcement of dispute resolutions and of monitoring have been developed over time in all trade agreements. The European directives to the negotiators of the TTIP indicated a further procedure directed to evaluate the sustainability impact (SIA) of the effects of the social chapter; the procedure was based on the Article 9 of the European treaty (TFUE)[15] and supposed to involve the social parties, the Nongovernmental Organizations (NGO) and the Social and economic committee of the EU.

Apart from many different details the procedures of the trade agreements have developed some common traits. The procedure is multistep and is activated by the negotiating parties, namely the States, through institutional channels. All necessary documents and arguments are submitted by the parties but also by various organizations. The case is treated through consultation between the parties possibly accompanied by hearings. Arbitration or judgment by panel of experts are sometimes provided but rarely used.

A model of procedure rather articulated is adopted by the TPP which distinguish two parallel tracks, one directed to favor the implementation of the various clauses and one finalized to resolve the disputes arising under the Treaty.

Two similar parallel procedures have been adopted by the CETA. This agreement innovates in some respects, in particular it provides not only bilateral consultations between the parties, but also a review panel of experts and civil society advisory groups entitled to submit opinions and recommendations. Moreover public authorities, in particular labor inspectors are in charge of controlling the implementation of the various contents of the social clauses. In case of nonacceptance of the judgment of the experts the claimant may suspend

---

14. Prislan and Zandvliet 2014 pp. 13 ff.
15. See Roccella-Treu 2016.

the obligations of the Treaty of an equivalent importance or may ask for monetary compensation of an amount indicated by the panel.

4.1 The Clause ISDS

A most discussed clause of the Treaties is the so-called Investor-State Dispute Settlement (ISDS).[16] The original model was promoted by the United States of America (USA) in the Treaties with some developing countries after the decolonization to protect the interests of the USA investors, avoiding the jurisdictions of those countries which were considered non reliable. In the process of time this clause has been widely used also beyond the original scope and is now present in over 2,750 treaties with a parallel growth of arbitrations: in 2015, they were over 600, but the number is underestimated because many arbitrations are not disclosed.

The ISDS clause has often been criticized for various reasons: because the criteria of the judgment of the arbitrators are left undefined and most important because the clause deprives the national jurisdictions of the power to judge important disputes, in favor of arbitrators who are held too close to the interests of the great multinational companies. The risk is great that the judgments of the arbitrators go against major State policies democratically decided, with possible negative and also financial consequences.

Some treaties like the CETA prevent this risk by stating that the States which are party to the agreement reaffirm their full sovereignty in the matters of labor standards. This statement implies that the State decisions on the labor standards cannot be considered an undue interference in the decisions of the foreign investors[17] and that the same investors cannot have any legitimate expectation that the standards existing at the time of the investment could not be changed subsequently (which is usually the claim of the investors using the ISDS clause). A justified claim could be raised only if the foreign investor was subject to discriminatory treatment vis-a-vis national investors.

In fact the past experience has suggested to fix specific rules to limit the power of the arbitrators, to pretend greater transparency in the procedures and the possible presence of independent experts. Similar requests were advanced by the European Council to the negotiators of the TTIP. And the CETA establishes a specialized Tribunal to adjudicate these disputes, composed of professional and impartial members, bound to decide according to the principles of international law and to follow the rules of transparency of the UNCITRAL. The decisions of the tribunal can be appealed (Article 18.8 and ff).

The reported decisions taken according to the ISDS procedure are rather few because most of them are not disclosed. Moreover many disputes of this kind are settled consensually by the parties.

---

16. Marchisiello 2016 pp. 129 ff; Faioli 2015 pp. 103 ff.
17. Prislan and Zandvliet 2014, p. 10; Faioli 2015 pp. 113 ff.

The two decisions most quoted concerning labor disputes, but known only in part, well demonstrate their potential impact on national labor laws. In the case *Centerra v. Kyrgyz Republic* the investor claimed that the law of that country which had raised workers' salaries caused an increase of labor costs (USD 6 million a year) and that this increase was not considered in the negotiation of the Treaty. The case appears to be decided in 2009.

In another case the French multinational Veolia accused Egypt of two violations of the treaty with France, one consisting in the anticipated breach of a commercial contract, one in the increase of minimum legal wage which reduced the profitability of the investments decided by Veolia.

4.2 The Weakness of the Procedures

In spite of the importance attributed to the procedures of the commercial Treaties these procedures are the weakest link of the agreements, particularly of the social clauses.

The weakness is in part due to the vagueness of the commitments written in the agreements. For example it is often unclear whether a violation of the clause to be relevant must concern an economic sector included in the treaty or it has to positively influence the investments or the commerce between the parties.[18]

Some agreements (CETA,TPP) state that the violations to be relevant must be serious and systematic or that they must depend on a recurring course of action or inaction. These provisions may reduce the impact of the social clause because in some Treaties with countries reluctant to respect the labor standards the sanctions for the violations has been avoided simply because the violating state has "taken steps" to remedy the violation or the monitoring procedures have decided to continue the review of the relevant behaviors.

Other limits of effectiveness depend on the fact that the instruments of enforcement are cumbersome and left to the initiative of the negotiating States and of their bureaucracy. Moreover the procedures relating to labor disputes are traditionally less rigorous than those applicable to the implementation of the commercial clauses of the treaties. The latter are followed by the public administrations dealing with trade and investment issues which particularly in the USA are more influential and better equipped than labor administrations.

The Obama Template of May 10, 2007 has declared that the procedures concerning labor matters must be examined according to the same procedural rules applicable to commercial disputes.

Another important difference between labor and commercial clauses concerns the sanctions for the violations of the obligations. The sanctions for the violations of the labor standards are generally applied with great caution, ranging from measures of moral suasion and of social pressure up to suspension

---

18. Vogt 2014, pp. 129 ff.

or loss of preferential treatments or even blockage of import. This latter sanction has been used in front of very serious violations of social and human rights, usually in GSP procedures.[19] The procedures for the enforcement of social clauses have usually provided not the suspension of treaty benefits but only monetary compensations within a maximum ceiling and with the possibility of reductions.[20]

Even after the 2007 Template this difference in the application of sanctions has continued due to the reluctance of the States to enforce effectively the social clauses. Both the CETA and TPP have reaffirmed the principle that all enforcement procedures must follow the same rules. But their effectiveness remains to be tested because the actual implementation still depends on the initiatives of the States and of their bureaucracies. This is a major difference with the ISDS clauses where the private investors have a right of their own to sue for the enforcement of the obligations under the treaty.

This weakness of the social clauses is often denounced by the trade unions and by other civil associations and is confirmed by the practical experience which shows that the implementation of social clauses is hardly pushed by State authorities. In general the impulse to the procedure is linked to political factors such as the strategic importance of the State involved or its political conditions, often in relation to the interest of the USA administration of a given period.[21]

As mentioned already the amount of public resources devoted to the monitoring and the enforcement of the social clauses is usually inferior to that devoted to the implementation of the commercial parts of the treaties. This difference is particularly important because the social regulations include in the treaties, differently from the commercial obligations are not directly actionable by the workers but depend exclusively on the state initiative.

5 UNCERTAIN OUTCOMES

Researches on the application of the Treaties have multiplied but are still insufficient, also due to the scarce transparency of the sources, to give a meaningful account of the various experiences. The results are at best uneven and variable according to the national contexts.[22]

The first surveys of the application of the GSP decided by the USA indicate a few cases of suspension and of abolition of benefits against violations of social rights by developing, usually poor or politically troubled countries. In some cases the sanctions have been revoked following partial or substantial improvements in the labor legislation.

The ILO reports indicate that the most effective commitments of the labor chapters, particularly by the developing countries, are those concerning capacity

---

19. Compa 1998, pp. 707 ff.
20. Vogt 2014, pp. 127 ff.
21. Compa, Vogt 2003, pp. 237 ff.
22. *See* ILO 2013, pp. 36 ff.; Compa 1998, pp. 174 ff., 2015 *a)* pp. 87 ff., 2015 *b)*.

building programs, exchange of good practices, promotional activities, social and public communications. The pre-ratification commitments have contributed to improve the legislation of some countries, particularly concerning trade union freedoms. More uncertain is the impact of the procedures of enforcement of social clauses on the actual improvement of labor standards.

The implementation of the CETA and TPP will be a particularly important test for the future of the social clauses in international trade because the clauses of these Treaties are called to function not only in developing countries but also in modern labor markets. And it will be possible to verify how this new social and economic context, so different from that of the first trade agreements, will, influence, positively or negatively, the effectiveness of the social commitments of the parties and in general the economy of the interested countries.

5.1 The (Possible) Pattern Setting Value of the CETA

The importance of the CETA is linked both to the central position of transatlantic trade and to the historic relations also in social traditions between the two areas. The importance of the TTIP would have been much greater, given the role of the USA and the very difference of its social system with the European model; but these negotiations are suspended with no chance to continue for the time being.

The value of well shaped treaties, like CETA and in different respects TPP, is so much greater in the present times when global trade seems to be stagnating and could be sustained by convergent regulations by major countries not only in labor but also in economic matters. A meaningful convergence will have to face quite a few obstacles not only between Europe and USA, where the differences are marked in both areas, but also with Canada. These differences have been quite visible during the negotiations of both the CETA and TTIP and in the process of ratification of the former. The judgment of the experts has been far from unanimous about their possible economic and social impact.[23] The attention is now concentrated on the implementation of the CETA as a testing ground for the future of trade agreements and their social clauses in the Atlantic hemisphere.

6 INTERNATIONAL EXCHANGES AMONG COMPANIES

Global trade has been growing not only by initiative of the States via commercial treaties but also because the new international organization of production has opened greater opportunities for exchanges between multinational firms. These enterprises have been able, due also to new technologies, to organize their activities in different countries through various channels: controlled companies

---

23. The impact of these Treaties on the economy of the interested countries is evaluated differently both by experts and by political representatives: *see* for the TTIP various opinions in the special issue of Economia e lavoro 2015, 2.

but also supplier firms which are legally autonomous but in fact linked to the multinationals by stable commercial ties.[24] This is a new vector of globalization which receives from the multinationals not only economic impulse but also contractual regulations.

These rules are of private nature and consequently separate from the contents of the commercial treaties between the states. In fact even when they include some labor issues these are concerned mostly with the economic conditions of employment. Social clauses are sometimes present and they usually confirm or possibly improve the standards included in the official treaties.

Specific clauses are particularly important in the matter of union rights, whose regulation is finalized to improve collective labor relations and to guarantee the social peace in the productive units. The private character of these clauses allows great flexibility and variety of contents. The procedures of enforcement are also different from those of the commercial treaties and rest mostly on the capacity of the companies and possibly of the unions to guarantee their effectiveness.

The multinational enterprises can exert wide discretion in these regulations for two reasons: (1), the weak presence of trade unions in international relations, (2), the reduced regulatory capacity of the national States. These empty spaces are filled by multinational companies with mainly soft types of regulations, like codes of conduct, guidelines, which are sometimes shaped in the context of international organizations (*see* the OECD guidelines and the Global compact).

6.1 Company Regulations and Corporate Social Responsibility

These soft regulations often make reference to the principles and conventions of the ILO. Usually they are based on the idea of the corporate social responsibility and reflect the culture and values of the enterprise.[25] But in spite of this, the content of these rules must take into account to some extent the characters and legislation of the national context where they are to be applied. The pressures of the public opinion and of the social organizations have often influenced the evolution of the conduct of these companies and sometimes managed to bloc their practices when in violation of core labor standards.

Some European multinationals influenced by the continental social model have agreed to consult or to negotiate these rules with the trade unions; in a few cases formal agreements have been concluded with the European works councils which are the only workers' representative channel recognized by the European Union and which have often exercised their power even beyond their official prerogatives.

---

24. Bellace 2014, pp. 176 ff.
25. Treu 2007; Perulli 2013; Rogowsky 2005; Schuler et al. 2017; Wettstein 2012 p. 739.

This network of rules negotiated or participated with the workers' representatives have become another vehicle of transnational diffusion of common social principles.

7 TRANSNATIONAL AGREEMENTS

Collective bargaining which has been historically linked to national constituencies has recently begun to go beyond the national borders, in different forms.

Framework agreements between the peak organizations of European employers and unions have regulated broad social issues, often finalized to shape European directives. Quite a few sectional agreements have set the basic rules for the enterprises and workers of specific industrial and service sectors. A growing number of agreements, more or less formalized, have been signed by large companies often multinational with the unions present in their plants and more often with the works councils.[26]

This variety of agreements confirms the plurality of instruments used to extend beyond the national borders the practices of industrial relations which were originally adopted at the national level but which now are losing ground within the original domain due to the effects of globalization. This extension of collective agreements beyond the national borders meets many obstacles both factual and legal. In fact the organization of the social parties are still nationally based and deprived of supranational powers. On the other hand supranational agreements have no defined legal status and consequently must base their effectiveness only on self-help.

The agreements concluded by the multinational firms have acquired greater diffusion also due to the trend to decentralize industrial relations force which is common to many countries. They can have more direct effects than sectional agreements because they can be implemented directly, also transnationally, by the decision of the companies which are party to the agreement.

The contents of transnational agreements are quite variable; they may concern only some relations between the negotiating parties or also the regulation of the individual employment relations. The agreements concluded by European multinationals often confirm the ILO basic labor standards but also fix broader and more favorable employment and social conditions.

When these agreements have binding regulations and not merely programmatic statements, the problem arises of defining their legal effects within the national borders and in countries different from that of the bargaining parties.

This question has received hardly any legal test, because the parties tend to solve their disputes under the agreements through their own channels without resorting to national tribunals, and because the national courts have been quite reluctant to decide labor cases arising or developed in other countries, i.e., to admit an extraterritorial application of national labor legislations.

---

26. Giubboni; Peruzzi 2013, pp. 131 ff. Sciarra 2009, p. 12; Rehfeld 2013.

8 PILOT CASES

Few cases are known, mainly originated in the USA and promoted by American lawyers, due to the great number of treaties concluded by the USA but also because the common law of torts and of contracts allows more than civil law innovative applications of the legal institutions. Innovative solutions have been adopted particularly in serious cases of violation of fundamental human and labor rights.[27]

These pilot cases are quite exceptional so far, but they show the potentials of some legal techniques to apply basic rules beyond national borders overcoming the principle of territoriality of the law which is valid also in the USA.[28]

One pilot case arises from an accusation by trade unions against the Dow Chemical for the use of pesticides in Costa Rica in violation of USA legislation. The Supreme Court of Texas admitted its jurisdiction and decided in favor of the unions on the ground that the firm decisions were taken in Texas, that the workers were American employed by an American company operating on land of its property for exporting bananas to American tables. In spite of these important principles the difficulty to bring sufficient evidence and the prospect of a lengthy procedure for the final decision suggested to the lawyers of the workers to settle the case for (a considerable amount of) damages.

A second case was originated by a collective dismissal of workers and of trade unionists by a company operating in Guatemala but owned by an American company. Given the refusal of the firm to respect the order of reinstatement of the court of Guatemala the workers' lawyers sued the USA company in Florida asking for the enforcement of the order of reinstatement on the basis of the traditional principle according to which the courts of different countries accept to apply their respective orders in their own jurisdiction. The suit plus the pressure of the public opinion and of the authorities of Guatemala forced the company to accept the judge's order. An extraterritorial application of the USA law can be found in an National Labor Relations Board (NLRB) decision which ordered an injunction in favor of an American employer (with damages) to stop a solidarity boycott organized by a trade union in a different State. But the U.S. Court of Appeal reversed the NLRB decision arguing that extraterritorial effects can be recognized only by the law itself not by the judges nor by the NLRB.[29]

An important solution drawn from the commercial treaties has been advanced in a dispute raised by the American Federation of Labor (AFL) against China, The union argued that the non-respect of fundamental labor rights amounts to an unfair labor practice and that it can give rise to commercial sanctions according to section 301 of the U.S. Trade Act of 1974.[30]

---

27. Arthurs 2001, p. 271.
28. Compa 2002, pp. 48 ff.
29. Compa 2002, pp. 51 ff.
30. Faioli 2015, pp. 116 ff.

Another decision (Filartiga) which demonstrate the potential of this case law concerned a case of violence and homicide perpetrated by the authorities of Burma. The decision of a U.S. Court of Appeal, based on an Act of 1789 against piracy, admitted its jurisdiction arguing that the torture perpetrated by public officials violates universal norms protecting human rights and consequently must be punished irrespective of the nationality of the persons affected. This precedent has been used to base a lawsuit against an American multinational operating in Burma with the argument that the local courts were not adequately protecting the workers victims of serious violations of their rights.[31]

A last case deals with a suit by a Korean union against a company decision (dismissal) taken in violation of a group agreement. The case was brought to a court in New York against the American mother company of the Korean firm accusing the violation of the collective agreement and the interference of the mother company on the local management. The judge had acknowledged the violation of the agreement, but had not decided for the responsibility of the mother company adducing a specific exception.

The first cases mentioned are based not on clauses of commercial treaties but on norms of the country of the mother company (the USA) which are held to be applicable also to fact occurred in another jurisdiction.

The last decision, in spite of the conclusion negative for the workers, opens the way to the possibility of enforcing contractual obligations against multinational firms based in the USA.[32] The arguments adopted here, if shared, can confirm the binding effects of collective agreements signed by multinationals not only for the signatory parties and their employees, but also for the various firm subsidiaries. The unitary legal relevance of the enterprise groups which has been recognized in various ways by many courts also Italian within the national borders would be extended across the borders. It could be an important innovation allowing collective agreements to operate also as a transnational source of labor regulations, and to follow the transnational projections of the enterprise, instead of being bypassed by the initiative of the multinationals.

A similar transnational consideration of the enterprise groups can hardly be relevant for the social clauses of the commercial treaties, because the rules of implementation of these treaties, as shown above, are controlled by the signatory States and the ensuing disputes are subtracted to the national courts' jurisdiction and reserved to internal conciliation and arbitration procedures.

9 POSSIBLE INNOVATIONS

The pilot cases just mentioned have a limited direct impact but might have the value as precedent for the future.

---

31. Compa 2002, p. 64.
32. Compa 2002, pp. 55–56; *see also* the Ruggie Report 2003, p. 301.

The importance of the issues considered by global treaties has raised a wide public attention and stimulated the search for innovative practical solutions directed to remedy to the weaknesses of their implementation, particularly that of the social clauses. Some of these solutions, advanced mainly in the Anglo-Saxon countries, deserve to be mentioned.

A general argument directed to justify the transnational effects of fundamental social rights has been advanced by A. Supiot (2016).The argument proceeds from the rule stated in the ILO declaration of 1998 whereby all States members of the ILO, even if they have not ratified the conventions, have the duty deriving from their membership to apply and promote the principles concerning the fundamental rights sanctioned by the same conventions. The violation of this duty by a Member State bound to observe it should legitimize other partner States to react with commercial countermeasures, such as the suspension of GSP and the non-application of specific clauses and benefits of the bilateral treaty.

This position which has been widely discussed is an attempt to justify the binding effects of fundamental social rights of the ILO even beyond and in absence of specific clauses of the Treaties, for all state members of the ILO including those, like the U.S., which have not ratified some of the core ILO conventions. The legal implications of this argument are wide-ranging even though the practical impact depend on the initiative of the States and on their interest to pretend the respect of the fundamental rights from their competitors in order to prevent them from taking advantage of practices of social dumping.

According to other commentators a broad interpretation of Article XX of GATT on the General Exceptions might allow the protection of human rights and of the basic social standards because it can legitimize the adoption of protective measures by the States not only internally but also in the commercial relations with other States.[33]

According to a similar type of arguments one could argue that, given the importance of labor conditions for competition, the nonobservance of basic labor standards by some States and the tolerance of their violations may hinder the observance also by other States, which do not want to suffer a competitive advantage.[34]

10 MULTIPLE INSTRUMENTS AND STRATEGIES FOR INTERNATIONAL SOCIAL REGULATION

The weakness of social clauses and of their enforcement procedures cannot be corrected only with some improvements of the existing system. A new perspective is necessary in order to pursue the objective of these clauses which is to contribute to a better social regulation of globalization. To this end are necessary not only more precise and consistent legal norms but a set of public policies and

---

33. Perulli 2014, p. 33; Benedek 2007, p. 137.
34. Perulli 2016.

administrative practices adopted by the national states vis-a-vis global trade and international markets.

The materials and the experiences accumulated in recent years may be useful, but need to be better finalized and harmonized. Innovative types of regulations are to be searched different from those adopted in the building of national legislations and also in the European community; the very dichotomy hard-soft law might not be exhaustive. Innovation is necessary because the scope of application of the rules is different from that of the national legislations, the parties are not those of the employment relations but public institutions which are also the sources of regulation and then responsible for the implementation of the standards.

The search for new solutions might have to reconsider not only the role of the legislators and of the representative bodies but also of the bureaucracies and the technical agencies which are decisive in the preparation of the dossiers and in the negotiation among States. In fact these negotiations last through the periods of many governments and parliaments, as shown by the seven years of negotiation of the CETA; and equally long lasting are the procedures of implementation of the agreements. The formation of the European directives and regulations gives full evidence of the importance of the technical and inter-institutional procedures and of their difference from the national parliamentary processes.

The diversity and complexity of negotiating international Treaties are even greater when the regulations must have a wider scope than the relatively homogeneous European space.

On the other hand the international rules created by the Treaties produce their effects only indirectly i.e., through the national institutions and consequently are influenced by this intermediation. Moreover the framing and application of the social clauses have to take into account, even more than other clauses of the treaties, the pressures of social actors and of multiple stakeholders.

The involvement of this variety of stakeholders is a necessary condition for framing acceptable regulations and for sustaining an effective implementation. The ILO recommendations confirm the importance of the fact that the stakeholders be fully involved both in the phase of negotiation and in the implementation of the social clauses.[35]

A second condition deriving from the experience has to do with transparency and information. A full knowledge of the possible alternatives of the negotiation and of the implications for the interested parties is important for winning the resistance to change and for reaching a true consensus. The lack of transparency and of information has proved to be a major obstacle in many negotiations, including those for the TTIP.

---

35. ILO 2013, pp. 103 ff.

The implementation of the social clauses equally requires continuous information through all the institutional and social channels. An active presence of these stakeholders, beginning with the unions and the NGO, in the procedures of implementation would greatly increase the effectiveness of the clauses, and compensate for the inertia of the negotiating states. Many experts have suggested to give powers of initiative to these stakeholders in the various steps of the procedures in order to reinforce their effectiveness.[36] This would give the stakeholders the same right of action that is recognized to private investors in the ISDS procedures. Such a right of initiative of social actors would also facilitate the courts' intervention in labor disputes, as shown by the pilot cases mentioned above.

The intervention of independent mediators and arbitrators has also been proposed as a means to improve the application of social clauses and make them more acceptable to the stakeholders and to the public at large.

Giving the power of initiative in these procedures to social and civic organizations may stimulate the public authorities to use all the available legal tools to implement the clauses of the treaty. But it cannot have a direct impact on the enterprise decisions concerning the respect of the social standards. In order to reach this result further steps are needed. The multinationals enterprises should accept more stringent social obligations than those resulting from the codes of practice; the States could require the enterprises to abide by the same social standards included in the trade agreements and/or to give binding force to the principles of corporate social responsibility.[37]

This solution would represent a profound change with respect to the present status of the social clauses because it would modify their exclusive interstate logic and make them directly actionable by the social parties.

The same result would be reached by the diffusion of transnational collective agreements concluded by multinational firms and containing not only economic and normative conditions but also the commitment of the firms to respect the core social standards fixed by the ILO.

The ILO, which is already involved in the implementation of social clauses with tasks of monitoring, fact-finding and mediation (so the CETA), could contribute directly to the enforcement of these clauses as arbitrator indicated by the parties to the treaties. Similar proposals have been advanced by some experts.[38]

The effective formation and implementation of social clause is not a merely technical question. It calls into question the role and the strategies of the States for the future of globalization.

The experience shows that improving the social rules of international economic relations is a difficult objective. In order to pursue this objective effectively the States should give it high priority in their political agenda. And

---

36. Compa 1993; Faioli, 2015; ILO 2013, p. 103.
37. M. Marchesiello, pp. 133 and ff.
38. Prislan; Zandvliet, p. 10; M. Faioli, pp. 113 ff.

they should use accordingly a variety of instruments and techniques with more continuity and consistency that it has been done so far. The same objective should have priority in the strategies of the social parties and of civic organizations which would project their actions beyond the national markets where they have been tested in the past.

The weak powers of the international organizations in our field need to be supported by the subsidiary intervention of organized groups of interest. They operate with private instruments of consensual origin: transnational collective agreements, partnership initiative, guidelines, investment and commercial agreements. The capacity of these private initiatives to influence and regulate the markets will depend on the social pressure which they will mobilize vis-a-vis all the stakeholders and the very various centers of public policy making.

The target should be to make the best use of these various instruments to build a network of social rules capable of operating effectively across and beyond the national borders. This will be a gradual process, which will not be immediately capable of taking labor costs out of global competition, as the national systems of labor law and industrial relations did in the last century for their national jurisdiction. But a multilevel network of social rules of different nature and origin, supported by social and institutional consensus, will contribute to that end avoiding that global competition takes advantage of the violation of basic human and social rights.

This innovative path for promoting transnational social regulations needs institutional ingenuity but must be supported and framed in a broader perspective as indicated above, namely in a political and social strategy finalized to promote a sustainable development and to correct the socially negative consequences of globalization.[39]

The defense of acquired social rights in some countries is not sufficient. If not framed in this broader perspective it may risk being accused of protectionism by less developed countries, as it has been already the case.[40] The sanction and promotion of social rights, in order to be accepted and credible, need to be inclusive, i.e., accompanied by positive measures conducive to balanced growth and by an equitable distribution of wealth between nations and social groups. Old and new groups need to be protected from the possible consequences of globalization. The losers of globalization can be found in different sectors of the population, from the traditional working class to some sectors of the once stable middle class and recently to the masses of migrants which are moving from poor to richer countries of the world.[41]

Europe and the United States, due to their economic importance and for their cultural and social traditions, could take the lead in pursuing these objectives. But this responsibility is being shared more and more by other emerging and newly central nations.

---

39. T. Treu 2016.
40. B. Hepple 2003, pp. 27 ff.
41. Compa 1993, pp. 100 ff.

References

Arthurs, H. (2001), Reinventing Labor Law for the Global Economy, in *Journal of Employment and Labor Law*, vol. 22, pp. 271-292.

Bellace, J.R. (2014), Human Rights at Work: The Need for Definitional Coherence in the Global Governance System, in *International Journal of Comparative Labour Law and Industrial Relations*, vol. 30, n. 2, pp. 175-198.

Benedek, W. (2007), The World Trade Organization and Human Rights, in W. Benedek, K. De Feyter, F. Marrella (a cura di), *Economic Globalization and Human Rights*, Cambridge: Cambridge University Press.

Blankett, A. e Trebilcock, A. (a cura di) (2015), *Research Handbook on Transnational Labor Law*, Glos: Edward Elgar Publishing.

Blanpain, R. (1979), *The OECD Guidelines Per Multinational Enterprises and Labor Relations*, Alphen aan den Rijn: Kluwer.

Blanpain, R. (2014), *Multinational Enterprises and Codes of Conduct: The OECD Guidelines for MNEs in Perspective*, in R. Blanpain (a cura di), *Comparative Labor Law and Industrial Relations in Industrialized Market Economies*, Alphen aan den Rijn: Kluwer Law International, pp. 195-221.

Ceruti, M. e Treu, T. (2010), *Organizzare l'altruismo. Globalizzazione e welfare*, Bari: Laterza.

Compa, L. (1993), Labor Rights and Labor Standards in International Trade, in *Law & Policy in International Business*, vol. 25, pp. 165-191.

Compa, L. (1998), The Multilateral Agreements on Investment (MAI) and International Labor Standards: A Failed Connection, in *Cornell International Law Journal*, vol. 31, pp. 683-712.

Compa, L. (2001), Workers' Freedom of Association in the United States under International Human Rights Standards, in *International Journal of Comparative Labour Law and Industrial Relations*, vol. 17, n. 3, pp. 289-308.

Compa, L. (2002), Pursing International Labor Rights in US Courts, New Uses for Old Tools, in *Industrial Relations*, vol. 57, n. 1, pp. 48-76.

Compa, L. (2015a), Labor Rights and Labor Standards in Transatlantic Trade and Investment Negotiations: A US Perspective, in *Economia & Lavoro*, vol. 49, n. 2, pp. 87-102.

Compa, L. (2015b), Labor Rights and Labor Standards in Transatlantic Trade Investment Negotiations: An American Perspective, in C. Scherrer (a cura di), *The Transatlantic Trade and Investment Partnership (TTIP): Implication for Labor*, 2014, Munchen-Merig: Rainer Hampp Verlag.

Compa, L., Vogt, J. (2003), Labor Rights in the Generalized System of Preferences: A 20 Year Review, in *Comparative Labor Law and Policy Journal*, vol. 22, pp. 199-238.

Ebert, F., Posthuma, A. (2011), *Labor Provisions in Trade Arrangements Current Trends and Perspectives*, International Institute for Labor Studies, Discussion Paper series.

European Parliament (2016), *TTIP and Jobs*, Directorate General for international policies, Policy Department.

Faioli, M. (2015), The Quest for a New Generation of Labor Chapter in the TTIP, in *Economia & Lavoro*, vol. 49.

Giubboni, S., Peruzzi, M. (2013), La contrattazione collettiva di livello europeo al tempo della crisi, in M. Carrieri, T. Treu (a cura di), *Verso nuove relazioni industriali*, Bologna: Il Mulino.

Hepple, B. (2003), *Diritto del lavoro, diseguaglianze e commercio globale*, in *DLRI*, nos. 3-4, pp. 341-372.

ILO, International Institute for Labor Studies (2013), *Social Dimension of Free Trade Agreements*, Geneva.

Marchesiello, M. (2016), L'arbitrato internazionale nelle dispute investitori-Stato: una nuova idea di giustizia o creazione di un suo mercato globale, in *Politica del diritto*, vol. 47, nos. 1-2, pp. 129-146.

OECD (1996), *Trade Employment and Labor Standards: A Story of Core Workers Rights and International Trade*.

Onida, F. (2009), Standard sociali e del lavoro nella rule of law internazionale, in G. Amato (a cura di), *Governare l'economia globale. Nella crisi e oltre la crisi*, Roma: Passigli.

Pantano, F., Salomone, R. (2008), *Trade and Labor within the European Union. Genaralized System of Preference*, J. Monnet working papers, New York University School of Law.

Perulli, A. (a cura di) (2013), *La responsabilità sociale dell'impresa: idee e prassi*, Bologna: Il Mulino.

Perulli, A. (2014), Fundamental Social Rights. Market Regulation and EU External Action, in *International Journal of Comparative Labour Law and Industrial Relations*, vol. 30, n. 1, pp. 27-47.

Perulli, A. (2015), *Commercio globale e diritti sociali. Novità e prospettive*, in *RGL*, n. 4.

Perulli, A. (2016), *Global Trade and Social Rights*, Changes and perspectives, International Society for Labor and Social Security Law, ISLSSL paper, nos. 4-5, in www.ISLSSL.org.

Prislan, V., Zandvliet, R. (2014), Mainstreaming Sustainable Development into International Investment Agreements: What Role for Labor Provisions?, in R. Hofmann, C. Tams, S. Schill (a cura di), *International Investment Law and Development*, Glos: Edward Elgar Publishing.

Rehfeldt, U. (2013), La posta in gioco nei canali multipli di rappresentanza. La contrattazione collettiva aziendale transnazionale, in M. Carrieri, T. Treu (a cura di), *Verso nuove relazioni industriali*, Bologna: Il Mulino.

Roccella, M., Treu, T. (2016), *Diritto del lavoro nell'Unione Europea*, Padova: CEDAM.

Rogowsky, N. (2005), *Socially Sensitive Enterprise Restructuring*, ILO Geneva.

Ruggie, J. (2003), The United Nations and Globalization. Patterns and Limits of Institutional Adaptation, in *Global Governance*, vol. 9, pp. 301-321.

Ruggie, J. (2013), *Just Business: Multinational Corporations and Human Rights*, New York: W.W. Norton & Company.

Schuler, R., Jackson, S.E., Tarique, I. (2007), Human Resource Management in Context, in R. Blanpain (a cura di), *Comparative Labour Law and Industrial Relations in Industrialized Market Economies*, Alphen aan den Rijn: Kluwer Law International, pp. 95–134.

Sciarra, S. (2009), *Transnational and European Ways Forward for Collective Bargaining*, Working papers Massimo D'Antona, n. 73.

Smit, P. (2016), The Future of Labor Law in a Globalized or Regionalized World, in *Bulletin of Comparative Labor Relations*, vol. 92, pp. 145–158.

Supiot, A. (2016), What International Justice in the Twenty-first Century?, in *Labor Law and Social Progress, Bulletin of Comparative Labor Relations*, n. 92, pp. 1–18.

Treu, T. (2007), Responsabilità sociale delle imprese: condizioni e forme di promozione, in A. Perulli (a cura di), *L'impresa responsabile*, Macerata: Halley.

Treu, T. (2016), *Labor Law and Sustainable Development*, Keynote Speech at the American Congress of the International Society for Labor and Social Security Law, Panama, in Working Papers M. D'Antona, n. 130/2.

Vogt, J.S. (2014), Trade and Investment Arrangements and Labor Rights, in L. Blecher, N.K. Stafford, G. Bellany (a cura di), *Corporate Responsibility for Human Rights Impact: New Expectations and Paradigms*, New York: ABA Book Publishing.

Wettstein, E. (2012), *CSR and the Debate on Business and Human Rights: Bridging the Great Divide*, Business Ethics Quarterly.

World Bank, *Doing Business, 2015, Going Beyond Efficiency*, Washington, DC: International Bank for Reconstruction and Development.

CHAPTER 7
The EU Generalised Scheme of Preferences and the Special Incentive Arrangement for Sustainable Development and Good Governance

Manfred Weiss

1 INTRODUCTION

The challenge for international labour law in the context of globalisation is the burning 'question of how global processes can be better regulated in order to deliver both economic growth and social justice embedded in the rule of law'.[1] This particularly means to find a fair balance between global trade and social standards. On the one side barriers to free trade have to be abolished, protectionist patterns are to be removed as far as possible. On the other hand, arrangements have to be established in order to make sure that free competition is not distorted by social dumping.

There are many attempts to promote this goal. A widespread strategy to combine free trade with respect for international labour standards are the social clauses inserted into free trade agreements, be they unilaterally imposed or the result of fair negotiations between different countries. Such social clauses in free trade agreements are also part of the European Union's (EU's) external policy since quite a long time.

But in addition to bilateral arrangements the EU (then the EEC) since 1995 has granted trade preferences to developing countries under its unilaterally

---
1. D. Held, Global Covenant: the Social Democratic Alternative to the Washington Consensus, Cambridge 2004, XV.

imposed scheme of generalised tariff preferences.² The basic idea of this scheme is to support developing countries in exporting their goods to the EU and thereby facilitate their integration into international markets.

The original scheme has often been amended. Since the beginning of the twenty-first century a 'carrot and stick'³ approach has been adopted by Council Regulation 250/2001 of December 2001.⁴ The carrot was the special incentive arrangement for the protection of labour rights. A beneficiary country requesting the tariff preferences had to show that national legislation incorporates the eight International Labour Organization (ILO) conventions on core labour standards and also had to show that it effectively implements these rules. The stick was the temporary withdrawal of the preferences in respect of all or of certain products originating in a beneficiary country. The temporary withdrawal not only was possible when these conventions were violated but also if products were made by slavery or by prison labour. This has remained to still be the basis of the present system.

2 THE LEGAL BASIS FOR THE PRESENT SYSTEM

The Treaty on the European Union (TEU) and the Treaty of the Functioning of the European Union (TFEU) not only contain a whole set of rules providing a legal basis for a scheme of preferences but also define the goals for such an arrangement.

According to Article 21 paragraph 1 TEU 'the Union's action on the international scene shall be guided by the principles which have inspired its own creation …'and according to paragraph 2 'the Union shall define and pursue common policies … in order to: (a) safeguard its values, fundamental interests … (b) consolidate and support democracy, the rule of law, human rights and principles of international law; (d) foster the sustainable economic, social and environmental development of developing countries, with the primary aim of eradicating poverty; (e) encourage the integration of all countries into the world economy, including through progressive abolition of restrictions on international trade and (h) promote an international system based on stronger multilateral cooperation and good global governance. Art. 21 EU has to be read together with Art. 3 TEU where the values of the EU are embedded. According to this article the EU In its relations with the wider world, the Union shall uphold and promote its values and interests … . It shall contribute to peace, security, the sustainable development of the Earth, … free and fair trade, eradication of poverty and the protection of human rights …' (paragraph 5). Since these articles refer to the values of the EU itself, it is evident that the fundamental

---

2. B. Hepple, Labour Laws and Global Trade, Oxford/Portland 2005, 102.
3. *Ibid.*
4. OJ 2001 L/346/1.

rights as embedded in the Charter of the Fundamental Rights for the EU also serve as a point of orientation.

The legal basis as contained in the TEU has to be linked to the TFEU where according to Article 208 TFEU 'Union policy in the field of development cooperation shall be conducted within the framework of the principles and objectives of the Union's external action … .

Union development cooperation policy shall have as its primary objective the reduction and, in the long term, the eradication of poverty … ' and according to Article 209 TFEU 'The EP and the Council … shall adopt measures necessary for the implementation of development-cooperation policy … .'

Based on this broad legal foundation and in line with its goals the scheme of generalised tariff preferences now is specified in Regulation No. 978/2012 of 25 October 2012.[5] It is in force since 1 January 2014.

3 THE DIFFERENT SCHEMES

The new Regulation significantly changes the number of countries addressed by the scheme. Before 176 beneficiaries were profiting from the tariff preferences. Now the focus is on ninety countries most in need. The idea is concentration instead of comprehensiveness to make sure that the scheme can be handled more effectively.

However, a closer look shows that countries which are no longer included are by no means left alone. Fifty-four countries profit from other arrangements as for example free trade agreements, covering about EUR 60 billion of imported goods in the EU. Another group of thirty-two countries stopped from benefiting from preferential access to the EU because these countries now are elevated into the group of high and upper middle-class income countries or overseas countries non-dependent on the EU. For them normal tariff for their exports is applied.

The Regulation distinguishes between three regimes: The general scheme of preferences (GSP), the special incentive arrangement for sustainable development (GSP+) and everything but the arms arrangement (EBA). GSP and GSP+ are in force for ten years, reviewed every three years, whereas EBA is open ended.

3.1 General Scheme of Preferences

This scheme is now regulated in Articles 4–8. The addressed developing countries profit of a significant reduction of tariff lines listed in an Annex to the regulation. Countries are only removed from the beneficiary lists if they become elevated to high or upper middle-class income countries three years in a row. It is important to stress that the European Parliament is involved in all changes affecting the GSP list of beneficiaries. Thereby democratic control is guaranteed.

---

5. OJ 2012 L 303/1.

As already indicated above: there is a trade-off for granting such preferences. The beneficiary countries have to abide to the principles laid down in United Nations (UN) / ILO conventions on core human and labour rights. These are the eight ILO conventions on core labour rights and seven UN conventions referring to the prevention and punishment of crime and genocide, to the elimination of all forms of racial discrimination, to civil and political rights, to the elimination of all forms of discrimination against women and to the rights of the child.

3.2 Special Incentive Arrangement for Sustainable Development (GSP+)

This scheme has been modified significantly by Articles 9–16 of the Regulation. It offers even deeper tariff cuts of the same tariff lines for vulnerable countries that ratified and implemented significant numbers of international conventions relating to human and labour rights, environment and good governance. The scheme now refers to twenty-seven international conventions, the seven UN conventions on human rights and the eight ILO conventions on core labour standards already covered by the GSP and in addition twelve further UN conventions, eight of them on environmental protection, the others on good governance, on the fight against corruption and on control of illegal drugs.

There are specific criteria to categorise a country has to meet to be vulnerable. The main preconditions are the facts that according to the import-share ratio the country is not competitive in the EU market and does not have a diversified export base.

According to these criteria of eligibility thirteen countries benefited from GSP+ preferences in 2014 and 2015: Armenia, Bolivia, Capo Verde, Ecuador, El Salvador, Georgia, Guatemala, Mongolia, Pakistan, Panama, Paraguay, Peru and Philippines. Five of them have now left the scheme: Costa Rica, El Salvador, Guatemala, Panama and Peru. They have concluded free trade agreements with the EU. This is considered to be a success and means progress for the respective countries.

3.3 Everything but Arms Arrangement

The third category of the scheme is contained in Articles 17–18 of the Regulation. It is a special arrangement for the least developed countries. They are granted full duty-free and quota-free access to the EU markets for all products except arms and ammunition. There is a special procedure in the context of the UN to identify the least developed countries. This list is continuously reviewed. These least developed countries are supposed to abide by the principles of the conventions covered by GSP.

4 SANCTIONS IN CASE OF VIOLATION

4.1 Temporary Withdrawal (Common to All Arrangements)

According to Articles 19–21 serious and systematic violation of the principles laid down in the mentioned conventions can be sanctioned by temporary withdrawal. The same is possible if goods made by prison labour are exported or if serious shortcomings in customs controls on the export and transit of drugs or failures to comply with international conventions on anti-terrorism and money laundering are observed. And it also applies if serious and systematic unfair trading practices which are prohibited or actionable under the World Trade Organization (WTO) agreements take place. Finally, serious and systematic infringement of the objectives adopted by Regional Fishery Organisations also can lead to temporary withdrawal of tariff preferences.

In order to find out whether there is a reason for temporary withdrawal, the beneficiary country has to communicate to the Commission in regular intervals and update the information necessary for the implementation of the rules of origin and the policing thereof. The country also has to assist the Union by carrying out the verification and carrying out or arranging for appropriate inquiries to identify or prevent contravention of the rules of origin. The Commission shall provide the beneficiary country concerned with every opportunity to cooperate during the monitoring and evaluation period. The information gained through this procedure is supplemented by additional information from local EU delegations, civil society, beneficiary authorities themselves, EU Parliament and EU Member States.

Preferential arrangements may be withdrawn temporarily in respect of all or of certain products originating in a beneficiary country. The temporary withdrawal shall not exceed six months.

It should be mentioned that so far the temporary withdrawal more or less has remained to be law in the books. Under the old regime it was applied only two times, namely first in the case of Myanmar which to a great extent was involved in the use of forced labour[6] and later on in 2010 against Sri Lanka which did not have a system of monitoring the observance of the conventions in a sustainable way.

4.2 Monitoring Mechanism for GPS+

There is a special monitoring mechanism for GSP+. It involves two interrelated tools: the so-called scorecard and the GSP+ dialogue.

---

6. See B. Hepple, *supra.*, 104.

4.2.1 'Scorecard'

The 'scorecard' means nothing else but an annual exchange of information on the beneficiaries' shortcomings. In order to evaluate possible violations the 'case law' developed by the monitoring bodies of the ILO and the UN is taken as a reference point for assessing whether the country has correctly implemented the principles contained in the conventions. This procedure is very interesting in view of the present debate on whether the case law of these bodies only has an internal or also an external effect.

4.2.2 'GSP+ Dialogue'

The GSP+ dialogue means a special engagement between EU and the beneficiary countries to support them to tackle their shortcomings and to discuss difficulties. The goal of this dialogue is to build a relationship based on trust and cooperation.

The first result of this dialogue is a joint report by the European Commission and the European External Action Service of 28 January 2016. It contains details of each country's progress and shortcomings in implementing the twenty-seven conventions. The report is a key part of the ongoing GSP+ monitoring process, a summary of how beneficiary countries have performed over the first monitoring period. Now the Member States and European Parliament's Committee on International Trade (INTA) are involved in screening the report. The monitoring takes place over two-year cycles in which the beneficiary countries must demonstrate a positive record of compliance.

5 GENERAL SAFEGUARDS

The general safeguards refer to all arrangements (Articles 22–28 of the Regulation). If a product originating in a beneficiary country is imported in volumes and/or prices which cause or threaten to cause serious difficulties to EU producers of like or competing products, normal Common Custom Tariff on that product may be introduced as long as necessary to counteract the deterioration.

Serious difficulties shall be considered to exist where Union producers suffer deterioration in their economic and/or financial situation. In order to make such an assessment specific factors are listed. These are market share, production, stocks, production capacity, insolvencies, profitability, capacity utilisation, employment, imports and prices.

An investigation is to be initiated upon request by a Member State, by any legal person or any association not having legal personality, acting on behalf of EU producers, or on the Commission's own initiative.

6 EVALUATION

All three schemes of the EU arrangement for tariff preferences are not the result of negotiations as free trade agreements normally are but a unilateral system. However, in comparison to other unilateral arrangements, as for example the United States of America's (USA) 'aggressive unilateralism', it is a rather 'soft unilateralism'[7] not primarily motivated by politics of protectionism but by the intention to provide developing countries access to the European market and combine free trade with protective standards, among them labour standards. The big difference to the system of the USA is the fact that the EU only requests obedience to conventions which were ratified by the EU Member States, whereas the USA refuses such ratification. This refusal, by the way, was now a big issue in the debates on a Transatlantic Trade and Investment Partnership (TTIP).

A remarkable feature of the generalised system of tariff preferences is the fact that in its monitoring system, again unlike the United States, it has established a clear link between the EU monitoring procedure and the 'case law' of the different monitoring bodies of the ILO and the UN. And unlike the USA the EU has to follow transparent and fair procedures before withdrawing or refusing preferences.

The generalised system of tariff preferences is understood to be a preliminary step. The goal is the conclusion of free trade agreements which are considered to be a progress since they are the result of negotiations.

Even if in principle a positive assessment of this arrangement can be made, it should not be ignored that in the very end it has its limits in blunt economic considerations. It only can work as long as it does not hurt the competitiveness of the EU economy. This is clearly demonstrated by the safeguard rules which are meant to protect the EU economy. This shows that protectionist considerations, even if they are not the dominant motif for the arrangement, nevertheless play a role.

---

7. *See also* B. Hepple, *supra.*, 105.

Part IV Investments, IMF, ISDS (Investor-State Dispute Settlement) Clauses and the Arbitral Procedures to Resolve a Conflict

CHAPTER 8

Social Rights and the Janus Face of International Investment: The Role of Commercial Banks and Project Finance

Sheldon Leader

This is an exploration of a particular strategy for regulating international investment in the light of the requirements of basic social rights. It is a strategy that aims to prevent investment from provoking serious social and environmental damage, intended to move societies along the path to sustainable development. At the same time, however, this is an investment technique that threatens to aggravate some of the same social damage it seeks to limit. It is, in short, a policy with two faces: one pointed towards and the other against the incorporation of human rights into investment decisions.

The strategy consists of lending principles to which many banks financing development projects have subscribed: the Equator Principles (EPs). We shall first examine the relevant parts of the strategy before then turning to its ambiguous legacy for social rights: a legacy that highlights the need for fundamental reform.

1 THE BASIC FRAMEWORK

1.1 What Are the EPs?

The *EPs* have their origin and function under the control of private financial institutions. They seek to provide banks, governments, and potentially affected populations with the assurance that the projects which are funded will respect basic social guarantees, many of which match the guarantees about development policy sought in the United Nations (UN's) sustainable development strategies. These principles have been adopted by more than eighty financial institutions in thirty-six countries worldwide covering over 70% of international Project Finance debt in emerging markets. They went into operation in 2003 and were revised in 2006 and again in 2013. They are modelled on equivalent project standards set by the International Finance Corporation (IFC), part of the World Bank. Group[1]

The EPs consist of requirements that borrowers satisfy the member lending institutions about their ability to assess and manage the following areas of concern:

Labor and Working Conditions; Resource Efficiency and Pollution Prevention; Community Health, Safety and Security; Land Acquisition and Involuntary Resettlement; Biodiversity Conservation and Sustainable Management of Living Natural Resources; Indigenous Peoples; Cultural Heritage[2]

The banks deploying these requirements are meant to assess the degree of risk that these standards will or will not be met for a project they are considering as an investment.

There are three categories of project specified:

Category A – Projects with potentially significant adverse environmental and social risks and/or impacts that are diverse, irreversible or unprecedented;
Category B – Projects with potentially limited adverse environmental and social risks and/or impacts that are few in number, generally site-specific, largely reversible and readily addressed through mitigation measures; and
Category C – Projects with minimal or no adverse environmental and social risks and/or impacts.

For all Category A and Category B Projects, the lender will require the client to conduct an assessment meant to address, to the lender's satisfaction, the relevant environmental and social risks and impacts of the proposed Project.[3]

1.2 The Discipline of Project Finance

The EPs developed initially, and still significantly, as a means of channelling the energies and ethics of lenders and borrowers of Project Finance (hereafter PF). PF is often attractive to the parties, and often controversial in the social climate

---

1. For the Equator Principles, *see* http://www.equator-principles.com For the performance standards set by the International Finance Corporation (IFC), part of the World Bank Group. http://www.ifc.org/wps/wcm/connect/Topics_Ext_Content/IFC_External_Corporate_Site/Sustainability-At-IFC/Policies-Standards/Performance-Standards.
2. *Ibid.*
3. *See* the EPs *supra* n. 2.

it encourages. How does it work?[4] Consider a corporate group consisting of a parent company and wholly owned subsidiaries. The group might wish to develop several projects simultaneously, each of which is independent of the other: each having its own financial profile and each promising a different prospect of success. At this point, the parent company might wish to limit its exposure arising from the failure of one or more of these projects. It can do this by allocating each project to a different wholly owned subsidiary, all of the subsidiaries being owned or de facto controlled by the parent. The subsidiary owns the assets that constitute the project, such as a dam or pipeline. The parent company in turn owns the shares of the subsidiary. At this point, a classic principle of corporate law – applied in many countries – can take hold. It separates the liability of a subsidiary for illegal activity from that of the parent.

This fragmentation of corporate liability provides fertile terrain for PF. It is a 'non-recourse' mode of finance. That is, the bank provides the loan directly to the subsidiary, not to the parent. What looks on the outside like a loan to e.g. Royal Dutch Shell or Vivendi Universal to finance a particular project, such as an oil pipeline or water installation, will often in fact be a loan to the subsidiary owning that project. That subsidiary is often called a Special Purpose Vehicle (SPV) signalling that its sole purpose is the development of the project which is the object of the loan. There is no recourse by the lender against the parent company in the event that the requirements of the loan are not met by the borrower.

This is a riskier proposition for the bank than is a loan to the parent, since the subsidiary is often kept at a low level of assets by regular transfers of those assets to the parent, particularly in less stable parts of the world. The bank will have as collateral only the assets of the subsidiary, which may well not be enough to cover the outstanding debt of a subsidiary that is in difficulty.

What does the bank do to compensate for these risks? It typically charges a higher rate of interest than it would for a more secure loan to the parent. In addition, it may well insist on stringent deadlines for loan repayment and hence will want to make sure that the construction of the project will proceed as quickly as possible so as to begin generating an income that will repay the loan.

2 EVALUATION

2.1 The Impact of PF on Social Rights and Sustainable Development

It is important to appreciate the positive and negative parts of this picture. It is here that we can see the Janus face of this significant species of international investment.

---

4. For more detail on the points made here *see* S. Leader, 'Project Finance and Human Rights' in Juan Pablo Bohoslavsky and Jernej Letnar Cernic (eds) *Making Sovereign Financing and Human Rights Work* (Hart, 2014).

Positive impacts: The needs for predictability of return on project investment may encourage a particularly careful calculation of environmental/social risks, given the impact these can have on steady cash flow. Where the lender has recourse against the project sponsor's assets, there can be less inducement to pay close attention to such factors. To focus attention onto the higher risks of non-recourse lending concentrates the minds of all who have risked assets in the loan, both for the lender and the borrower. The assessment of these risks is called for by the performance standards set by the EPs. These will call for social and environmental impact assessments, often in the hands of experts. Alongside these points, it is clear that there are some needs in development for poorer countries that would not be met were there not the security provided to parent companies by non-recourse PF investment.

Negative Impacts: On the other side, there is the possibility that risks of certain types of damage to local populations might be heightened by some of the pressures on project timing and performance, as well as techniques of risk management, in PF. This may be so, for example, when unrealistic completion deadlines for construction are set; stringent stabilization requirements freezing regulatory change are placed on host governments; or the possibility exists for project sponsors to abandon a project that is underperforming, allowing the SPV to collapse with potential loss to third parties. As an important study has shown, the concern for stability might even be intense enough remove an investor's enthusiasm for democracy in the country hosting the project in favor of the more predictable environment that a strong non-democratic form of government can provide.[5]

In this mix of positive and negative social impacts, where do basic social rights fit? Here we need to compare and contrast the human rights obligations of the state hosting a project in which there is an investment and the equivalent obligations of private investors operating within the same country under the EPs.

Host states for investment have obligations to respect, protect, and fulfil human rights of their populations, and these in turn have been woven into the guidelines for rights-based development: guidelines developed by the UN High Commissioner for Human Rights.[6] Alongside these state obligations, what are those of the commercial EP banks? The banks can come under an overlapping, but also diverging, set of obligations corresponding to the same rights. The difference between the two sets of duties is one of scope.

---

5. This is one possible explanation for the correlations between forms of government and the price of loans discussed in S. Leader and D. Ong, *Global Project Finance and Human Rights* (Cambridge University Press, 2011) Chapter 8. cf n. 17 *infra.*
6. For the UN's approach to rights-based development, *see* UN High Commissioner on Human Rights, Rights-based approaches, available at http://www.fes-globalization.org/geneva/GCSPF.htm (Accessed 10 August 2017).

This can be seen if we consider the example of the right of access to water.[7] Consider an investment in a pipeline project that uses water to such an extent that the supply to the local population falls below minimal standards set by international instruments. The host state could legitimately impose, in fulfilment of its obligation to protect this basic right, regulations requiring the pipeline not to block this access to water for the local population. If the private investor is an EP lender or borrower, they are not likely to find this regulation fundamentally objectionable. At that point, the obligations (if not the interests) of the investor and those of the host state converge: both aim at a portion of the guarantees involved in rights-based development.

Not only that, but were the host state to fail to enforce protection of this right in its own domestic rules, there would nevertheless be independent grounds on which the investor could be held responsible for the damage done to the water supply. It could, for example, be held to have broken a basic condition of its loan from an EP bank.

The same would be true were the project company to violate fundamental labour rights as defined in certain International Labour Organization (ILO) conventions. These are conventions which bind the host states, but also form part of the lending conditions set by the EP banks.[8] Both state and EP financed enterprises have a basic obligation to recognize ILO standards governing, for example, trade union rights and worker health and safety.

When we look closer, however, things appear to be somewhat different. Even though the private investor might acknowledge, at a general level, that it has to respect many of the same social rights that the state must respect, it may aim to determine their *content* and *weight* in a way that weakens their protective potential. It may do this in the name of respecting the principles of project finance. How might this clash of standards arise?

2.2 Risk to Basic Rights and Risk to Profit

The cost, timing, and other features of lending to a project under PF are themselves determined by principles of risk management. It is here that two agendas may clash: that of managing risk to the basic rights of those in society affected by a project, and that of managing risk to the objectives of those investing in a project. PF is potentially a locus for negotiation over both types of risk. However, too often the parties to the bargain are those focused on the commercial variables, while those representing civil society are left to pick up the pieces: reacting to features of a project that have been set between banks and

---

7. *See* 'Note: What Price for the Priceless? Implementing the Justiciability of the Right to Water', 120 Harv. L. Rev. 1067 (2007).
8. For example, ILO Conventions No. 182 on Worst Forms of Child Labour, No. 176 on Health and Safety in Mines, No. 167 on Health and Safety in Construction, or No. 154 on Collective Bargaining, available at http://www.ilo.org/ilolex/english/convdisp1.htm, last reviewed 3 March 2008.

corporate borrowers sometime before the project takes shape on the ground. Those concerned about the project's social effects may try to intervene in order to avoid the worst damage to their environments, health or allied interests, via insisting on their rights to be consulted before land is expropriated, or a potentially polluting measure is implemented. While the obligations to consult on these matters are formally part of the agenda that the Equator Banks set when they lend, the logic of risk management in PF can get in the way of giving these social obligations their proper weight.

2.3 Two Examples

Damage Avoidance versus Damage Compensation
When a project risks producing damage to the health and safety of workers or local populations, there are one of two courses of action to take: either to prepare to pay compensation to the injured as and when the company is found to have caused the damage, or to take measures that will permit the damage to be avoided in the first place. It seems to make ethical sense to prefer the avoidance solution over the compensation solution.

This is the view taken by the IFC. It says in its project standards that:

> The measures and actions to address identified impacts and risks will favor the avoidance and prevention of impacts over minimization, mitigation, or compensation, wherever technically and financially feasible.[9]

It is only when it is not feasible to do this, that the compensation option appears legitimate:

> Where risks and impacts cannot be avoided or prevented, mitigation measures and actions will be identified so that the project operates in compliance with applicable laws and regulations ... .[10]

The EPs echo this priority, saying in the Preamble that:

> We recognise the importance of climate change, biodiversity, and human rights, and believe negative impacts on project-affected ecosystems, communities, and the climate should be avoided where possible. If these impacts are unavoidable they should be minimised, mitigated, and/or offset.[11]

This is a clear commitment to a policy of avoidance of damage over compensation for that damage, where it is possible to choose between the two. It is important to have both in place for any project, and many project companies have substantial funds in their treasuries in the event that compensation proves

---

9. International Finance Corporation, Performance Standard 1: Social and Environmental Assessment and Management Systems, April 2006, paragraph 14, available at http://www.ifc.org/ifcext/enviro.nsf/AttachmentsByTitle/pol_PerformanceStandards2006_full/$FILE/IFC + Performance + Standards.pdf.
10. *Ibid.*
11. http://www.equator-principles.com/resources/equator_principles_III.pdf.

necessary. The avoidance of damage, however, calls for a different approach. It can save lives, not simply compensate for their loss. It may require slowing or stopping a project so as to make alterations that will guarantee worker safety. At this point, the choice between the two approaches calls for special attention to the social impact of PF. It may be a choice between allowing a risk to continue without abatement while standing ready to pay compensation, as opposed to taking the more substantial measures required to avoid the same damage.

Everything here turns on where we draw the line between what is or is not 'financially feasible', in accord with the IFC principle. It is here that PF can have a substantial negative impact. Recall that lenders under PF arrangements often demand tight development schedules so that the project can begin to generate income to pay back the loan. This is the only source of income that the banks can demand from the borrower under the non-recourse principle. The banks will therefore be inclined to declare that it is not financially feasible to delay the project in order to avoid the damage. Their critics, including those concerned to give social rights the scope and weight that they enjoy when dealing with the obligation of the state, are inclined to draw the line at what is and is not financially feasible in a way that comes closer to the state's obligation to avoid serious damage. The consequences of this PF policy for worker safety are significant.

Stabilization Requirements and Social Rights[12]

The EPs are rightly tested against their ambition to make bank lending a progressive force. That ambition has two levels of strength. One aims to move to societies that are able in a sustained way to enjoy economic growth while preventing well-recognized types of damage, such as various forms of discrimination, labour abuse, loss of livelihood or civil liberties. A second ambition that the host society might well have goes further: it is to fundamentally transform certain of its features. It might, for example, aim to nationalize certain key sectors of the economy or to introduce wide-ranging worker control of enterprises. While in principle there would be no obstacle to either types of change contained in the EPs per se, once they are placed alongside the financial discipline of project finance, the picture can change dramatically. We need to consider both types of social change and the PF investors' response.

2.3.1 *Social Change as a Transition to Sustained Prevention of Serious Social Damage*

Based on the author's experience and that of his colleagues on the Essex Business and Human Rights Project[13] there are several concrete issues that test

---

12. This portion of this chapter draws on the author's essay on the 'Equator Principles as Soft and Hard Law – Facilitators Of and Obstacles To Social Change', prepared for the University of Pretoria and due to appear in a volume edited by Prof. Danny Bradlow and Prof. David Hunter.
13. http://www.essex.ac.uk/ebhr/.

the robustness and equity of the Principles. These show that what the EPs give with the right hand of commitment to social responsibility is sometimes taken back with the left hand of commercial bank priorities and pressures. We can see this in several places.

2.3.1.1 No-Go for a Proposed Project

Implicit in the EPs is the need to draw a boundary line between projects that are viable, while risky, and those which are not viable because the risk is simply too great. The risk assessment called for can orient the investigation in two different directions. One is to treat the social and environmental requirements in the EPs as means to an end: preserving and possibly enhancing commercial return if they are respected or hurting the bottom line if they are not. The second approach treats the damage the EPs are concerned to avoid – such as harm to labor rights, or health and safety in the local community – as objectives distinct from commercial ones, and if the impact on the former is too severe it should be avoided by e.g. refusing to go ahead with the project despite an indisputable commercial gain to the borrower of carrying on.

Given that the weight assigned to the EPs is under the sole control of the relevant financial institutions, with no authoritative input from other stakeholders, there is little prospect of the second approach to risk having much of a hearing. As a result, certain notoriously high-risk projects are allowed to go through despite their heavy potential for damage – the banks hoping that the EP procedures for Category A projects will be enough to avoid the worst. It is only if stakeholder participation is widened that this might change. This would represent a 'hardening' of the EPs in the sense that they would be open to more systematic interpretation, no longer at the sole discretion of each lender, and could serve as the basis for empowering third parties to make the case for avoiding a project that poses too great a threat of social or environmental damage quite independently of the fact that it could earn a high profit.

2.3.1.2 Lack of Transparency

This is a further instance in which the left hand of lender practice takes back what the right hand of the EPs promise. The Principles now clearly require reporting on the Environmental and Social Impact Assessment carried out on the project. This is qualified by an exemption for client confidentiality requirements. The latter has led Non-governmental organizations (NGOs) to complain that certain banks '… hide behind excessive interpretations of "client confidentiality" to withhold information to stakeholders and the public.'[14]

---

14. Manuel Wörsdörfer, *10 Years 'Equator Principles': A Critical Economic-Ethical Analysis*, Osgoode CLPE Research Paper No. 54/2013.

2.3.1.3 *Competition among Banks Affecting the Categorization Process*

Given that it is up to each lender to decide whether the risk of damage produced by a given project is high, medium or low, a potential conflict arises between the competition among lenders to secure business at a lucrative rate and the aim of preventing social and environmental damage. This could lead some banks to rank the risk of damage among Categories A, B, and C lower than they otherwise would. Given that the EPs are under the sole control of individual lenders there is no countervailing voice that would challenge any given risk assessment.

2.3.2 *Social Change as Fundamental Transformation*

Here, we are dealing with changes in society that lead to fundamental alterations of priorities – and in the norms reflecting those priorities. As indicated earlier, these changes can be reflected in new forms of social control over certain types of property, as happens when a project is nationalized, or a changed profile of forms of democracy, leading to a stronger role for employees or local communities in making key decisions. To what extent can the strategy of international project finance help to promote such fundamental change? Here we find barriers. The obstacles emerge from a dominant concern that lenders have: stability. This is, of course, a feature of all lending. In the types of finance that is focused on by the EPs, however, the lender's anxiety is heightened by its reliance on the single stream of revenue from a given project. This leads, as indicated earlier, to support by the financial community for stringent stabilization clauses in legally enforceable contracts, whereby a host government promises the enterprise that it will not apply to its project any new law – though there are sometimes exceptions drawn around certain state initiatives depending on negotiations. If the host government goes ahead and applies new law, it will have to make up for lost revenue arising from the changes. This can include changes that the host government makes in accord with its own ongoing and evolving human and social rights requirements. The result is that workers in an industry in which there is PF investment might face weaker standards of protection than are enjoyed by their counterparts working on other projects that have not been covered by this stabilization requirement.

Furthermore, the undertaking to compensate investors for loss of revenue resulting from applying changed law can damage poorer countries, facing stretched resources already committed so as to bring about fundamental social change, such an undertaking can push the cost of such change too high for the national treasury to bear.[15] This can provoke costly battles, pitting host governments pushing ahead with a plan for change – often with the strong support from public opinion – against the lending community wanting the bill for such change

---

15. This is a problem that is receiving a large amount of critical attention. *See Human Rights on the Line, supra* n. 11.

to be paid along the way. The change might be abandoned, or if a government presses ahead while not paying the compensation due, it might find itself frozen out of future dealings with the international lending community. This might help explain the surprising finding by researchers that interest rates charged by international lenders tend to be higher the greater is a regime's commitment to democracy as part of its strategy for development.[16]

3 CONCLUSION

This has been an exploration of a potential path to sustainable development: one that is built on a fundamental tension. It is a tension arising from the fact that investment can contribute to the protection of values that make development 'sustainable' for a given society, while that potential might be undermined by the instruments for protection that lenders typically seek. These are protections that make sense in some situations, but not in others. The investor's search for an unchanging legal framework protecting its property makes sense when there are no basic social rights at stake in a given project, but it makes much less sense when the well-being of a population is at stake in the successful functioning of such a project. If investment is truly to serve the society which it purports to help develop – which the EPs aim to do – then connections must be forged between private lending and its social function. This social function will only be secure if public bodies play role in regulating this contribution from private sources: which can then become contributions to truly sustainable development.

---

16. Girardone and Snaith 'Project Finance Investments and Political Risk' in Leader and Ong (eds) *Global Project Finance, Human Rights, and Sustainable Development* (Cambridge University Press, 2011) p. 213.

CHAPTER 9
Stabilization Clauses in State-Investor Agreements: A Brief Overview

Vania Brino

1 FRAMING THE ISSUE

The controversial dilemma in order to the interdependencies between foreign direct investment and human rights poses new tensions and challenges for states, companies, communities and human beings.[1]

Adopting a historical point of view, it emerges that 'the links between human rights and international investments have, over the past decade, evolved from being a niche subject of the human rights community to dominating international investment negotiations and making headline news'.[2] Consequentlythe legal regime of foreign investment has also gained new relevance in the eyes of scholars specialized in human rights.

---

1. On that issue the literature is enormous. *See* among others De Schutter O., Swinnen J., Wouters J. (edited by), *Foreign Direct Investment and Human Development – the Law and Economics of International Investment Agreements*, Routledge, 2013; Leader S., *Human Rights, Risks, and New Strategies for Global Investment*(2006) 9 Journal of International Economic Law 657–705; Leader S., *The Place of Labour Rights in Foreign Direct Investment*, in A. Morris and S. Estreicher (edited by), *Global Labor and Employment Law for the Practicing Lawyer*, Kluwer, 2010; Wouters J., Hachez N., *When Rules and Values Collide: How Can a Balanced Application of Investor Protection Provisions and Human Rights Be Ensured?*(2009) 3 Human Rights & International Legal Discourse, 2, 316; Sornarajah M., The International Law on Foreign Investment, Cambridge University Press, 2010, 293; Jacobs M., *International Investment Agreements and Human Rights*, INEF Research Paper Series, 3, 2010; Francioni F., Petersmann E.U., Dupuy P.-M. (edited by), *Human Rights in International Investment Law and Arbitration*, Oxford University Press, 2009.
2. Report 'Principles for Responsible Contracts: Integrating the Management of Human Rights Risks into State-Investor Contract Negotiations: Guidance for Negotiators Addendum 3 to

The complex question posed above could be inserted within 'an increasingly privatized conception of the political economy'[3] as a result of which 'foreign investment agreements seem to encompass the idea that the states' policy choices on the environment, work, development, etc., cannot compromise with that goal'.[4] In that framework 'the dynamics of foreign investment recognizes companies as a veto player'[5] in the sense that businesses can condition the political choices of the host state that conflict with their interests.

On the background there is a dangerous trade-off for countries: rather than the arrival of foreign direct investments creating winners as well as losers, countries should decide how to 'reconcile the participation of local communities in determining the conditions according to which investment should be allowed to proceed with other values'.[6] As it will be seen this trade-off is particularly difficult for developing countries due to their weakness at economic but also at juridical level.

So the key issue regards, in particular, the risks for human rights, includinglabour rights,[7] where investment agreements are alleged to restrict the ability of States to fulfil their obligations in such fundamental field. This critical point is strictly linked to the fact that 'host government agreements and stabilization clauses are largely developed in isolation from states' obligations relative to human rights'.[8]

Empirical evidences recognized this problem but at the same time, as it will be seen below, the recent trends show a sort of reaction by governments and international organizations with the purpose to 'balance' investor's interest with public needs and human rights.

If this is the core of an ongoing debate and the scenario of the investigation, the analysis should move within a nuance territory characterized by light and shadow.[9] The study intends to analyse only one part of that more complex picture such as the stabilization clauses in State-Investor Agreements governing

---

the Report,' A/HRC/17/31/Add.3, 2011, 4, http://www.ohchr.org/Documents/Publications/Principles_ResponsibleContracts_HR_PUB_15_1_EN.pdf.
3. Ferrarese M.R., Sulla governance paragiudiziaria. Arbitrati investimenti esteri, in Pol. Dir., n.3, 2014, 394.
4. *Ibid.*, 400.
5. *Ibid.*, 394.
6. *See* De Schutter O. et. Al., *Id.*, 179.
7. Leader S., *The Place of Labour Rights*, *Id.*, 1, who proposed a reflection on the labour rights through the prism of investment instruments. In particular the author questions on what is the relative weight of worker rights – ranging from trade union through to non- discrimination entitlements – as they compete with other interests and rights that investment norms aim to protect.
8. Shemberg A., Stabilization Clauses and Human Rights. A research project conducted for IFC and the United Nations Special Representative of the Secretary-General on Business and Human Rights, Consultation Summary, 2008, Annex 1, 3, http://www.ifc.org/wps/wcm/connect/9feb5b00488555eab8c4fa6a6515bb18/Stabilization%2BPaper.pdf?MOD=AJPERES.
9. Leader S., Human Rights, Risks, and New Strategies for Global Investment, *Id.*

foreign direct investment. The Bilateral and International Investment Treaties stipulated by States are out of the scope of the article.

However, it is evident that all these kind of tools could have strong implications on the social matter, especially in terms of restraint of the regulatory powers of governments. As scholars said the clauses contained in such agreements or treaties could prevent states from pursuing their economic and social policies, and even have a 'chilling effect'[10] due to the exposure to claims of breach of contract, especially before arbitral tribunals.[11] If we take the example of a host state which wants improve the working conditions it is evident that 'the prospect of having to pay the bill for imposing a strengthening of employee rights has the potential to deter a host state from implementing such a change'.[12]

In the same critical perspective the *ETUC Resolution on EU Investment Policy*, adopted at the Executive Committee meeting of 5–6 March 2013, states that 'investment treaties should not contain clauses which import investors' contractual rights into the treaties, giving it far stronger protection. A common issue arising in this context is a contractual stabilisation clause, which attempts to insulate investors from changes in law or governmental decisions taken after the effective date of the agreement. Of course, EU investment policy should never itself include a stabilisation clause'.

Finally, as last point of this brief introduction, it could be stressed that the increasing number of State-Investor Agreements reflects a 'diversification process' that involves both states and businesses. The first one became more and more 'contracting parties'[13] in order to attract capital while enterprises became important regulatory agent able to create rules and to influence the evolution of national juridical regimes.[14] The issue is strictly linked with the multiplication of

---

10. Tienhaara K., *Regulatory Chill and the Threat of Arbitration: A View from Political Science*, in Ch. Brown, K. Miles (edited by), *Evolution in Investment Treaty Law*, Cambridge University Press, 2011, 606.
11. Gazzini T., *Beware of Freezing Clauses in International Investment Agreements*, Columbia FI Perspectives, N.191, 16 January 2017, 1. In the spatial limit of this study the author cannot go more in detail on the arbitration case law concerning the interpretation and the enforcement of stabilization clauses. Normally stabilization clauses are enforced by international arbitration rather than national courts. Doing so the contract is internationalized in the sense that 'business tend to assure that states won't affect the process and outcome of dispute settlement through their own judicial system', *United Nations Global Compact, the Human Rights and Business Dilemmas Forum, Dilemmas and Case studies: Stabilization Clauses*, https://hrbdf.org/dilemmas/stabilization-clauses/#.Wf7i-IjSI2w. As observed in the Study just mentioned 'there are only a few known examples of arbitral awards on stabilization clauses in international investment agreements' also because 'the more flexible – "economic equilibrium", "balancing" or "adaptation" clauses have not yet been the subject of review by arbitral tribunals'.
12. Leader S., *The Place of Labour Rights*, supra n.7.
13. Ferrarese M.R., Le organizzazioni internazionali e gli stati 'contraenti, in Rassegna italiana di Sociologia, n.2, 2003, 197.
14. Cafaggi F. (edited by), *Transnational Private Regulation*, Edward Elgar, 331; *see also* Ferrarese M.R., Transnational private regulation con atri mezzi. Arbitrati, investimenti

regulatory agents combined with a process of privatization of law in the global scenario.[15]

2 THE INCREASING ROLE OF MULTINATIONAL ENTERPRISES IN THE RULE MAKING PROCESS AT GLOBAL LEVEL

As scholars said transnational corporate networks pose a regulatory challenge to the international legal systems.[16] Corporations are the cardinal actors in the global scenario not only according to an economic perspective but also adopting a juridical viewpoint. It is enough to mention, just to do some examples, the strong regulatory power assumed by corporation thanks to the so-called soft law instruments (such as code of conducts or the other Corporate social responsibility tools).

As we know multinational enterprises have been described as 'an economic entity operating in more than one country or as a group of economic entities operating in two or more countries, independently from their juridical form, both in the origin country and the country where the activity actually takes place, and whether they are individually or collectively considered'.[17]

The juridical literature identified multinational enterprise as a group composed of several entities that are juridically distinguished but economically linked to each other. In most cases, the group of enterprises' nationality is the same to the one related to the leading firm (usually in developed countries) and it is operational through some linked subsidiaries, located in a plurality of States mainly individuated on the basis of the economic convenience (which results in lower labour and raw material costs, in fiscal benefits, lower obligations from the environmental point of view, etc.)

Therefore, the enterprise is presented as internationalized in its field of action, but conditioned to the compliance with the different juridical regimes of the countries where it carries out its activity. There is, in this sense, a gap between the transnational dimension of its business, in view of the functional

---

esteri e lotte sulla regulation, in F. Cafaggi (edited by), Regolazione transnazionale e trasformazioni dello stato, Bologna: Il Mulino, 2016.
15. Arato J., *Corporations as Lawmakers*, in *Harvard International Law Journal*, 2015, Volume 56, n.2; Kolben K., *Integrative Linkage: Combining Public and Private Regulatory Approaches in the Design of Trade and Labour Regimes*, in *Harvard International Law Journal*, 2007, 48, 203; Robè J.P., A. Lyon-Caen, Vernac S (edited by), *Multinationals and the constitutionalization of the world power system*, Routledge, 2016; Martin J., Bravo K.E., *The Business and Human Rights Landscape: Moving Forward, Looking Back*, 2017, Cambridge University Press.
16. Ruggie J., Business and Human Rights: The evolving international agenda, Corporate Social Responsibility Initiative, Working Paper n.31, 2007, 7.
17. *See*, in this sense, what is provided for the 'Norms on the Responsibilities of Trans-national Enterprises and other Enterprises with regards to Human Rights', UN Docs, E/CN. 4/Sub. 2/2003/12/Rev. 2 (2003), paragraph 20, http://hrlibrary.umn.edu/links/res2003-16.html.

integration between segments of the productive process distributed at global level, and the national dimension of the applicable norms.

Starting from the early 1970s, the paths of internationalization of enterprises were already mainly characterized by strategies of exploitation of advantages deriving from the production in areas where the normative systems were particularly weak or underdeveloped. The processes of liberalization of the markets and the pressure of international markets have then further intensified the attempts of enterprises to free themselves from the normative regimes of the States also through the adoption of opportunistic and non-transparent behaviours to the detriment of any consideration related to values.

If the multinational has acquired an undeniable ability of controlling the global market, States, on the contrary, have lost power, being able to intervene only in one fragment of the space where economic actors operate and, in most cases, resulting themselves as accomplices of entrepreneurial initiatives. In other terms, multinationals make use of their status of stateless enterprises in order to exploit the gaps of the law and the governments' weakness. There is on this issue a sort of *mismatch* between the modern forms of violation of human and labour rights carried out by *corporations*, and the regulative instruments of the past to limit the deviations of *free trade*.

The crisis of juridical systems, which is particularly explained in the inability to carry out efficient measures of control of the entrepreneurial behaviours has highlighted the centrality of the matter related to regulation at global level as well as the problems raised by the domination of economic rationality over the issues of social justice.

At the same time, and sometimes as a substitute of the typical regulative agent that becomes inactive and/or accomplice, we have the economic actor that, differently, becomes the protagonist of the scene. Above all two issues are really interesting in our perspective.

First of all economic freedoms and markets are the point of reference for enterprises and states which are increasingly crushed under the weight of deregulatory competition. Enterprises run their business in the most convenient areas of the world while States are forced to compete sharply to attract foreign investors by acting in particular on regulatory frameworks. The increase of Export Processing Zones is a good example to describe this phenomenon.

Second, it is actually within the normative gaps, utilized as vectors of the notorious processes of outsourcing and internationalization of economic activities, that new mechanisms of regulation have gained prominence and cannot surely be considered as secondary. Multinational enterprises become a key regulatory actor able not only to choose the most favourable law but also to define the rules useful for their business. As we said before codes of conduit or other corporate social responsibility tools could highlight this trend. But in this light we could also interpret the State-Investor Agreements, especially if they contain stabilization clauses. In other terms, we could identify multiple ways in which corporations influence laws and public policy and institutions to advance their private interests over the protection of human rights.[18]

3 STABILIZATION CLAUSES: MEANING AND PROBLEMS

The State-Investor Contract could be described 'as a contract made between the state, or an entity of the state, which for present purposes, may be defined as anyorganisation created by statute within a state that is given control over an economic activity, and a foreign national or a legal person of foreign nationality'.[19] Such contract 'can cover a wide range of issues, including loan agreements, purchase contracts for suppliers or services, contracts of employment or large infrastructure projects'.[20]

If in the past the enterprises were worried about the risk of expropriations after the signature of the contract with host state,[21] more recently the question is strictly linked to the so-calledindirect expropriations such as the possibility that new laws reduce the value of investment or compromise the economic interest of investor. Enterprises could protect their interests through several actions. If there is a Bilateral Investment Treaty between the host state and the enterprise's home state companies may invoke its content to receive a compensation through the Investor-State Dispute Settlement.[22] But companies could also insert a stabilization clause in the agreement with the host state to reduce that risk due to changes in law.

Briefly, stabilization clauses 'protect foreign investors against subsequent unilateral action by host countries in the form of total or partial exemption from regulations enacted during the term of a contract'.[23] The aim is to ensure a

---

18. *See* Amnesty International, Injustice Incorporated. Corporate Abuses and the Human Right to Remedy, 2014, https://www.amnesty.org/en/documents/pol30/001/2014/en/ according to which 'the multiple ways in which corporations unduly influence laws and public policy and institutions to advance their private interests over the protection of human rights, is often referred to as "corporate capture"', 173.
19. UNCTAD, 'State Contracts', UNCTAD Series on Issues in International Investment Agreements, United Nations, New York and Geneva, 2004.
20. UNCTAD, 'State Contracts', UNCTAD Series on Issues in International Investment Agreements, United Nations, New York and Geneva, 2004.
21. Cotula L.,Regulatory Takings, Stabilization Clauses and Sustainable Development, OECD Global Forum on International Investment, 2008.
22. As examples we could mention the case of French multinational Veolia which is currently attempting to sue the Egyptian government, among other things, over recent increases in the minimum wage. And earlier in June 2012, Vattenfall filed a case against the German government for restricting the use of nuclear power. In this way, multinational companies are using investor protection rules and investor-state dispute settlement as a means of achieving corporate aims, increasing the cost to the taxpayer of defending public policy and rules. *See* ETUC Resolution on EU Investment Policy, 2013. *See also* Cagnin V., *New Generations Treaties and the Attempts for a Renewal of the Investor State Dispute Settlement (ISDS)*, in this book.
23. Gazzini T., Beware of Freezing Clauses in International Investment Agreements, *id.*, 1.

degree of legal predictability and security for the investments in the host countries. In this perspective 'the state undertakes not to apply *any* new legal regulation to a project, whatever the degree of its impact, without the consent of the company that is party to the contract. If this provision is violated, then compensation to the company for the higher costs resulting from the change is required'.[24]

The debate on stabilization clauses is rather new if we consider the literature specialized in human rights[25] but the increasing number of foreign investment agreements in the last years has imposed new reflections at political and juridical level due to the potential negative implications of these clauses in the social field.

The key point regards the fact that 'the protection of investors' rights in investment contracts and agreements by insulating them from new regulations is not being balanced with companies' responsibility to respect human rights'.[26] For contract negotiators, these clauses create some perplexing questions based on unclear allocation of transaction's risk between an investor and a host state.

Moreover the problem of stabilization clauses consists on a 'trade off between the need of developing countries for capital, which leads to a willingness to make such commitments to investors, and the policy autonomy that such governments would prefer in order to implement the social and environmental and other regulatory measures that respond to the needs of their citizens over time'.[27] To sum up the critical question regards the effects of stabilization clauses in the area of government lawmaking power, especially if we consider the social policy finalized to guarantee human rights.

3.1 Stabilization Clauses: Aims, Effects and Models

When we discuss of stabilization clauses we have to face with a heterogeneous category of provisions with several peculiarities.

First, focusing on the aims of these clauses, they vary according to the viewpoint adopted.

If we take the part of the investor, stabilization clauses could be important tools to mitigate the risk especially due to the internal instability of the host country. The investments in developing countries could be really at risk for business. In fact 'developing-country governments are perceived by investors as

---

24. Leader S., *The Place of Labour Rights*, id., 4.
25. The issue has become well known to human rights and labour lawyers since the famous case of BP Oil Company (2003). *See* in particular the study elaborated by John Ruggie and the International Financial Corporation (IFC) of the World Bank in 2008 which represents the first empirical research on stabilization clauses.
26. Office of the High Commissioner for Human Rights (OHCHR), *Resolution in Human Rights, Trade and Investment*, E/CN.4/SUB.2/RES/2002/11.
27. Howse R., *Freezing Government Policy: Stabilization Clauses in Investment Contracts* (2011) 1 Investment Treaty News, 3.

more likely to change laws unexpectedly, to impose unforeseen regulatory changes, to breach contracts or even to expropriate property and offer inadequate compensation'.[28] In other words stabilization clauses are used 'to deal with the risk of arbitrary or discriminatory legislation against the investor, nationalization, or expropriation, but they also are likely to guard against physical or creeping expropriation by the host state'.[29] Moreover they could be used to avoid costs related to a national policy which, for instance, could improve social or environmental rights in the host state.

Instead, if we adopt the host state's viewpoint stabilization clauses could create a friendly investment terrain for the foreign investors. In other words they could represent a 'favourable investment climate' or 'red carpet' provision that host states lay out for foreign investors'.[30]

But, at the same time, these clauses limit the application of new laws in the host country and consequently they compromise the regulatory power of states. They also hinder the State's ability to fulfil their duty under international law adversely affecting the development of protection of human rights. As Leader observed it emerges a potential tension with the commitments made by a host state to conform to international standards and their evolution.[31]

Second, stabilization's clause impact could vary according to the legal, economic and political context of the state partner. Many experiences point out that the problems occur especially when developing countries are involved. There are several reasons to explain that. The negotiating power of host states may be weaker than that of investors. Moreover the human rights framework is usually not so developed in these countries. Finally, as we said before, the host states want to be attractive for enterprises to receive investments and to achieve this aim state could maintain a very low normative level.

According to the Report by Ruggie and International Finance Corporation (IFC) there is a strong difference between Organisation of Economic Cooperation and Development (OECD) and Non-OECD countries in the implementation of these clauses. It also depends on the fact that the nature of stabilization clauses contained in the investment contracts with OECD member countries are much more balanced compares with these stipulated by Non-OECD countries due to the uncertaintywhich characterized the developing countries' political and juridical systems.

As observed before these clauses influence the national regulatory sovereignty and the state's autonomy to decide whethertomodify or not the normative

---

28. United Nations Global Compact, the Human Rights and Business Dilemmas Forum, Dilemmas and Case studies: Stabilization Clauses, https://hrbdf.org/dilemmas/stabilization-clauses/#.Wf7i-IjSI2w.
29. Schemberg A., Stabilization Clauses and Human Rights, *id. See also* De Schutter O. et. Al., Foreign Direct Investment and Human Development, *Id.*
30. *Ibid.*, 5.
31. Leader S., *The Place of Labour Rights*, supra n. 7.

internal system. Even if the international case law largely supports the propositions that 'stabilisation clauses are lawful and legally binding under international law and parties treat stabilisation clauses as binding',[32] the question is still open.

Mainly the controversial issue regards the variety of clauses (*see* below) and the possibility of compressing the state's obligations on human rights based on national and international legal sources.

On one side stabilization clauses are emphasized as vector of stability for the contractual relations. On the other side the stability is important but it couldn't justify a limitation of human rights obligations of states.[33] In this perspective 'it may be suggested that whenever a stabilization clause conflicts with fundamental human rights obligations it can be considered as null and void as fundamental human rights trump all the other corporate and state obligations'.[34] In the same perspective we could mention the arbitral decision Libyan American Oil Company (LIAMCO) which 'confirmed the principle of State sovereignty, stating that it is impossible to prevent a State to change the law despite contractual provisions such as freezing clauses'.[35] But 'if the freezing clause is considered as valid in a contract, the State would be responsible for a breach of contract before a court and thus the private party may claim for compensation on the legal grounds of real damages and loss of profits'.[36]

Thirdly, the stabilization clauses could vary according the models adopted. As suggested by literature we could identify three models.[37]

The first one, named 'freezing clause', is 'designed to make new laws inapplicable to the investment' so it freezes 'the law of the host state with the respect to the investment project'.[38] As defined in the *Amoco v. Iran case* this clause freezes 'the provisions of a national system of law chosen as the law of the

---

32. Halabi S., *Efficient Contracting Between Foreign Investors and Host States: Evidence from Stabilization Clauses*, (2011) 31 *Northwestern Journal of International Law & Business* 261 (2011), 31.
33. Černič J. L., *Corporate Human Rights Obligations under Stabilization Clauses*, in *German Law Journal*, 2010, 215. See also U.N. High Commissioner for Human Rights, Report on Human Rights, Trade, Investment, E/CN.4/Sub.2/2003/9, 2 July 2003, paragraph 24. See also Shemberg A., *id.* paragraphs 34–37 available at:http://www.ifc.org/ifcext/sustainability.nsf/AttachmentsByTitle/p_StabilizationClausesandHumanRights/$FILE/Stabilization+Paper.pdf.
34. Černič J.L., Corporate Human Rights Obligations under Stabilization Clauses International Law Association, *ID*.
35. *Libyan American Oil Company (LIAMCO) v. The Libyan Arab Republic*, 1977, https://www.biicl.org/files/3939_1977_liamco_v_libya.pdf https://www.biicl.org/files/3939_1977_liamco_v_libya.pdf.
36. Marco C., Berthier C., Bihr C., Lagrange M., *Applicable Law to a Contract: What Happens When the Law Changes?*, 2015.
37. Sheppard A., Crockett A., *Are Stabilization Clauses a Threat to Sustainable Development?*, in Segger Cordonier M. et al., (edited by),*Sustainable Development in World Investment Law*, Kluwer, 2010, 333–350.
38. Schemberg A., *id.*, 5.

contract as of the date of the contract, in order to prevent the application to the contract of any future alterations of this system'.[39]

The 'full freezing clause' is the most controversial because the state couldn't introduce new rules in all fields (social, fiscal, political, etc.) while in case of 'limited freezing clause' the investor is protected only from a restrict set of legislative actions. An example of a freezing clause would be Syria's model production contract, which states that 'Contractor and Operating Company shall be subject to all laws and regulations of local application in force in the S.A.R. provided that no laws, regulations or modifications thereof shall be contrary to or inconsistent with the provisions of this Contract.'[40]

This type of clause was widespread in the past while nowadays it is present especially in the contracts from Sub-Saharan Africa, the Middle East and North Africa, and Eastern, Southern Europe and Central Asia Regions.[41] It is also important to stress that some states exclude the legitimacy of such clause (common law states as United Kingdom (UK), some Middle Eastern States)[42] while in other cases the clause is not considered applicable to human rights field.

The second one, so-calledeconomic equilibrium clause, aims to maintain the economic equilibrium of the investment and guarantee the business interests. To realize that it states a compensation for enterprise for any additional costs due to the introduction of a new law.Also this type of statement could be full or limited as the case of freezing clause.

An example could be the provision contained in the 1997 Model Production Sharing Agreement for Petroleum Exploration and Production in Turkmenistan according to which 'where present or future laws or regulations of Turkmenistan or any requirements imposed on Contractor or its subcontractors by any Turkmen authorities contain any provisions not expressly provided for under this Agreement and the implementation of which adversely affects Contractor's net economic benefits hereunder, the Parties shall introduce the necessary amendments to this Agreement to ensure that Contractor obtains the economic results anticipated under the terms and conditions of this Agreement'.[43]

Finally, it could be the case of 'hybrid clause' which 'share some aspects of both of the other categories and require the state to restore the investor to the

---

39. *Amoco International Finance Corporations v. The Government of Islamic Republic of Iran*, et al., Partial Award No. 310-56-3, 14 July 1987, reprinted in 15 Iran-US CTR at paragraph 239.
40. Article 18.1, Syria's model production sharing contract from the late 1980s.
41. Shemberg A., *id*, 19.
42. *See* Walde T., George N., Stabilizing International Investment Commitments: International Law Versus Contract Interpretation, 31 Texas International Law Journal, 215, 236.
43. Model Production Sharing Agreement for Petroleum Exploration and Production in Turkmenistan 1997, Article 16.1, available at faolex.fao.org/docs/texts/tuk81989e.doc.

same position it was in prior to any changes in law – including by exemption from new laws'.[44]

4 WHAT ABOUT THE TRENDS FOR THE FUTURE?

If the aim of stabilization clauses is the mitigation of the risks for enterprises at the same time it is also important to recognize that these clauses should not compromise the improvement of social standards and the social development of the countries.

What kind of model investment agreement should be introduced to affirm the investor interest without compromising the fundamental human rights? How is it possible to promote a responsible contracting as feature through which investor rebalances a purely commercial vision recognizing their impacts on communities and on the environment?

On that profile the doctrine observes a positive evolution both at institutional and enterprise level due to thanks to a general consensus in order to the need to improve the deficient investment contracts[45]. Otherwise, it emerges the need to balance the investors' rights and their 'legitimate expectation' to protect their interests with the investor's obligations in the human rights context and with the state's right to improve their internal policy.

This new 'sound' is particularly evident if we consider the *'Principles for Responsible Contracts: Integrating the Management of Human Rights Risks into State-Investor Contract Negotiations: Guidance for Negotiators'*[46] according to which investment contracts are an important instrument through which States and business enterprises could affect the human rights impact of business activities and investments. It stressed the need 'to find ways to ensure that investor protection recognizes and reinforces both the State's duty to protect human rights and the corporate responsibility to respect human rights'.[47]

The *Principles for Responsible Contracts* should be read in conjunction with the *UN Guidelines Principles on Business and Human Rights* (which emphasize the effort to combine economic interests with human rights) and with the State's obligations set out in international human rights law.

We could mention also the document *'A Turn to Responsible Contracting: Harnessing Human Rights Transform Investment. E15 Initiative'* produced by Office of the High Commissioner for Human Rights (OHCHR) in 2016 which

---

44. United Nations Global Compact, the Human Rights and Business Dilemmas Forum, Dilemmas and Case studies: Stabilization Clauses, https://hrbdf.org/dilemmas/stabilization-clauses/#.Wf7i-IjSI2w.
45. Office of the High Commissioner for Human Rights (OHCHR), *A Turn to Responsible Contracting: Harnessing Human Rights to Transform Investment. E15 Initiative*, Geneva: International Centre for Trade and Sustainable Development (ICTSD) and World Economic Forum, 2015. www.e15initiative.org, 8.
46. Id.
47. Id.

contains a strategic analysis and recommendations for government, business, and civil society geared towards strengthening the global trade and investment system for sustainable development.[48]

Of course the debate is still open in order to the actions necessary to realize this 'new generation on investment policies'.[49]

According to someone the Investment-State Agreements – but generally speaking also International or Bilateral Investment Treaties – should refer to fundamental human rights obligations and international standards.[50] In this lightthe *European Network on Debt and Development* introduced a *Responsible Finance Charter*[51] which recognized, above all, the duty to apply and interpret the agreement complaining withnational and international law, including human rights treaties.

The recognition of human rights obligations should regard not only states but also companies. As observed by the UN Human Rights Council 'the responsibility to respect human rights is the baseline norm for all companies in all situations'.[52]

One other useful action could be to design a sort of standardized model of clauses mainly addressed to balance all the interests involved in the agreements. A good example could be the stabilization clause which cannot apply to human rights legislation as in the case of Production Sharing Agreements between Tullow Oil and the Uganda Government[53] or in the case of 'Human Rights Undertaking' of the Baku-Tbilisi-Ceyhan pipeline consortium.[54]

The first one was renegotiated by providing that government is free to modify social and environmental legislation without paying compensation. The second one states that the consortium 'shall not seek compensation under the

---

48. *See* in this perspective Mann H., Foreign Investment Contracts and Sustainable Development: The New Foundations Begin to Emerge, in Investment Treaty News, 2011.
49. UNCTAD, World Investment Report 2012: *Toward a New Generation on Investment Policies*, http://unctad.org/en/PublicationsLibrary/wir2012_embargoed_en.pdf. *See also* the *World Investment Report 2016* according to which the investment policies should be based on the paradigm of sustainable development.
50. *See* Cotula L., *Reconciling Regulatory Stability and Evolution of Environmental Standards in Investment Contracts: Towards a Rethink of Stabilization Clauses* (2008) 1 Journal of World Energy Law & Business 2, 158–179.
51. http://eurodad.org/files/const/responsible_finance.pdf.
52. U.N. Human Rights Council [HRC], Promotion and Protection of All Human Rights, Civil, Political, Economic, Social and Cultural Rights, Including the Right to Development: Protect, Respect and Remedy: A Framework for Business and Human Rights, U.N. Doc. A/HRC/11/13/, 22 April 2009. paragraph 46.
53. Agreement drafted in 2010 and then renegotiated in 2011, http://www.tullowoil.com/media/press-releases/government-of-uganda-and-tullow-sign-production-sharing-agreements.
54. *Human Rights Undertaking*, 22 September 2003, http://subsites.bp.com/caspian/Human%20Rights%20Undertaking.pdf. *See* the Report elaborated by Amnesty International UK, Human Rights on the Line: The Baku-Tbilisi-Ceyhan Pipeline Project, 2003, http://www.amnesty.org.uk/images/ul/H/Human_Rights_on_the_Line.pdf. *See also* the analysis in Schemberg A., *Id.*, 1.

"economic equilibrium" clause or other similar provision (...) in such manner as to preclude any action or inaction by the relevant Host Government that is reasonably required to fulfil the obligations of that Host Government under any international treaty on human rights (including the European Convention on Human Rights), labor or HSE (health, safety, environment) in force in the relevant Project State from time to time to which such Project State is then a party'.[55]

On this point the Principle 4 contained in *the Principles for Responsible Contracts* (*see* above) could be really important because it points out that 'contractual stabilization clauses should be carefully drafted so that any protections for investors against future changes in law do not interfere with the State's bona fide efforts to implement laws, regulations or policies, in a non-discriminatory manner, in order to meet its human rights obligations'.

In particular 'stabilisation clauses that freeze laws applicable to the project or that create exemptions for investors with respect to future laws are unlikely to satisfy the objectives of this principle if they include areas such as labour, health, safety, the environment or other legal measures that serve to meet the State's human rights obligations'. So if it is legitimate for investors to seek protection against unlawful actions by states at the same time the contractual partners cannot forget their responsibility relating to human rights field.

As suggested in a Report by Amnesty international 'to tackle this pervasive problem, future draft texts should elaborate further on the scope and implications of this duty. It should be clear that the duty entails refraining from seeking or accepting exemptions from existing standards related to the protection of the environment, labour or human rights; entering into agreements with governments that restrain the latter's ability to strengthen the protection of human rights (for example, through stabilization clauses) and opposing legislation aimed at bringing the national law in line with international human rights standards'.[56]

Of course, to take this 'new direction', it is necessary to redefine the negotiation processes introducing a common guideline for business community and governments involved in investment project contract. In this light the *Principles for responsible contracts* mentioned above could have a very important role. The contractual partners need support during the negotiation to understand how to formulate the clause, to know what provisions should be inserted to reduce the negative externalities produced by the agreements in the human rights field and which international sources should be introduced to complain with human rights obligations for states and companies. These guidelines could also improve the state's capacity to negotiate. As pointed out in the *Ruggie/IFC*

---

55. Point 2.d, Human Rights Undertaking, 22 September 2003, *ibid*.
56. Amnesty International, Preliminary Observations and Recommendations, Elements for the draft legally binding instrument on transnational corporations and other business enterprises with respect to human rights, 20 October 2017, https://www.amnesty.org/.../IOR5173232017ENGLISH.PDF.

report governments with sophisticated negotiating capacity are able to come to terms with investors while avoiding freezing clauses.

To conclude this partial reconstruction of a very intricate scenario the roadmap to navigate in the future could be identified in the Ruggie's statement: first of all 'the human rights policies of states in relation to business need to be pushed beyond their narrow institutional confines'; second, 'governments need to ensure that human rights compliance becomes part of defining an ethical corporate culture'; finally, states 'need to consider human rights impacts when they sign trade agreements and investment treaties, and when governments provide export credit or investment guarantees for overseas projects in contexts where the risk of human rights challenges is known to be high'.[57]

In the background, the idea according to which investment agreements must be considered as 'microcosm' which have to coexist with other microcosms into a more complicated landscape and cannot ignore the social context where it is added.

---

57. Schemberg A., *Id.*, 3.

CHAPTER 10
New Generations Treaties and the Attempts for a Renewal of the ISDS

Valentina Cagnin

1 INVESTOR-STATE DISPUTE SETTLEMENT: A CONTROVERSIAL TOOL FOR DISPUTE RESOLUTION

Since the 1950s, disputes between foreign investors and the host States of their investments are solved through the Investor-State Dispute Settlement (ISDS): a neutral, private, international arbitration procedure which allows foreign investors to sue the host government for alleged discriminatory practices against them or other violations of international investment law before ad hoc tribunals.

The ISDS was initially designed to assist foreign direct investments to obtain compensation for direct expropriation of private property by national governments in developing countries with poorly functioning court systems, but over time a number of abuses have arisen through the use of ISDS, as the original concept behind this tool has long since departed: as we will see, it has grown into a mechanism which shifts the balance of power between investors, states and other affected parties and priorities corporate rights over the right of government to regulate and to sovereign right of nations to determine their own affairs,[1] representing an effective menace of regulatory chill for States also in the field of social rights and national labour law.

ISDS is usually contained on standalone agreements (Bilateral Investment Treaties – BITs) or investment chapters in Free Trade Agreements (FTAs) and it is nowadays at the centre of the debate in the context of the new most recent

---

1. *See* Opinion of the European Economic and Social Committee on investor protection and investor to state dispute settlement in EU trade and investment agreements with third countries (2015/C 332/06), 8.10.2015, Official Journal of the European Union, C 332/45.

mega treaties which are now on the table of negotiations in the most developed economies, such as European Union (EU) and United States (US).[2]

According to United Nations Conference on Trade and Development (UNCTAD) there are 3,328 such agreements in existence internationally[3] and the EU Member States have already signed more than 1,400 trade agreements providing for this mechanism of dispute resolution.

The rate of new treaty-based ISDS cases continued unabated. According to *UNCTAD Report, Investor-State Dispute Settlement: Review of Developments in 2016 (May 2017)*, last year 62 new cases were initiated pursuant to international investment agreements (IIAs), bringing the total number of known cases to 767, but the precise number of cases cannot be stated with full certainty as it could be underestimated because there is no legal obligation in these treaties to disclose the initiation of proceedings.

Figure 10.1   Trends in Known Treaty-Based ISDS Cases, 1987–2016

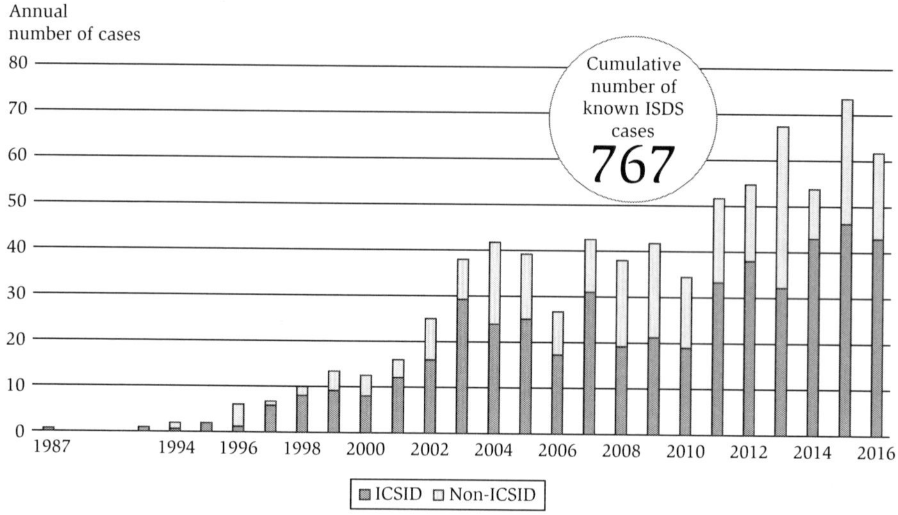

Source: ©UNCTAD, ISDS Navigator.

Hence 259 of them are currently pending, whereas 495 have been concluded.

Looking at the totality of decisions on the merits by the end of 2016, about 60% were decided in favour of the investor and 40% in favour of the State.

About two-thirds of ISDS cases in 2016 were brought under BITs, most of them dating back to the 1980s and 1990s. The remaining arbitrations were based on treaties with investment provisions (TIPs). The IIAs most frequently invoked

---

2. *See* paragraph 3.
3. UNCTAD International Investment Agreements Navigator. Data accurate on 13 April 2017.

Chapter 10: New Generations Treaties and the Attempts for a Renewal of the ISDS

in 2016 were the Energy Charter Treaty (ECT[4]) (with ten cases), the North American Free Trade Agreement (NAFTA[5]) and the Russian Federation–Ukraine BIT[6] (three each).

On the one hand, ISDS is based to a large extent on the argument that it could enforce the provisions regarding the protection of investors contained in the majority of trade agreements among states, playing a key role in the growth of international investments, granting freedom from discrimination and a general protection against denial of justice. Second, it could lead – in theory[7] – to a speedy resolution of disputes ensuring fairness of treatment between governments and foreign investors. Moreover, companies could resolve problems affecting their investments which domestic courts systems are not always able to effectively deal with. This mechanism ensures an award rendered by *super-partes* arbitrators, whereas before national courts judges may, it is argued, be tempted to decide in favour of the state.

On the other hand, opponents of ISDS underline all the critical aspects of this mechanism and outline that it needs substantial improvements towards a more balanced relationship between governments' right to regulate and investments protection, in order to guarantee the corporations' interests do not prevail on States' and citizens' interests. As a matter of fact, the power vested in corporations – to sue the government in case the law is considered a threat to its own investment – could have a massive effect on the capacity of the governments to enact and enforce reforms and rules that protect public health, safety and welfare, assure worker health and safety and protect the environment. This

---

4. The most important and famous International Investment Agreement is the Energy Charter Treaty (ECT). The Energy Charter Treaty provides a multilateral framework for energy cooperation that is unique under international law. It is designed to promote energy security through the operation of more open and competitive energy markets, while respecting the principles of sustainable development and sovereignty over energy resources. It was signed in December 1994 and entered into legal force in April 1998. To date the Treaty has been signed or acceded to by fifty-four states (also European Union signed it). Italy for example has at the moment several pending ISDS cases, as respondent state, under the ECT (five cases started in 2015, two cases in 2016 and one in 2017): all those cases are still pending and regards investments in renewable energy generation enterprise and some solar power projects. For more information, http://investmentpolicyhub.unctad.org/ISDS/Country Cases/103?partyRole=2 (accessed in November, 2017).
5. NAFTA, the North American Free Trade Agreement signed by Canada, Mexico and United States creating a trilateral trade bloc in North America, came into force on 1 January 1994. It is one of the most important mega treaties which contains the ISDS, (Chapter 11) according to which, investors of one NAFTA party are allowed to bring claims directly against the government of another NAFTA party before an international arbitral. The first instance of an ISDS provision receiving widespread public attention in the wake of the famous *Methanex case* (*Methanex Corporation v. United States of America*) was started under NAFTA.
6. Agreement between the Government of the Russian Federation and the Cabinet of Ministers of the Ukraine on the encouragement and mutual protection of investments (Moscow, 27 November 1998).
7. Some cases can take several years to conclude.

menace is strictly linked to the fact that ISDS, being traditionally arbitration instead of judicial settlement, lacks coherence and therefore predictability.

What we risk is a 'freezing' of the legislative power, or the 'regulatory chill': in considering any new law, governments would consider consequences in the relationship with corporations and may moderate, or even reject, drafts before they are approved,[8] failing to enact or enforcing bona fide regulatory measures because of a perceived or actual threat for investment arbitration.

Other causes of concern are related to the procedure and regard lack of transparency[9] – many decisions and awards in ISDS cases are not publicly available, or just little information is made available to the public: in 2016, ISDS tribunals rendered at least fifty-seven substantive decisions in investor-State disputes, forty-one of which are in the public domain (at the time of writing).[10]

ISDS is also criticized for the lack of independence of arbitrators: with regard to the latter aspect, highly paid corporate lawyers[11] might represent corporations one day and sit as arbitrators the day after, they sit in closed session and are appointed on an ad hoc basis. Their decision is final and not subject to any formal appeal process. Furthermore, they are often named by the corporations involved in the case, and they tend to support their interests,[12] a situation that might lead to the violation of the duty to be and remain independent and impartial throughout the arbitration proceedings, the duty of confidentiality and the duty of behaving diligently in the conduct of the arbitration proceedings.[13] Moreover, there is a risk of concentration of decisional power in the hands of few people: just fifteen arbitrators, nearly all from Europe, the US or Canada, have decided 55% of all known investment-treaty disputes. This small group of

---

8. M. Volcansek, *Constitutional Courts as Veto Players: Divorce and Decrees in Italy*, European Journal of Political Research, 39, no. 3 (2001), pp. 347–372.
9. See generally J. Nakagawa (ed.), *Transparency in International Trade and Investment Dispute Settlement, USA and Canada* (Routledge, 2013) (arguing that transparency in international trade dispute settlement procedures should be enhanced so that they may be accountable to a wider range of stakeholders); R. Sappideen & L. Ling He, *Dispute Resolution in Investment Treaties: Balancing the Rights of Investors and Host States*, Journal of World Trade, 49, no. 1 (2015), pp. 85–116.
10. UNCTAD Report, Investor-State Dispute Settlement: Review of Developments in 2016, May 2017.
11. Lawyers are paid more than USD 1,000 by the hours (even USD 1,000 p/h), so we could suppose the lack of interest in ending quickly the arbitration as the profit creates an incentive for cases to go on for years, even if they have no merit. The *Philip Morris v. Uruguay* Case, started in February 2010, according to which corporation filed ISDS claim arguing that Uruguay's law requiring warning labels on cigarette packets devalued its trademark and investments, was dismissed after six years of proceedings, in July 2016 in favour of Uruguay.
12. S. Dumanoir, *Vers une renégotiation de l'accord économique et commercial global (AECG) entre l'Union Européenne et le Canada? Le mécanisme de règlement des différends par l'arbitrage entre investisseur et Etat en question*, in Revue de L'Union Européenne, n. 596/mars 2016, p. 141.
13. U. Draetta, *Internal Conflicts among Arbitrators in International Arbitration*, Diritto del Commercio Internazionale n. 1 (2016), p. 48.

lawyers sit on the same arbitration panels, act as both arbitrators and counsels and even call on each other as witnesses in arbitration cases.[14] This has led to growing concerns, including within the broader legal community, over conflicts of interest: three corporate lawyers unaccountable to any electorate decide ISDS cases, adjudicating and making binding decisions on areas of fundamental public interest. This is why it is essential that arbitrators on ISDS tribunals must be fully impartial and not open to conflict of interests.

Then, it is necessary to consider the risk of huge compensation awards for States:[15] according to the Unctad Report 2017, the amounts claimed ranged from USD 10 million (*Grot and others v. Moldova* and *Görkem Insaat v. Turkmenistan*) to USD 16.5 billion (*Cosigo Resources and others v. Colombia*). If we consider the cases decided in favour of the investor, the average amount claimed was USD 1.4 billion and the median USD 100 million. The average amount awarded was USD 545 million and the median USD 20 million.[16] In terms of costs, we need to consider that the defence for an ISDS case costs an average of USD 8 million,[17] which is obviously paid by taxpayers; or, even if they emerge victorious from the proceedings, they may have to pay a large legal bill, although the possibility to condemn in costs when the claim is unfounded is increasing.[18]

Further, the ISDS mechanism is not considered as necessary if the countries have already an efficient and functional judicial system and investment protection as the case for example of EU and US.[19] It is thus necessary to consider that the need for foreign investment protection varies from country to country: in countries with a functioning and mature legal system investment disputes could be dealt with by mediation, domestic courts and State to State resolution, so the ISDS should not be considered as necessary.

Finally, it seems to be a unilateral power given to multinational corporations: affected communities citizens, domestic entrepreneurs, trade unions and governments cannot make use of the same mechanisms.

---

14. P. Eberhardt & C. Olivet, *Profiting from Injustice How Law Firms, Arbitrators and Financiers Are Fueling an Investment Arbitration Boom*, Corporate Europe Observatory and the Transnational Institute, Brussels / Amsterdam, November 2012.
15. While USA never lost a case, Australia spent $50 million defending its legislation on cigarette packet warnings against a challenge from Philip Morris (Case *Australia v. Philip Morris*) dismissed on 15 December 2015 on procedural grounds).
16. The amount claimed or awarded refers to the amount of monetary compensation awarded by the arbitral tribunal to the claimant, not including interest, legal costs or costs of arbitration.
17. T. Fritz, *Accordi internazionali sugli investimenti al vaglio*, Traidcraft, 2015, p. 8.
18. M. Casas, *Nationalities of Convenience, Personal Jurisdiction, and Access to Investor-State Dispute Settlement*, New York University Journal of International Law and Politics, 49, 63, p. 17.
19. In this sense, Carvalho points out that the same 'high-quality-legal-system' argument could be used to exempt disputes among developed countries from any form of international adjudication forum, including from the International Court of Justice or the WTO Panels. See P. Carvalho, *The Sword of Damocles, Investor-State Dispute Settlement and the Rule of Law*, Policy, 32, no. 2 (Winter 2016), p. 26.

Given the above, there are a lot of critical issues on this mechanism of controversial resolution of disputes.

2 ISDS AND SOCIAL RIGHTS: THE RISK OF FREEZING THE LAW

Even if most of the ISDS cases concern health and environmental protection, there are some interesting cases affecting labour law, and in particular, the topic of legal minimum wage (*Veolia Propreté v. Egypt* case and *Centerra v. Kyrgyz Republic* case) and that of discrimination of workers (*Piero Foresti & others v. South Africa* case), which clearly demonstrate the possible implications of ISDS for social rights and national labour law. As a matter of fact, from the one hand the risk is that of a freezing of the law – because the state does not want to be sued by a multinational enterprise for a new law – and from the other hand, the risk is to pay a gross compensation to the investors whose investments have been damaged by this new law provisions.[20]

2.1 *Veolia Propreté v. Egypt* Case

The *Veolia Propreté v. Egypt* case is the most representative and cited ISDS case in the field of labour law. Veolia Propreté, a French multinational corporation with investments in Egypt, filed a complaint against Egypt in 2012, demanding USD 110 million under the France-Egypt Bilateral Investment Treaty over disputes relating to a fifteen-year contract for waste management in the city of Alexandria. The corporation claims that the government violated its contractual commitments to Veolia due to changes in Egyptian laws, Veolia said that changes in Egyptian labour laws – including the increase in minimum wages from EUR 41 per month to EUR 72 per month – have negatively affected the company's investment, and that Egypt has violated its contract and the protection of investments granted by the BIT by not helping the corporation to offset such costs. An investor-state tribunal was established in 2013 and the case is still pending with no news on proceedings, but even if the arbitrators rule in favour of Veolia, the result will be a damage award, not a repeal of Egypt's minimum wage law: the claimant (in this case Veolia Propreté) is required to prove that the measures in questions caused to her significant damage but if the case is upheld, the host country (Egypt) is required to provide compensation for the damage caused. Unlike the World Trade Organization (WTO) Dispute Settlement Procedure, if a state loses a case, it is not bound to change its legislation.

---

20. V. Cagnin, *Investor-State Dispute Settlement (ISDS) from a Labour Law Perspective*, ELLJ (2017).

2.2 Centerra v. Kyrgyz Republic

Another well-known case with potential consequences for labour law and social rights is the *Centerra v. Kyrgyz Republic* case, which is referred to an arbitration that Centerra (a Canadian company) commenced against the Kyrgyz Republic. The facts are based on a labour reform that the Kyrgyz Republic implemented in order to improve the salary of workers operating at high altitude. Centerra, a multinational operating in the gold mines, alleged that, given the implementation of such a reform, its labour costs in the Kyrgyz Republic would have significantly increased (approximately USD 6 million per year), and at the bargaining stage of the treaty among the States involved, the salary conditions were not expected to change. The arbitration was settled in 2009: the Parties have amicably settled the disputes and they have formally withdrawn their respective claims and counterclaims, and request that the proceedings in this arbitration be terminated, sharing the arbitration costs of USD 200,000 in equal share.[21] This decision had for sure a serious impact on the public budget of a country where 32% of the population lives below the poverty line[22] and demonstrated how the government regulation power is menaced by ISDS.

2.3 *Piero Foresti & Others v. South Africa* Case

Another case in matter of workers' discriminations and fair treatment is the *Piero Foresti & others v. South Africa* case, started under the Italy-South Africa and Belgium-Luxembourg-South Africa BIT. In 2004, South Africa's new, post-apartheid Mineral and Petroleum Resources Development Act (MPRDA) came into force. Along with a new mining charter, the act sought to redress historical inequalities in the mining sector, in part by requiring companies to partner with citizens who had suffered under the apartheid regime, facilitating meaningful participation of Black people in the mining and minerals industry. The new system terminated all previously held mining rights, and required companies to reapply for licences to continue their operations. It also instituted a mandatory 26% ownership stake in the country's mining companies for black South Africans. Two years later, a group of Italian investors, members of the Foresti and Conti families, prominent Tuscan industrialists and a Luxembourg-based holding company, Finstone, who together control most of the South African granite industry, filed a landmark investor-state claim against South Africa.[23] The country's new mining regime, they argued, had unlawfully expropriated their investments and treated them unfairly. They demanded USD 350 million in compensation. The companies' case against South Africa dragged on for four years, before ending abruptly when the Italian group dropped its claims and the

---

21. Case available at http://www.italaw.com/cases/4191 (accessed on 4 November 2017).
22. R. Knottnerus & R. Satke, *Kyrgyz Republic's Experience with Investment Treaties and Arbitration Cases*, Transnational Institute Amsterdam (July 2017).
23. Case available at http://www.italaw.com/cases/446. (accessed on 4 November 2017).

tribunal ordered them to contribute EUR 400,000 towards South Africa's costs and the investors received new licences requiring a much lower divestment of shares (only 5% of their ownership to black South Africans, rather than the 26% mandated by the state mining authority).

3 NEW GENERATION TREATIES (CETA, TTIP, TPP AND EUSFTA) AND THE PROGRESS MADE IN DEVELOPING A BALANCED AND FORWARD-LOOKING APPROACH IN THE INTERNATIONAL INVESTMENT POLICY

With the continuing use of the ISDS mechanism and its discussion in numerous negotiations for mega treaties and IIAs, investment arbitration is nowadays at the centre of public attention. As a matter of fact, the inclusion of ISDS in trade and investment agreements has become subject to increased public scrutiny and questioning: this issue has prompted a huge public debate on the need for an ISDS mechanism in any investment chapter, with a strong opposition mainly voiced by trade unions, scholars, Non-governmental Organizations (NGOs), consumers, environmental and public health organizations.

Concerns around ISDS have been raised particularly in the context of the negotiations of some recent mega treaties, in particular Comprehensive and Economic Trade Agreement (CETA), EU-Singapore Free Trade Agreements (EUFSTA), Transatlantic Trade and Investment Partnership (TTIP), Trans-Pacific Partnership (TPP), called *'new generations treaties'*, as they are extensive and more complex than ever before, going beyond just lowering tariffs. Those agreements deal with not only the abolition of tariffs and duties but also the regulatory *'non-tariff barriers'* which cover bureaucratic procedures for regulating trade, social, environmental, privacy, and food safety issues, encouraging strong trans-collaboration among parties by promoting mutual recognition, harmonization and cooperation between regulators on important global regulation issues, such as in respect of energy, environment, agriculture, privacy, health and safety, sustainable development, food and financial security, social standards, privacy standards and investments.

With regards to this last issue, the protection of investments, the ISDS, as it was conceived in the NAFTA agreement,[24] was originally inserted in all those named treaty but due to the strong opposition to this mechanism of dispute resolution, the negotiations have been even in certain cases even stopped, or, more commonly, they led to a modification of the ISDS, demonstrating a certain progress in developing a balanced and forward-looking approach in the international investment policy.

CETA, the Comprehensive and Economic Trade Agreement negotiated by Canada and the EU since 2009, which aims to boost trade and help generate

---

24. NAFTA, Chapter 11.

growth and jobs, lowering customs tariffs and other barriers to trade between the parties, is one of the agreement concerned by ISDS.

The European Commission's decision to include the ISDS in the agreement text has generated such a big opposition to negotiations to lead the signatories' parties to change the mechanism in the final version of the text, with a new, improved and more democratic transparent and independent system for resolving disputes between investors and state: the Investment Court System (ICS). The agreement thus entered into force provisionally[25] on 21 September 2017 but it will be fully implemented once all EU Member States ratify the deal according to their respective constitutional requirements. At the time CETA will take full effect, the new ICS will replace the current ISDS mechanism (that exists however in many bilateral trade agreements negotiated in the past by EU Member States' governments).

How does the new ICS work? CETA moves decisively away from the traditional approach of investment dispute resolution and establishes independent, impartial and permanent investment Tribunals. Accordingly, the members of these Tribunals will be individuals qualified for judicial office in their respective countries, and these will be appointed by the EU and Canada, and not arbitrators nominated by the investor and the defending state (as foreseen in the ISDS). Contrary to the traditional investment dispute settlement approach, cases will be heard by three randomly selected members. Strict ethical rules for these individuals have been set to ensure their independence and impartiality, the absence of conflict of interest, bias or appearance of bias. The Tribunal will be composed of fifteen members nominated by the European Union and Canada (the signatories parties) and not by arbitrators nominated by the investor and the defending state. The tribunal will hear cases in divisions of three members appointed via a randomized procedure. CETA is then the first agreement to include an Appeal mechanism (Article 8.28 of the Treaty) which will allow the correction of errors and ensure the consistency of the decisions of the Tribunal of first instance.[26] Further (Article 8.36), CETA introduces full transparency in investment dispute settlement proceedings: all documents (submissions by the parties, decisions of the tribunal) will be publicly available on a United Nations website which the EU will finance and all hearings will be open to the public. Interested parties (NGO's, trade unions) will be able to make submissions. This will be binding and cannot be waived by the tribunal or the parties to a dispute.[27] This new ICS, according to the agreement text, should have all the requirements to represent an alternative dispute settlement procedure which could better

---

25. National parliaments in EU countries – and in some cases regional ones too – will then need to approve CETA before it can take full effect.
26. Council of the European Union, Joint Interpretative Instrument on the Comprehensive Economic and Trade Agreement (CETA) between Canada and the European Union and its Member States, Brussels, 27 October 2016.
27. European Commission, Investment provisions in the EU-Canada free trade agreement (CETA), February 2016.

reconcile the legitimate demand of investors with the legitimate concerns of civil society and it has been incorporated also into the EU-Vietnam FTA.[28]

Another comprehensive agreement in limbo due to the ISDS provision is the EUSFTA,[29] the free trade agreement signed by the EU and Singapore.[30]

Its negotiation, started in September 2013 was (quite quickly) concluded on 17 October 2014, but its entering into force has been recently stopped by the historical European Court of Justice (ECJ) pronouncement dated 16 May 2017,[31] holding that the EUSFTA covers shared competences with respect to: (i) non-direct foreign investment, (ii) investor-state dispute settlement (ISDS), and (iii) state-to-state dispute settlement and therefore, in its current form, the European Commission cannot finalize a free trade agreement with Singapore without Member States approval.[32] Even if the 'double track' of ratification imposed by Bruxelles could 'freeze' the agreements negotiations,[33] and those agreements could result 'old', compared to the economic framework that could be in the meantime modified, this decision could help the revision process of the ISDS, as the consent of all the European Member States could be difficultly reached if the ISDS will not be removed or modified from the actual version.

Following the Court's Opinion, the debate on the best architecture for EU trade agreements and investment protection agreements is ongoing.[34]

The ISDS debate concerns also the TTIP (Transatlantic Trade and Investment Partnership between US and EU[35]), a deal being negotiated between the EU and the US since 2013, which should create, if concluded, the world's largest free-trade zone, as the two areas combined account for 40% of world GDP, and

---

28. http://trade.ec.europa.eu/doclib/docs/2016/february/tradoc_154210.pdf.
29. CETA, together with the EU-Singapore FTA, contain the first ever investment chapters negotiated by the EU in any agreement since the EU gained competence for investments under the Lisbon Treaty, in 2009.
30. The EU-Singapore agreement was the first EU trade agreement after the entry into force of the Lisbon Treaty for which a complete draft text was available.
31. In 2015 the EU sought an opinion of the European Court of Justice to clarify the EU competence to sign and ratify the free trade agreement with Singapore. The Court delivered its opinion on the division of competences in May 2017, see CJEU, Press Release n. 52/2017, Luxembourg, 16 May 2017.
32. The sentence is consolidating a recent trend: also the CETA has been considered as a 'mixed' agreement by the Commission, this is why at the moment it is at the ratification at national levels. See also M.R. Calamita, *Sulla competenza dell'Unione europea a siglare accordi di libero scambio: il caso dell'EU-Singapore Free Trade Agreement*, in Parere 2/15 CGUE –DPCE on line, 2017/3.
33. This decision risks to weaken the competence of the European Commission in the field of trade, in a moment on which Bruxelles is trying to relaunch the free trade against new protectionist trends, at the US ones and this could also limit the third countries' interest to conclude agreements with the EU.
34. European Commission, The Opinion of the European Court of Justice on the EU-Singapore Trade Agreement and the Division of Competences in Trade Policy, Factsheet, September 2017.
35. *See U.S.-EU Joint Report on TTIP Progress to Date*, available at http://trade.ec.europa.eu/doclib/docs/2017/january/tradoc_155242.pdf.

Chapter 10: New Generations Treaties and the Attempts for a Renewal of the ISDS

1/3 of the globe's total trade exchanges.[36] For the duration of its negotiations, ISDS has been a dominant issue for EU and US stakeholders, in particular for the worries (mostly from the EU side) linked to the risk of a race to the bottom of labour standards for the European workers, view that historically, US labour law is weaker.[37]

For this reason, given the strong public interest in the issue of investment protection and ISDS, the European Commission launched a public consultation,[38] open to all interested EU citizens and stakeholders, between 27 March and 13 July 2014 to develop further the EU approach on these important issues that matter to Europeans and the collective submissions reflect a wide-spread opposition to ISDS in TTIP (and also quite a majority of replies opposing TTIP in general). The same position has been taken by the European Parliament which recommended to the European Commission *'to ensure that foreign investors are treated in a non-discriminatory fashion, while benefiting from no greater rights than domestic investors, and to replace the ISDS system with a new system for resolving disputes between investors and states which is subject to democratic principles and scrutiny, where potential cases are treated in a transparent manner by publicly appointed, independent professional judges in public hearings and which includes an appellate mechanism, where consistency of judicial decisions is ensured, the jurisdiction of courts of the EU and of the Member States*

---

36. For details, *see* V. Cagnin, *La convergenza normativa in tema di diritto del lavoro tra Ue e Usa nell'accordo commerciale geopolitico Ttip*, in Lavoro e Diritto, n. 1/2016; V. Cagnin, *What Future for Social Rights under the New Transatlantic Trade and Investment Partnership (TTIP)? Some Reflections on TTIP*, Economia e Lavoro, n. 2 (2015), pp. 77–86; G. Celi, *How Beneficial Is TTIP for EU Countries? Economic Gains and Social Costs of an Ambitious Project*, Economia & Lavoro (2015), 2; M. Di Pietro, Il TTIP (Partenariato transatlantico per il commercio e gli investimenti) e la cooperazione normativa, Economia & Lavoro, 2015, 2; M. Faioli, *The Quest for a New Generation of Labor Chapter in the TTIP*, Economia & Lavoro (2015), 2; M. Faioli, The Quest for a New Generation of Labour Charter in the TTIP, Economia & Lavoro, n. 2 (2015); A. Perulli, *Sostenibilità, diritti sociali e commercio internazionale: la prospettiva del Trans-Atlantic Trade and Investments Partnership (TTIP)*, in WP C.S.D.L.E. 'Massimo D'Antona'.INT – 115/2015; A. Perulli, *Sustainability, Social Rights and International Trade: The TTIP*, International Journal of Comparative Labour Law and Industrial Relations, 32 (2015), pp. 473–495.
37. EU labour law usually acknowledges better labour standards and working conditions and social rights compared to the USA system. Discrepancies between US and EU labour and social law are huge: just to give an example, EU countries have all ratified the eight Core Labour Conventions in full, while the US has only ratified two and its labour law deviate considerably from the core labour conventions in several aspects. For a more details about the USA labour law system, *see* L. Compa, *Labor Rights and Labor Standards in Transatlantic Trade and Investment Negotiations: An American Perspective*, Transatlantic Stakeholder Forum, Working Paper Series, July 2014; L. Compa, *The North American Free Trade Agreement (NAFTA) and the North American Agreement on Labor Cooperation (NAALC)*, International Encyclopedia of Laws, Labour Law and Industrial Relations (2008), 110.
38. European Commission, Online public consultation on investment protection and investor-to-state dispute settlement (ISDS) in the Transatlantic Trade and Investment Partnership Agreement, Brussels, 13.1.2015 SWD (2015) 3 final.

is respected, and where private interests cannot undermine public policy objectives'.[39]

Starting from those important documents, detailed discussions had taken place on the EU's reform proposals for investment protection and ICS adopted for CETA, but, for the moment, significant gaps remained between the positions of both sides.[40] Moreover, the same TTIP future is uncertain because the last round of negotiations dates back to October 2016 and are currently on hold following the change of US Administration.

The debate on ISDS has raised not only in Europe but also in the context of the TPP (Trans-Pacific Partnership) negotiations.

TPP is a trade partnership initially thought among twelve countries (US, Japan, Malaysia, Vietnam, Singapore, Brunei, Australia, New Zealand, Canada, Mexico, Chile and Peru), which has been recently publicly considered almost dead (after ten years of negotiations) due to the Donald Trump's decision (on January 2017) to sign an executive order removing the US from the agreement. The future of this agreement, now called TPP-11, has been recently (November 2017) thrown again after the US exit because the new government of New Zealand lobbied for the removal, or at least some amendments, of the ISDS,[41] leading to a further block of negotiations.

ISDS is thus leaving a critical phase as it represents a reason for blocking the FTA's negotiations.

4 THE QUESTIONS ON THE COMPATIBILITY OF THE INVESTMENT COURT SYSTEM (ICS) WITH THE EU LAW

Recent studies demonstrate that both industrialized countries' and emerging markets' trade volumes have plateaued and in reply to the general stagnation of global trade,[42] in the last decades, several countries started negotiations of new FTAs, accepting also the insertion of the ISDS in order to attract investors and thus investments in their territory, even if this provision could lead to serious implications for social rights and national sovereignty in this field, particularly in terms of labour law regulatory chill. As we saw for example in *Veolia Propreté v. Egypt* case, the ISDS has been invoked in order to protect investment from new social policies (the rise in the minimum wage). In this sense, ISDS (contained in

---

39. European Parliament resolution of 8 July 2015 containing the European Parliament's recommendations to the European Commission on the negotiations for the Transatlantic Trade and Investment Partnership (TTIP) (2014/2228(INI)), p. xv.
40. European Commission, Transatlantic Trade & Investment Partnership Advisory Group Meeting report, 9 March 2017.
41. R. Bermingham, *TPP Faces Fresh Crisis over New Zealand Opposition to ISDS*, Global Trade Review (1 November 2017), available at https://www.gtreview.com/news/asia/tpp-faces-fresh-crisis-over-new-zealand-opposition-to-isds/ (last access on 4 November 2017).
42. T. Treu, Globalizzazione e diritti umani e clausole sociali dei trattati commerciali negli scambi internazionali fra imprese, in WP C.S.D.L.E. 'Massimo D'Antona'.INT – 133/2017, p. 30.

FTAs, or BIT, or IIAs) might be used by investors to challenge the national regulation, to dismantle social protection and to extend the general trend of deregulation, lowering wages or other labour conditions standards, in favour of global trade.

At the same time, however, ISDS is facing 'a new crisis of legitimacy':[43] there is a general agreement that ISDS cannot continue in its present form,[44] as it is commonly perceived as an unacceptable mechanism which is strongly resisted by an increasing number of important global player and this is largely demonstrated by the opposition to its inclusion in the treaties mentioned (CETA, TTIP, EUSFTA and TPP). This lack of legitimacy is also linked to the big concerns raised about the potential effects of this mechanism in the social field and in general, on domestic labour law, even if, looking at the past ISDS cases on average States were significantly more successful than investors.

In response to stark criticism from civil society, which perceives these mechanisms to be undemocratic, the European Commission has seized the opportunity to reform the traditional arbitration-based system and replace it with the ICS.[45] The mechanism of the Investment Court incorporates many innovative features and addresses some of the core criticism, as it is intended to correct the flaws of traditional ISDS mechanisms, solving many problems like to the ISDS as the lack of the right to appeal, the lack of transparency or the lack of independence of arbitrators.

The ICS effectively addresses a number of the prominent concerns through an innovative structural reform of the traditional, arbitration-based, ISDS system but this mechanism fails to respond to internal constitutional challenges.[46] As a matter of fact, on 6 September 2017, Belgium officially submitted[47] it to the Court of Justice of the European Union (CJEU) for an opinion about the compatibility of the ICS with EU law, in particular regarding the compatibility of the ICS with: (i) the exclusive competence of the CJEU to provide the definitive interpretation of EU law; (ii) the general principle of equality and the 'practical effect' requirement of EU law; (iii) the right of access to the courts; (iv) the right to an independent and impartial judiciary. As a matter of fact, the ICS gives exclusive

---

43. C. Brower & S. Schill, *Is Arbitration a Threat or a Boon to the Legitimacy of International Investment Law?*, Chicago Journal of International Law, n. 9 (2009), p. 472.
44. Even UNCTAD defined five valid options for reforming ISDS: tailoring existing systems through IIAs, limiting investor access to ISDS, Promoting Alternative State Resolution (ASR), Introducing an appeals facility and Creating a standing International Investment Court.
45. UNCTAD, Reform of Investor-State Dispute Settlement: in search of a roadmap updated for the launching of the World Investment Report (WIR), 26 June 2013.
46. H. Lenk, *Investment Court System for the New Generation of EU Trade and Investment Agreements: A Discussion of the Free Trade Agreement with Vietnam and the Comprehensive Economic and Trade Agreement with Canada*, European Papers, 1, no. 2 (2016), European Forum, Insight of 14 August 2016, pp. 665–677.
47. https://diplomatie.belgium.be/sites/default/files/downloads/ceta_summary.pdf.

jurisdiction to EU Member States courts, and above all, the ECJ to decide challenges that concern the EU law.[48]

The EU Court of Justice has not yet ruled on the compatibility of an ICS system with EU law. Hence, whether positive or negative, the CJEU's opinion will definitely constitute a landmark decision for the future of the EU investment policy and the institution of the ICS.

Without an explicit prior involvement of the CJEU in investment disputes under the FTA, which concern the interpretation or appreciation of EU law, the future of all agreements, and thus the future of national social rights, remains uncertain.

---

48. E. Biel & M. Wheeler, *The Uncertain Future of the European Investment Court System*, Yale Journal of International Law (1 December 2016).

PART V   The ILO Perspective

CHAPTER 11
An Overview of the Main ILO Policies and Tools in the Organization of Promotional Activities on Social Rights

Giuseppe Casale & Mario Fasani

1 INTRODUCTION

The aspiration for social justice, through which every working man and woman can claim freely and on the basis of equality of opportunity their fair share of the wealth which they have helped to generate, is as great today as it was when the International Labour Organization (ILO) was created in 1919.[1] The current global economy has grown to a scale unprecedented in history. Aided by new technologies, people, capital and goods are moving between countries with an ease and at a speed that has created an interdependent global economic network affecting virtually every person on the planet.

While globalization has created opportunities and benefits for many, at the same time millions of workers and employers worldwide have had to face new challenges. The globalized economy has displaced workers and enterprises to new locations, resulted in the sudden accumulation or flight of capital, and caused financial instability which in turn led to the 2008 global economic crisis. Despite the clear benefits, globalization has not ushered in an era of prosperity for all. In fact, despite strong economic growth that had produced millions of new jobs since the early 1990s until the 2008 crisis, income inequality also grew dramatically in most regions of the world. The personal distribution of wages has become more unequal, with a growing gap between the top 10% and the

---

1. ILO, *A Fair Globalization: Creating opportunities for all, Report of the World Commission on the Social Dimension of Globalization*, Geneva, 2008.

bottom 10% of wage earners. Moreover, nine years after the 2008 economic and social crisis, the global employment situation remains uneven: if certain advanced economies have managed to recover some of the jobs lost, other economies are still confronted with significant challenges with respect to their labour market and social prospects continue to deteriorate.[2] From the economic point of view, indicators show that profitability and stock markets have recovered in most countries. Executive pay is also on the rise, following a pause in the immediate aftermath of the crisis. Therefore, the key issue is how to translate these profits into productive investment. Over 30 million jobs are still needed to return employment to pre-crisis levels. The fact that the global crisis has had significant negative repercussions for labour markets and that recovery is proving uncertain and elusive has further highlighted the necessity of inclusive growth.[3]

Inequality not only leads to a decline in productivity but also breeds poverty, social instability and even conflict. In view of this, the international community has recognized the need to establish some basic rules of the game to ensure that globalization offers a fair chance at prosperity for everyone.

The ILO Declaration on Social Justice for a Fair Globalization of 2008 and the Global Job Pact of 2009 both reaffirmed the relevance of the ILO's mandate to promote social justice using all the means available to it, including the promotion of international labour standards.

The United Nations (UN) 2030 Agenda for Sustainable Development identified decent work for all women and men, and lower inequality, as among the key objectives of a new universal policy agenda.

2 THE ROLE OF INTERNATIONAL LABOUR STANDARDS

In 1919, the signatory nations to the Treaty of Versailles created the International Labour Organization (ILO) in recognition of the fact that 'conditions of labour exist involving such injustice, hardship and privation to large numbers of people as to produce unrest so great that the peace and harmony of the world are imperilled.' To tackle this problem, the newly founded organization established a system of international labour standards – international Conventions and Recommendations drawn up by representatives of governments, employers and workers from around the world – covering all matters related to work. In the ILO's Declaration of Philadelphia of 1944, the international community recognized that 'labour is not a commodity' and set out basic human and economic rights under the principle that 'poverty anywhere constitutes a danger to prosperity everywhere'. The ILO has adopted 189 Conventions and 205 Recommendations covering all aspects of the world of work.[4]

---

2. Global Wage Report 2016/17, Wage inequality in the workplace.
3. World Employment and Social Outlook: Trends 2017.
4. Last updated 2 January 2018.

A supervisory system, that is unique at the international level, helps to ensure that countries apply the Conventions they ratify. The ILO also provides advice in the drafting of national labour laws. It regularly examines the application of standards in Member States and points out areas where they could be better applied. If there are any problems in the application of standards, the ILO seeks to assist countries through social dialogue and technical assistance.

3 AN INTERNATIONAL LEGAL FRAMEWORK FOR A FAIR GLOBALIZATION

In 1998, the ILO created a special promotional measure to strengthen the application of the four principles and associated rights that are considered fundamental for social justice. By adopting the *Declaration on Fundamental Principles and Rights at Work* and its Follow-up, ILO Member States recognized that they have an obligation to work towards realizing certain basic values that are inherent in ILO membership, namely freedom of association and the effective recognition of the right to collective bargaining; the elimination of all forms of forced or compulsory labour; the effective abolition of child labour; and the elimination of discrimination in respect of employment and occupation.

This obligation exists regardless of whether the States had ratified the relevant Conventions which embody these principles. At the same time, the ILO itself has an obligation to provide assistance needed to achieve these objectives.

After ten years, in 2008, at the 97th International Labour Conference, by acclamation of Member States, workers and employers, the *'Declaration on Social Justice for a Fair Globalization'* together with a Resolution on strengthening the ILO's capacity to assist its Members' efforts to reach its objectives in the context of globalization were adopted.

This was the third major statement of principles and policies adopted by the International Labour Conference since the ILO's Constitution of 1919. It built on the Philadelphia Declaration of 1944 and the Declaration on Fundamental Principles and Rights at Work of 1998. The 2008 Declaration expresses the contemporary vision of the ILO's mandate in the era of globalization.

Through the Social Justice Declaration governments, employers and workers from all Member States call for a new strategy to sustain open economies and open societies based on social justice, full and productive employment, sustainable enterprises and social cohesion. The Declaration acknowledges the benefits of globalization but calls for renewed efforts to implement decent work policies as the means to achieve improved and fair outcomes for all.

Specifically, the Declaration establishes a new foundation on which the ILO can effectively support the efforts of its constituents to promote and achieve progress and social justice. The basis is composed of four strategic objectives of the ILO which represents the *Decent Work Agenda* – employment, social protection, social dialogue and tripartism, and fundamental principles and rights at work. The Declaration also underscores the fact that failure to promote any one of these objectives would hinder progress towards promoting the others by stressing their mutually supportive nature and interdependence.

At the same time, it gives ILO constituents a key responsibility to contribute, through their social and economic policy, to the realization of a global and integrated strategy for the implementation of the Decent Work Agenda. The Declaration also asks the ILO to invite other international and regional organizations to promote decent work, adding 'as trade and financial market policy both affect employment, it is the ILO's role to evaluate these employment effects to achieve its aim of placing employment at the heart of economic policies'.

The Declaration highlights that globalization is reshaping the world of work in profound ways. It states that on the one hand, it has helped a number of countries to benefit from high rates of economic growth and employment creation, to absorb many of the rural poor into the modern urban economy, to advance their developmental goals, and to foster innovation in product development and the circulation of ideas. On the other hand, it has caused many countries and sectors to face major challenges of income inequality, continuing high levels of unemployment and poverty, vulnerability of economies to external shocks, and the growth of both unprotected work and the informal economy, which impact on the employment relationship and the protections it can offer.

The Declaration on Social Justice for a Fair Globalization marks the most important renewal of the Organization since the adoption of the historic 'Declaration of Philadelphia' in 1944. In addition, it marks a significant step forward in respecting, promoting and realizing the Declaration on Fundamental Principles and Rights at Work adopted by the ILO in 1998.

The 1998 Declaration stresses the fundamental principles of freedom of association and the right to collective bargaining, the elimination of all forms of forced labour, the effective abolition of child labour and the elimination of discrimination in employment and occupation as the Organization's bedrock principles.

It includes a follow-up mechanism to ensure the means by which the Organization will assist the Member States in their efforts to promote the Decent Work Agenda, including a review of the ILO's institutional practices and governance; regular discussion by the International Labour Conference responding to realities and needs in Member States and assessing the results of ILO activities; voluntary country reviews, technical assistance and advisory services; and strengthening research capacities, information collection and sharing.

As mentioned above, the Declaration covers several areas:

3.1 Freedom of Association

The right of workers and employers to form and join organizations of their choice is an integral part of a free and open society. It is a basic civil liberty that serves as a building block for social and economic progress. Linked to this is the effective recognition of the right to collective bargaining. Freedom of expression and representation are an important part of decent work.

3.2 Forced Labour

The ILO presses for effective national laws and stronger enforcement mechanisms, such as legal sanctions and vigorous prosecution against those who exploit forced labourers. By raising public awareness, the ILO seeks to shine a spotlight on such human and labour rights violations.

3.3 Discrimination

Hundreds of millions of people suffer from discrimination in the world of work. This not only violates a most basic human right, but has wider social and economic consequences. Discrimination stifles opportunities, wasting the human talent needed for economic progress and accentuating social tensions and inequalities. Combating discrimination is an essential part of promoting decent work, and success on this front is felt well beyond the workplace.

3.4 Child Labour

There are more than 200 million children working throughout the world, many full-time. They are deprived of adequate education, good health and basic freedoms. Of these, 126 million – or one in every 12 children worldwide – are exposed to hazardous forms of child labour, work that endangers their physical, mental or moral well-being. As with other aspects of decent work, eliminating child labour is a development as well as human rights issue. ILO policies and programmes aim to help ensure that children receive the education and training they need to become productive adults in decent employment.

3.5 Fair Globalization

Globalization – the interlinking of economies in the world – provokes a wide variety of opinions. Some people argue that it worsens unemployment and poverty. Others see it as a way of solving these problems. But the ILO and other international organizations agree on one thing: that in the current wave of globalization not enough attention is being paid to the social consequences of the phenomena. There is inadequate focus on the human side of globalization which creates a gap in understanding the forces of change and how people react to them.

One of the ILO's strategies for promoting fairer globalization was to launch the World Commission on the Social Dimension of Globalization in 2002. The Commission explored innovative, sustainable ways of combining economic, social and environmental objectives to make globalization work for all. In its report 'A Fair Globalization – The Role of the ILO' the Commission said: 'The quest for a fair globalization that creates opportunities for all will dominate international affairs in the next decade. Whether seen from the angle of social and political stability and security concerns or through the eyes of the many people for whom the benefits of globalization are today a mirage, real concerns about fairness and opportunities cannot be wished away.' To address these concerns, the Commission's report offered proposals for making decent work a global goal, creating national policies to address globalization, and establishing decent work in production systems. It also discussed social dialogue and global policy coherence for growth, investment and employment, globalization, the cross-border movement of people, strengthening the international labour standards system, and improving the capability of the ILO in mobilizing action for change. In accepting the Commission's Report on behalf of the ILO, the then Director-General Juan Somavia, said: 'The stakes are high. We all know that if we don't solve the employment challenge, global stability is at risk.' He proposed three clear challenges for the ILO to create a fair globalization and make its contribution to meeting the UN's Millennium Development Goal of reducing poverty by half by 2015. The challenges he outlined were: making decent work a global goal, making the ILO a global player in shaping globalization and mobilizing tripartism for global action.

4 A PATH TO DECENT WORK

'The primary goal of the ILO today is to promote opportunities for women and men to obtain decent and productive work, in conditions of freedom, equity, security and human dignity.'[5]

Decent work sums up the aspirations of people in their working lives – their aspirations for opportunity and income; rights, voice and recognition; family stability and personal development; and fairness and gender equality. Ultimately these various dimensions of decent work underpin peace in communities and society.

Decent work is addressed by four strategic ILO objectives: fundamental principles and rights at work and international labour standards; employment and income opportunities; social protection and social security; and social dialogue and tripartism. These objectives hold for all workers, in both formal and informal economies; in wage employment or working on their own account; in fields, factories and offices; in homes or in the community.

Decent work is central to efforts to reduce poverty, and is a means for achieving equitable, inclusive and sustainable development. The ILO works to develop Decent Work-oriented approaches to economic and social policy in

---

5. Statement of the ILO's Director-General, Juan Somavia.

partnership with the principal institutions and actors of the multilateral system and the global economy.

5 THE 2030 AGENDA ON SUSTAINABLE DEVELOPMENT AND DECENT WORK

During the UN General Assembly in September 2015,[6] decent work for all women and men and the four pillars of the Decent Work Agenda – employment creation, social protection, rights at work, and social dialogue – became integral elements of the new 2030 Agenda for Sustainable Development.[7]

The 2030 Agenda puts people and planet at its centre and gives the international community the impetus it needs to work together to tackle the formidable challenges confronting humanity, including those in the world of work.

The 2030 Agenda embraces the three dimensions of sustainability – economic, social and environmental. It has seventeen Sustainable Development Goals (SDGs) that will build on the progress achieved under the Millennium Development Goals (MDGs).

The very first goal of the Agenda is to end poverty by 2030 'in all its forms everywhere'.[8]

In addition, the Agenda devotes significant attention to the importance of decent work. In particular, SDG 8 calls for the promotion of sustained, inclusive and sustainable economic growth, full and productive employment and decent work. This represents a key area of engagement for the ILO and its constituents. Furthermore, key aspects of decent work are widely embedded in the targets of the other sixteen goals of the UN's new development vision.

5.1 Targets for SDG 8: Decent Work and Economic Growth

The following are the main targets of Goal No. 8:

- 8.1 Sustain per capita economic growth in accordance with national circumstances and, in particular, at least *7 per cent gross domestic product growth per annum in the least developed* countries;
- 8.2 Achieve *higher levels of economic productivity through diversification, technological upgrading and innovation,* including through a focus on high-value added and labour-intensive sectors;

---

6. The Agenda was formally adopted by 193 world leaders gathering at a United Nations special summit in September 2015 in New York.
7. 'Promoting jobs and enterprise, guaranteeing rights at work, extending social protection and promoting social dialogue are the four pillars of the ILO Decent Work Agenda with gender as a cross-cutting theme.' Guy Ryder, ILO Director-General.
8. As far back as 1944, the Declaration of Philadelphia noted that 'poverty anywhere constitutes a threat to prosperity everywhere'.

8.3 Promote *development-oriented policies* that support productive activities, decent job creation, entrepreneurship, creativity and innovation, and encourage the *formalization and growth of micro-, small- and medium-sized enterprises*, including through access to financial services;

8.4 Improve progressively, through 2030, *global resource efficiency in consumption and production and endeavour to decouple economic growth from environmental degradation*, in accordance with the 10-year framework of programmes on sustainable consumption and production, with developed countries taking the lead;

8.5 By 2030, achieve *full and productive employment and decent work for all women and men, including for young people and persons with disabilities*, and equal pay for work of equal value;

8.6 By 2020, substantially *reduce the proportion of youth not in employment, education or training*;

8.7 Take immediate and effective measures to *eradicate forced labour, end modern slavery and human trafficking* and secure the prohibition and elimination of the worst forms of child labour, including recruitment and use of child soldiers, and *by 2025 end child labour in all its forms*;

8.8 *Protect labour rights and promote safe and secure working environments for all workers, including migrant workers*, in particular women migrants, and those in precarious employment;

8.9 By 2030, devise and implement *policies to promote sustainable tourism that creates jobs* and promotes local culture and products;

8.10 Strengthen the *capacity of domestic financial institutions to encourage and expand access to banking*, insurance and financial services for all;

    8.10.1.1 Increase *Aid for Trade support for developing countries*, in particular least developed countries, including through the Enhanced Integrated Framework for Trade-Related Technical Assistance to Least Developed Countries;

    8.10.1.2 By 2020, develop and operationalize a global strategy for youth employment and implement the Global Jobs Pact of the International Labour Organization.

5.2 Evaluation of the Impact of the ILO Declaration on Social Justice for a Fair Globalization

Within the context of further promoting decent work in a globalized economy, the International Labour Conference (ILC) at its 105th session of June 2016, having undertaken an evaluation of the impact of the ILO Declaration on Social Justice for a Fair Globalization, adopted the following resolution:

Significance of the Declaration. The Organization and its Members renewed their commitment to implement the ILO's constitutional mandate on the four strategic objectives for Decent Work and placed full and productive employment and decent work at the centre of economic and social policies at the national and regional levels, and in the multilateral system.

The Declaration is more relevant today than ever. Decent work deficits and incomplete progress in poverty reduction persist. In light of rising inequality, the achievement of fair globalization requires sustained efforts by Members, supported by an increasingly effective and efficient ILO.

The ILO, taking advantage of its unique tripartite structure and standard system, has a vital role to play in promoting progress toward social justice. This evaluation of the Declaration should inform the ILO actions in pursuit of its Centenary Initiatives leading up to and beyond the 100th Anniversary of the ILO in 2019.

Impact of the Declaration. Eight years after the adoption of the Declaration, decent work is now widely recognized as a global goal. The 2030 Agenda represents an opportunity for Members to reinforce a fully integrated approach to decent work in the design and financing their sustainable development plans based on national consultations. The Sustainable Development Goals cannot be achieved without the integration of the Decent Work Agenda into development policies at the national, regional and international levels.

The Declaration has served the basis for the Global Jobs Pact adopted by the ILC in 2009. In addition, through the follow-up to the Declaration, the ILC has adopted the Social Protection Floors Recommendation (Rec. No. 202) and the Protocol of 2014 to the Forced Labour Convention (P29).

At the same time, achieving policy coherence leading to decent work is still a challenge in many parts of the world. More work is needed to raise awareness and promote a better understanding of the Declaration as an instrument for a holistic approach.

ILO Decent Work Country Programme has proven a useful tool, yet these programmes need to be owned by the constituents and should include all four strategic objectives.

Needless to say, the Declaration has helped to increase policy coherence, coordination and collaboration between the ILO and other UN agencies and the global economic institutions, with the G20 playing an important role in this regard. However, it continues to be a challenge to translate high-level commitment into policies and programmes at country level.

5.3 Priority Areas for Action

(1) *Principles and policies to achieve the full potential of the Declaration.* Concrete action is needed to achieve the full potential of the Declaration, with specific attention to advancing decent work in the framework of the implementation of the 2030 Agenda, in particular by integrating decent work into national sustainable development strategies.

Member States should continue to stress the urgent priority to promote employment by creating a sustainable institutional and economic environment; the critical role of social protection to ensure a just share of the fruits of progress for all; the importance of social dialogue and tripartism as crucial means for the effective achievement of the strategic objectives at national, regional and international levels; the universal and immutable nature of fundamental principles and rights at work and their particular significance both as rights and enabling conditions; the imperative of gender equality and non-discrimination as cross cutting issues; the need for greater policy coherence, complementarity and coordination of national, regional and international contributions for the full implementation of the Declaration and the 2030 Agenda.

(2) *ILO action to effectively assist its Members:* Standard system: (a) strengthen through appropriate modalities the coordination between the recurrent discussions and the implementation of the Standards Review Mechanism to ensure that the ILO has a clear, robust and up-to-date body of international labour standards; (b) further adapt the modalities of Article 19, paragraphs 5(c) and 6(d) of the ILO Constitution, to make the best use, without increasing the reporting obligations of Member States, of its two functions: (i) to encourage Members to take into account in their legislation and practice the standards adopted by the Conference; and (ii) to enable the ILO assess the relevance of its standards to the needs of the world of work and to take appropriate action.

(3) *Recurrent discussion:* strengthen recurrent discussions so as to provide constituents and the general public with a regular update review of Members' diverse need and realities; ensure effective contribution to the general survey of the recurrent discussions; adopt a specific set of rule for the recurrent discussions in order to give them a distinct status and the appropriate visibility within the context of the ILC; examine the possibility of a shorter cycle of recurrent discussions taking into account the specific requirements for the ILO, the cycle of discussions, and the ILO contribution to the follow-up and review by the UN of the implementation of the 2030 Agenda.

(4) *Strengthening results-based framework and Decent Work Country Programmes (DWCP):* develop a strategic plan for 2018–2021 based on the integrated approach to decent work covering all four strategic objectives and with a coherent intervention model that makes the best use of the ILO tripartite structure and standards system and supports the capacity development of constituents; ensure that the DWCP comprise an integrated approach and address issues identified by the constituents, contain measurable, realistic and achievable outcomes, and should be overseen by tripartite governance structures to ensure ownership and increase impact; better align the DWCP with national sustainable development strategies and the 2030 Agenda and its decent work components, as well as with UN planning frameworks at the country level.

(5) *Institutional capacity building:* further strengthen the institutional capacity of Member States and workers and employers to pursue coherent social, economic and environmental policies; strengthen the awareness, understanding and capacity of constituents (including through the International Training Centre of the ILO in Turin) to

achieve the aims of the Declaration, and measure and monitor the results of such capacity-development efforts in a systematic and coherent manner.

(6) *Research, information collection and sharing*: continue its policy-oriented and evidence-based research to enable informed policy dialogue; further enhance capacity of constituents to produce and use the necessary statics; assist in establishing and measure decent work indicators.

(7) *Partnership and policy coherence for decent work:* develop a strategy for promoting decent work through partnership based on the principles of complementarity and mutual reinforcement with selected international and regional organizations that have mandates in closely related fields; include in such a strategy a special focus on promoting inclusive growth and decent work; strengthen its capacity and that of its constituents to contribute to the achievement of decent work and related goals of the 2030 Agenda based on the integrated approach of the declaration; foster policy coherence by offering evidence-based policy advice and closely working with relevant government ministries and departments; lead or engage on innovative issue-based alliances related to Goal 8 on decent work and other decent work-related goals with the active involvement of tripartite partners and within the framework of the declaration; contribute to the follow-up and review of the 2030 Agenda through inputs concerning decent work trends and indicators to global reports that will feed into the annual reviews by the High-Level Political Forum on Sustainable Development; in the context of the Enterprise Centenary Initiative, further develop its engagement with the private sector, the Tripartite Declaration of Principles concerning Multinational Enterprises and Social Policy (1977) and the UN guiding principles on Human Rights in Business Practices; promote strategic partnerships with non-state actors (academia, foundations, religious organizations) consistent with the principles of tripartism and social dialogue; attract additional resources for the implementation of the declaration further diversify funding resources (south- south and triangular cooperation, larger development projects and programmes).

Lastly, the Resolution invites the Governing Body members of the ILO and the Director-General to follow-up with an awareness campaign; better coordination of technical programmes; improve the communication to the UN High-Level Political Forum on Sustainable Development, and to relevant organizations.

As stated above, one of the major concerns for the ILO is to make sure that Member States are developing employment policies for decent work.

5.4 Productive and Decent Jobs

There is a need for many more productive and decent jobs in the world, but the pace in creating decent work worldwide is insufficient. Employment has to be put at the centre of economic and social policies. Greater international coordination of macroeconomic policies, as well as active labour market policies at the national level are needed.

The ILO is committed to full employment – productive and freely chosen employment is at the core of its mandate. In pursuing this goal, the ILO identifies policies that help create and maintain decent work and income – policies that are formulated in a comprehensive Global Employment Agenda worked out in a tripartite way by governments, workers' and employers'.

To carry out its mandate the ILO produces employment analysis and research, and takes part in international discussions of employment strategies. It promotes employment-intensive investment and helps formulate and implement employment policy. It also provides technical support and advice in areas ranging from training and skills to microfinance, job creation, cooperatives, enterprise and small business development.

Not only employment, but also social security systems are fundamental for implementing the 2030 Agenda.

5.5 Social Protection

Only 20% of the world's population has adequate social security coverage, and more than half lack any coverage at all. They face dangers in the workplace and poor or non-existent pension and health insurance coverage. The situation reflects levels of economic development, with fewer than 10% of workers in least-developed countries covered by social security. In middle-income countries, coverage ranges from 20% to 60%, while in most industrial nations, it is close to 100%.

Access to an adequate level of social protection is recognized by international labour standards and the UN as a basic right of all individuals. It is also widely considered to be instrumental in promoting human welfare and social consensus on a broad scale, and to be conducive to and indispensable for social peace and thus improved economic growth and performance.

Social Protection is one of the four strategic objectives of the Decent Work agenda. The ILO has always actively promoted policies and provided its Member States with tools and assistance aimed at improving and expanding the coverage of social protection to all members of the community across the full range of contingencies: basic income security in case of need, healthcare, sickness, old age and invalidity, unemployment, employment injury, maternity, family responsibilities and death. Many activities are also designed to improve the social protection of migrant workers.

At a closer look, all the above-mentioned policies and tools can effectively be achieved if there is in place a sound system of social tripartite dialogue.

5.6 Social Dialogue and Tripartism

The ILO defines social dialogue to include all types of negotiation, consultation and exchange of information between, or among, representatives of governments, employers and workers (the social partners) on issues of common interest. How social dialogue actually operates varies from country to country and from region to region. Effective social dialogue depends on:

- Strong, independent workers' and employers' organizations with the technical capacity and knowledge required to participate in social dialogue.
- Political will and commitment to engage in social dialogue on the part of all parties.
- Respect for the fundamental rights of freedom of association and collective bargaining.
- Appropriate institutional support.

The main goal of social dialogue itself is to promote consensus building and democratic involvement among the main stakeholders in the world of work. Successful social dialogue structures and processes have the potential to resolve important economic and social issues, encourage good governance, advance social and industrial peace and stability and boost economic progress.

The world of work is diverse and is constantly adapting to meet new challenges. Elements within it, such as the health and safety environment, the impact of globalization and technology, what training and skills are needed, as well as the aspirations of workers and employers, are constantly changing. These changes can bring about opportunities as well as conflicts for workers and employers. Ensuring that these changes are managed in the most effective and mutually beneficial manner requires relevant labour laws, effective social dialogue and efficient and responsive labour administration. These are essential in order to meet the needs of workers, employers and their representative organizations. The process of continuous change in the world of work poses challenges to institutions, legal frameworks, collective bargaining and other practices and procedures that govern the workplace and the labour market.

The ILO aims to ensure that it serves the needs of working men and women in a tripartite way by bringing together governments, employers and workers to set labour standards develop policies and devise programmes. Its tripartite structure makes the ILO unique among world organizations because employers' and workers' organizations have an equal voice with governments in its deliberations.

Achieving fair terms of employment, decent working conditions, and development for the benefit of all cannot be achieved without the consent of workers, employers and governments, including a broad-based effort by all of them. To encourage that effort, a strategic objective of the ILO is to strengthen social dialogue among the tripartite constituents. It helps governments, employers' and workers' organizations to establish sound labour relations, adapt labour laws to meet changing economic and social needs and improve labour administration.

Among the ILO promotional tools for a fair globalization, mention should be made of the Tripartite Declaration Concerning Multinational Enterprises and Social Policy (MNE Declaration).

5.7 MNE Declaration

The MNE Declaration is the only ILO instrument that provides direct guidance to multinational enterprises on social policy and inclusive, responsible and sustainable workplace practices. It is the only global instrument in this area that was elaborated and adopted by governments, employers and workers from around the world. It was adopted in 1977 and amended in 2000, 2006, 2014 and 2016 but its aims remain highly relevant in the context of the 2030 Agenda for Sustainable Development. Its principles are addressed to MNEs, governments, and employers' and workers' organizations and cover areas such as employment, training, conditions of work and life, and industrial relations as well as general policies.

The MNE Declaration facilitates outreach and understanding of the Decent Work Agenda in the private sector, as highlighted in the ILO Declaration on Social Justice for a Fair Globalization.

The MNE Declaration's approach to social and labour issues has directly influenced and guided policies of international and regional organizations, many multi-stakeholder initiatives as well as codes of conduct of enterprises of all sizes and structures.

Multinational enterprises are the principal drivers of globalization and through their operations influence the working and living conditions of millions of people worldwide. They have a vital role to play in promoting economic and social progress. Today, businesses increasingly realize the benefits of referring to internationally- accepted labour standards and principles in their operations. They set the stage for sustainable growth and development. Moreover, they are a foundation on which to expand productivity and business success in the enterprise itself.

Experience shows that partnership and social dialogue among employers, workers, and governments can help create decent jobs, point the way to genuine labour and social progress and – at the same time – enhance enterprise competitiveness.

This declaration is aimed at inspiring effective, socially responsible labour relations policies and practices in the world of work. In fact, the MNE Declaration is rooted in social dialogue at the international and national levels; it sets core labour principles and promotes effective practices for both multinational and domestic enterprises in the areas of employment, skills training, conditions of work and life, and industrial relations, and recognizes the responsibility of governments in promoting good social practices.

5.8 2014 Follow-Up Mechanism and 2016 Revision of the MNE Declaration

A new follow-up mechanism to the MNE Declaration has been adopted by the ILO Governing Body in 2014, focusing on increased promotional and capacity building activities and a data gathering mechanism allowing for further policy discussions among governments, employers' and workers' organizations especially in the context of the ILO Regional Meetings.

At its 326th session in March 2016, the ILO Governing Body decided to establish a tripartite ad hoc working group of eight members representing Governments, four members representing Workers and four members representing Employers that will meet twice before March 2017 to review the text of the MNE Declaration including its annex and addenda and the interpretation procedure. The recommendations of the working group, arrived at through consensus, will be presented for possible adoption at the 329th Session (March 2017) of the Governing Body.

In a nutshell, the qualities of the ILO MNE Declaration can be summarized as follows:

> *Importance of the Declaration.* The MNE Declaration is important because it expresses a very broad, international tripartite consensus on the proper conduct of enterprises with respect to work and social policy.
>
> *Purpose of the Declaration.* The aims of the Declaration are to encourage the positive contributions of MNEs to economic and social progress and minimize and resolve the difficulties to which their operations may give rise. The principles enshrined in the ILO's Declaration are intended to help multinationals, governments, and employers' and workers' organizations craft their social policy and to inspire multinational enterprises to introduce good practices.
>
> *Relationship with other elements of the normative framework.* The MNE Declaration integrates the ILO's other most important declarations and conventions and, consequently, its fundamental labour standards. The Declaration specifies what is expected from MNEs within this context. It contains the most comprehensive summary of rights at work of relevance to MNEs. The most important points have also been incorporated into the OECD Guidelines for Multinational Enterprises, Part IV (employment and industrial relations).

Who does the Declaration address? The Declaration makes recommendations to both governments and MNEs. Paragraph 6 of the Declaration states that 'To serve its purpose this Declaration does not require a precise legal definition of multinational enterprises.' In general, the Declaration defines a multinational enterprise as an enterprise that owns or controls production, distribution, service or other facilities outside the country in which it is based. The form of ownership is of no relevance. The recommendations are intended for all the various entities of an MNE (parent company and/or local entities). Depending on the actual distribution of responsibilities, the various entities are deemed to cooperate and provide assistance to one another as necessary to facilitate observance of the principles laid down in the Declaration.

The Declaration does not aim to impose stricter standards on multinational enterprises than on national ones, as that could undermine their competitiveness. The Declaration therefore states explicitly that 'the principles laid down in this Declaration do not aim at introducing or maintaining inequalities of treatment between multinational and national enterprises': the expectations and principles laid down in the Declaration pertain to all enterprises.

What the Declaration says about the conduct of MNEs. General principles and human rights: Obey national laws and respect international standards, such as the UN's Universal Declaration of Human Rights. Contribute to the realization of the fundamental principles and rights at work. Consult with government, employers' and workers' organizations to ensure that operations are consistent with national development priorities.

Moreover, the MNE Declaration looks at the major following areas:

Employment: Endeavour to increase employment opportunities and standards, work security and the company's long-term future. Give priority to the employment, occupational development, promotion and advancement of the nationals of the host country. Hire local contractors whenever possible. Extend equality of opportunity and treatment in employment. Assume a leading role in promoting security of employment. Provide reasonable notice of intended changes in personnel and avoid arbitrary dismissal.

Training: Provide training for all levels of employees to meet the needs of enterprises as well as the development policies of the host country. Participate in programmes to encourage training, skill formation and career choices. Afford opportunities within the MNE for local management to broaden their experience in such fields as industrial relations.

Conditions of work and life: Do not provide wages, benefits and conditions of work that are less favourable than those observed by comparable employers in the host country. If there are no comparable employers, endeavour to provide the best possible wages, benefits and conditions of work, within the framework of government MNE policies, to meet the basic needs of employees and their families. Respect the minimum age for admission to employment. Do everything possible to eradicate the worst forms of child labour. Maintain the highest standards of safety and health at work; provide transparent information about the standards maintained and investigate potential risks.

Industrial relations: Observe industrial relations no less favourable than those observed by comparable employers in the host country. Respect workers' freedom of association and the right to collective bargaining and protect them against anti-union discrimination. Support representative local employers' organizations. Do not threaten to transfer workers or operating units in order to influence unfairly bona fide negotiations or prevent workers from organizing. Provide worker representatives with information required for meaningful negotiations and to obtain a true and fair view of the performance of the enterprise. Consult regularly with employees on matters of mutual concern. Make sure that a proper grievance procedure is introduced.

In order to follow-up on the implementation of the MNE Declaration, already in 1993, the ILO's Governing Body installed the Subcommittee on Multinational Enterprises within the framework of the Committee on Legal Issues and International Labour Standards. The Committee's mandate is to conduct periodic surveys on the effect given to the MNE Declaration and to consider requests for the interpretation of the provisions of the MNE Declaration.

Before concluding, it is worthwhile to recall that the MNE Declaration addresses specific principles directed to governments and enterprises. They are:

5.9 Principles Directed to Governments

5.9.1 *General Policies*

- Ratify all the Fundamental Conventions and apply to the greatest extent possible, through their national policies, the principles embodied therein.
- Promote good social practice in accordance with the MNE Declaration and be prepared to have consultations with other governments whenever the need arises.

5.9.2 Employment

- Declare and pursue, as a major goal, an active policy designed to promote full, productive and freely chosen employment.
- Pursue policies designed to promote equality of opportunity and treatment in employment, with a view to eliminating any discrimination based on race, colour, sex, religion, political opinion, national extraction or social origin.
- Never require or encourage multinational enterprises to discriminate and provide guidance, where appropriate, on the avoidance of discrimination.
- Study the impact of multinational enterprises on employment in different industrial sectors.
- In cooperation with multinational and national enterprises, provide income protection for workers whose employment has been terminated.

5.9.3 Training

- Develop national policies for vocational training and guidance, closely linked with employment in cooperation with all the parties concerned.

5.9.4 Conditions of Work and Life

- Endeavour to adopt suitable measures to ensure that lower income groups and less developed areas benefit as much as possible from the activities of multinational enterprises.
- Ensure that both multinational and national enterprises provide adequate safety and health standards for their employees.

5.9.5 Industrial Relations

- Apply the principles of Convention No. 87, Article 5, in view of the importance, in relation to multinational enterprises, of permitting organizations representing such enterprises or the workers in their employment to affiliate with international organizations of employers and workers of their own choosing.
- Not include in their incentives to attract foreign investment any limitation of the workers' freedom of association or the right to organize and bargain collectively.

5.10 Principles Directed to Enterprises

5.10.1 *General Policies*

- Obey national laws and respect international standards.
- Contribute to the realization of the fundamental principles and rights at work.
- Consult with government, employers' and workers' organizations to ensure that operations are consistent with national development priorities.

5.10.2 *Employment*

- Endeavour to increase employment opportunities and standards, taking the employment policies and objectives of governments into account.
- Give priority to the employment, occupational development, promotion and advancement of nationals of the host country.
- Use technologies which generate employment, both directly and indirectly.
- Build linkages with local enterprises by sourcing local inputs, promoting the local processing of raw materials and local manufacturing of parts and equipment.
- Extend equality of opportunity and treatment in employment.
- Promote security of employment, providing reasonable notice of intended changes in operations and avoiding arbitrary dismissal.

5.10.3 *Training*

- Provide training for all levels of employees to meet needs of enterprises as well as development policies of the country.
- Participate in programmes to encourage skill formation and development.
- Afford opportunities within MNE for local management to broaden their experience.

5.10.4 *Conditions of Work and Life*

- Provide wages, benefits and conditions of work not less favourable than those offered by comparable employers in the country concerned.
- Provide the best possible wages, benefits and conditions of work, within the framework of government policies, to meet basic needs of employees and their families.
- Respect the minimum age for admission to employment.

- Maintain highest standards of safety and health at work.
- Examine the causes of industrial safety and health hazards, provide information on good practice observed in other countries, and effect necessary improvements.

5.10.5 *Industrial Relations*

- Observe industrial relations no less favourable than those observed by comparable employers.
- Respect freedom of association and the right to collective bargaining, providing the facilities and information required for meaningful negotiations.
- Support representative employers' organizations.
- Provide for regular consultation on matters of mutual concern.
- Examine the grievances of worker(s), pursuant to an appropriate procedure.

References

Arrigo, G.; Casale, G., *International Labour Law Handbook (from A to Z)*, Giappichelli, Forthcoming 2017.

Casale, G.; Fasani, M., *International Labour Standards and Guiding Principles on Labour Administration and Labour Inspection*, Working Document No. 22, ILO, Geneva, 2012.

ILO Agenda, *Report of the ILO Director General to the International Labour Conference*, 2014.

ILO, *A Fair Globalization: Creating Opportunities for All, Report of the World Commission on the Social Dimension of Globalization*, ILO, Geneva, 2004.

ILO, *Declaration on Fundamental Principles and Rights at Work*, ILO, Geneva, 1998.

ILO, *Declaration on Social Justice for a Fair Globalization*, ILO, Geneva, 2008.

ILO, *Global Wage Report 2016/17, Wage Inequality in the Workplace*, ILO, Geneva, 2016.

ILO, *Labour Migration: Facts and Figures*, Fact sheet, March 2014.

ILO, *Recovering from the Crisis: A Global Jobs Pact*, ILO, Geneva, 2009.

ILO, *Transitioning from the Informal to the Formal Economy*, Report V(1), International Labour Conference, 103rd Session, ILO, Geneva, 2014.

ILO, *Tripartite Declaration of Principles Concerning Multinational Enterprises and Social Policy (MNE Declaration)* – 4th Edition, ILO, Geneva, 2014.

ILO, *World Employment and Social Outlook: Trends 2017*, ILO, Geneva, 2017.

ILO, *World of Work Report 2014: Repairing the Economic and Social Fabric*, ILO, Geneva, 2014.

UN Secretary-General, *Message for the World Day of Social Justice*, 20 February 2014.

UN, *Transforming Our World: The 2030 Agenda for Sustainable Development (A/RES/70/1)*, UN, New York, 2015.

Index

1998 Declaration on Fundamental Principles and Rights, 10, 61, 87, 173, 174
2030 Agenda, 11, 18, 172, 177–190

A

Accidents and diseases, 44
Aggressive unilateralism, 127
Amoco v. Iran case, 149
Appeal mechanism, 83, 163
Arbitral tribunals, 54, 143
Arbitration, 9, 66– 68, 81, 83, 87, 90, 105, 106, 113, 155–159, 161, 162, 167
Arbitrators, 7, 83, 106, 116, 157–160, 163, 167
Argentina, 4, 5, 41–55, 86
Article XX of GATT, 114
Asia, 60, 65, 72, 73, 104, 150
Aspirational language, 6, 84, 86
ATS, 27

B

Balance, 3, 9, 10, 16, 19, 20, 34, 37, 88, 102, 117, 121, 142, 147, 148, 151, 152, 155, 157, 162–166
Bank(s), 2, 8, 9, 20, 28, 36, 67, 131–140
Beneficiary, 55, 122–126
Bilateral investments agreements (BITs), 84, 100, 155, 156
Brazil, 4, 5, 41–55, 73, 75
Brexit, 2

C

CAFTA, 66
Cambodia, 21, 28, 29, 31, 64
CAMFEBA, 64, 65
Canada, 6, 61, 67, 72, 76, 78, 83, 85, 109, 158, 162, 163, 166
Capital, 4, 10, 35, 73–75, 143, 147, 171
Centerra v. Kyrgyz Republic, 9, 107, 160, 161
CETA (Comprehensive Economic and Trade Agreement), 2, 6, 9, 71–91, 100, 103–109, 115, 116, 162–167
Child labour, 5, 49, 50, 53, 62, 63, 66, 173–175, 178, 187
Chilling effect, 143
China, 2, 6, 27, 59, 72, 73, 75, 112
CJEU (Court of Justice of the European Union), 82, 167, 168
Code(s) of conduct, 7, 21, 83, 87, 101, 110, 144, 184
Collective agreement(s), 7, 87, 100, 101, 111, 113, 116, 117
Collective bargaining, 10, 26, 27, 47–49, 53, 61–63, 65, 79, 87, 111, 173–175, 183, 187, 190
Commerce, 1, 100, 107
Commercial bank, 8, 131–140
Commitment(s), 2, 5–7, 24, 25, 30, 42, 52, 54, 61, 72, 84–86, 103–105, 107–109, 116, 136, 138, 140, 147, 148, 160, 178, 179, 183

Index

Common Market Group, 51, 54
Comparative advantages, 1, 3, 16–18, 34, 101
Compensation, 4, 9, 89, 106, 108, 136, 137, 140, 146–150, 152, 155, 159–161
Competition, 1, 3, 4, 9, 16–18, 21, 23, 27, 33–36, 52, 75, 76, 80, 91, 101, 102, 114, 117, 121, 139, 145
Competition law, 16, 18, 23
Competitive advantage(s), 16, 34, 102, 114
Competitiveness, 1, 8, 49, 127, 184, 186
Compliance, 3, 4, 17, 18, 21–23, 29–31, 36, 54, 64, 65, 76, 87, 126, 136, 144, 154
Compulsory labour, 63, 173
Conditionality, 1–3, 7, 17, 20, 27, 28, 36, 104
Constitutionalization, 37, 38
Consumers, 9, 25, 37, 162
Contingent work, 80
Convergence, 47, 77–80, 109
Core conventions, 7, 8, 58, 62–64, 66, 67, 105
Core labour standards, 24, 122, 124
Corporate responsibility, 62, 151
Corporate Social Responsibility (CSR), 21
Corporations, 6, 9, 10, 42, 67, 74, 76, 78, 81, 88, 101, 131, 132, 144–146, 148, 157–160
Crisis, 2, 10, 29, 45, 100, 145, 167, 171, 172

D

Damage avoidance, 136–137
Damage compensation, 136–137, 160
David Ricardo, 17
De-globalization, 2
Decent work, 5 2, 10, 11, 18, 19, 24, 25, 41–42, 49, 86, 105, 172–176, 190
Decent Work Agenda, 11, 24, 105, 173, 174, 177, 179, 182, 184

Decent Work Country Programmes (DWCP), 179, 180
Declaration of Philadelphia, 172, 174
Democracy, 20, 25, 42, 86, 122, 134, 139, 140
Derogations, 2, 6, 75, 85
Developing countries, 1, 4, 8, 9, 17, 22, 43, 100, 106, 108, 109, 121–123, 127, 142, 147, 148, 155, 178
Discriminatory practices, 9, 155
Dismissal regime, 80
Dispute Resolution, 6, 7, 9, 51, 66, 67, 105, 155–160, 162, 163
Domestic labor systems, 71
Domestic law, 6, 26, 74, 79
Domestic regulation, 2, 26
Dumping, 16–18, 27, 52, 114, 121
Duty of care, 26

E

EBA, 8, 123
Economic equilibrium clause, 150, 153
Economic freedom, 145
Economic growth, 3, 11, 18, 19, 31, 34, 41, 53, 73, 121, 137, 171, 174, 177–178, 182
Economic rationality, 145
Effectiveness, 3, 4, 29, 30, 45, 53, 79, 88, 104, 105, 107–111, 116
Emerging countries, 104
Employers' associations, 65
Enforceability, 27, 81, 89
Enforceable, 6, 58, 59, 74, 88, 139
Enforcement, 5, 7, 23, 65–68, 76, 78, 79, 81, 83, 85, 86, 104–110, 112, 114, 116, 175
Environmental conditionality, 4, 17, 36
Equal, 5, 25, 28, 31, 35, 47, 52, 53, 79, 89, 161, 178, 183
Equal remuneration, 62
Equator Principles (EPs), 8, 9, 131–132, 134, 136–140
Equity within trade, 17

EU Court of Justice, 10, 167, 168
EU external action, 25, 99-127
EU external relations, 16, 17
EU Member States, 9, 58, 125, 127, 156, 163, 168
EU-Korea agreements, 86
EU-Vietnam FTA, 164
EUFSTA, 9, 162
Europe, 4, 24, 26, 43, 50, 75, 91, 103, 109, 117, 150, 158, 166
European Convention on Human Rights (ECHR), 101
European Social Model, 4, 44, 102
European Union, 2, 7, 8, 16, 43, 45, 51, 58, 72, 99-127, 156, 163
Everything but arms arrangement (EBA), 8, 123
Export Processing Zones, 145
External action, 25, 99- 127

F

Fair trade, 16, 17, 19, 61, 101, 122
Fairness, 16, 18, 74, 157, 176
Finance, 8, 9, 52, 131-140, 148, 163, 182
Financial responsibility, 81, 82
Forced labour, 49, 53, 62, 125, 174, 175, 178, 179
Foreign investors, 9, 26, 73, 76, 80-83, 106, 145, 146, 148, 155, 157, 165
Free trade, 1, 2, 6, 8, 16, 17, 42, 57, 61, 65, 121, 123, 124, 127, 145, 164
Free trade agreements (FTAs), 5, 6, 8, 15, 21, 24, 27, 57-67, 72, 78, 84, 85, 121, 123, 124, 127, 155, 164, 168
Freedom of association, 5, 10, 24, 47, 49, 50, 53, 61-66, 87, 173-175, 183, 187, 188, 190
Freezing, 6, 9, 88, 89, 134, 149, 150, 154, 157, 160-162
FTAs. See Free trade agreements (FTAs)
Full freezing clause, 150

Fundamental rights, 4, 24, 26, 45, 61-66, 101, 114, 123, 183

G

GATT, 1, 21, 60, 114
Generalised Scheme of Preferences, 7, 121-127
Generalized preference system(s), 2
Generations, 3, 5, 6, 35, 67-68, 88, 152, 155-168
Global Compact, 62, 101, 110
Global players, 16, 17, 167, 176
Global scale, 16
Global trade, 1-3, 7, 15-31, 99, 100, 102, 103, 109, 115, 121, 152, 166, 167
Globalized economy, 171, 178
Good Governance, 7, 8, 19, 22, 121-127, 183
Group of enterprises, 144
Group(s), 5, 25, 36, 47, 51, 54, 103, 105, 113, 117, 123, 132, 133, 144, 158, 161, 185, 188
GSP, 7, 8, 19, 100, 108, 114, 123-124
GSP+, 2, 8, 22, 123-126
Guatemala, 66, 68, 88, 112, 124
Guidelines, 2, 7, 29, 30, 60, 64, 78, 90, 101, 103, 110, 117, 134, 151, 153, 185

H

Havana Chart (Charter), 1, 31
Home country, 104
Host country, 147, 148, 160, 186, 187, 189
Human being, 4, 45, 102, 141

I

ICS (Investment Court System), 9, 10, 71, 163, 166-168
IFAs, 27

Index

ILO Convention(s), 4, 5, 8, 22, 24, 27, 28, 45, 49, 61, 63, 65, 66, 114, 122, 124, 135
ILO core labour standards, 7, 24, 104, 110
ILO Declaration on Social Justice for a Fair Globalization, 87, 172, 178–179, 184
ILO Fundamental Principle, 62–64
ILO Recommendation, 115
ILO standards, 16, 17, 135
IMF (International Monetary Fund), 20, 90
Immigrant workers, 74
Implementation, 3, 21, 28–31, 35, 45, 47, 54–55, 62, 64, 71, 78, 87, 103–105, 107–109, 113–116, 123, 125, 148, 150, 161, 174, 179, 180, 181, 187
Incentive, 6–8, 22, 84, 101, 121–127, 188
Inclusive growth, 10, 172, 181
India, 6, 27, 72, 73, 75
Indicators, 48, 172, 181
Indirect expropriation(s), 83, 146
Industrial relation, 3, 6, 26–27, 48, 72–75, 77–80, 111, 117, 184–188, 190
Industry/ industries, 21, 26–27, 44, 46, 48, 58–60, 64, 72–75, 77–80, 111, 117, 139, 161, 166, 182–188, 190
Inequality, 10, 17, 161, 171, 172, 174, 175, 178, 186
Influenced right, 43
Informal economy, 174, 176
Informal work, 4, 45
Informality, 48
Information and consultation, 26
International competition, 3, 17, 23, 33–35
International cooperation, 2, 31
International exchange(s), 36, 99–117
International Finance Corporation (IFC), 132, 136, 137, 148, 153

International Framework Agreements (IFAs), 27
International Investments Agreements-IIAS, 100
International Labour Standard, 121, 172–173, 176, 180, 182, 187
International law, 3, 22, 23, 67, 76, 79, 84, 106, 122, 148, 152
International organizations, 1, 10, 37, 38, 100, 109, 110, 117, 142, 175, 188
International standards, 27, 104, 148, 152, 186, 189
International trade, 1–4, 15–18, 21, 22, 25, 27, 31, 33–38, 59, 60, 86, 99–102, 109, 122
Internormativity, 21–23
Interrelation, 3, 23
Investor protection, 151
Investor-State Dispute Resolution, 66, 67

J

Job losses, 59, 60
Jobs, 2, 6, 19, 28, 52, 58–61, 73, 75, 77, 89, 103, 163, 171, 172, 178, 179, 182, 184
Juridical system, 34, 37, 145, 148
Jus cogens, 51
Justification, 9, 16, 17–19

K

Kyrgyz Republic, 161

L

Labor clauses, 5, 58–68, 85
Labour cost(s), 10, 79, 102, 117, 161
Labour Law, 1, 4, 6, 15, 17, 19, 22, 23, 25–27, 41, 43, 44, 46, 52, 60, 64, 66, 67, 71, 74, 76–78, 80, 81, 84–88, 90, 107, 117, 121, 155, 160, 161, 165–167, 173, 183, 184

Labour market(s), 10, 19, 29, 59, 74, 79, 80, 102, 109, 172, 182, 183
Labor provisions, 3, 6, 15, 24, 25, 71, 84, 85, 87
Labor reforms, 7, 104
Labour relations, 4, 25, 46, 48, 53, 67, 73, 110, 112, 184
Labor relationship, 25
Labour right(s), 4-8, 5, 7, 10, 18, 19, 20, 43-47, 49, 66, 71, 76, 77, 78, 80, 84, 86, 88-90, 104, 112, 122, 124, 135, 138, 142, 145, 175, 178, 178
Labour Standard(s), 24, 64, 121, 122, 124, 127, 165, 172-173, 176, 180, 182-185, 187
Labor violation, 6, 66, 88
Lack of transparency, 7, 115, 138, 158, 167
Least developed countries, 8, 19, 124, 177, 178, 182
Level playing field, 16-18
Levels of regulation, 3, 33, 34
Liberalization of exchanges, 36
Liberalization of the markets, 145
Liberalizing, 59-60
Limited freezing clause, 150
Lisbon, 19
Litigations, 26, 79, 87
Localization, 34

M

Manager(s), 33
Manufacturing industries, 59
Market(s), 4, 7, 8, 10, 15-17, 19, 21, 36-38, 41-55, 72, 74, 79, 80, 102, 109, 115, 117, 122, 124, 126, 127, 132, 145, 166, 172, 174, 182, 183
Maternity protection, 44
Mega trade treaties, 3
Mega-treaties, 2, 6, 9, 71, 73-76, 81, 82, 84, 85, 88, 90
Mercosur, 2, 4-6, 41-55, 73

Millennium Development Goals (MDGs), 177
Minimum wage, 53, 79, 160, 166
MNE Declaration, 11, 184-187
MNEs, 11, 184-187, 189
Monitoring, 7, 29, 30, 31, 36, 65-67, 104, 105, 107, 108, 116, 125-127
Monitoring activity, 31, 65-66, 125-126
Monopoly, 47
Multinational companies, 2, 3, 25, 26, 60, 74, 106, 110
Multinational enterprises, 4, 7, 10, 11, 36, 37, 101, 110, 144-146
Multinational firms, 109, 111, 113, 116

N

NAFTA, 2, 22, 23, 59-61, 88, 100, 157, 162
National Juridical regimes, 10, 143
Nationalization, 148
Natural resources, 3, 24, 25, 34, 132
Negotiations, 1, 2, 6-9, 19, 24-27, 29, 35, 57-59, 61, 72, 73, 103, 107, 109, 115, 121, 127, 135, 141, 151, 153, 156, 163-166, 183, 187, 190
Neo-protectionism, 2
Network, 24, 89, 111, 117, 144, 171
New generations treaties, 155-168
New Zealand, 27, 166
NGO's, 9, 30, 83, 105, 116, 138, 162, 163
Non-discrimination, 47, 52, 180
Non-tariff barriers, 58, 162
Norm(s), 3, 4, 7, 21, 23, 26, 33-37, 85, 90, 100, 113, 114, 139, 145

O

Obligations, 3, 5-7, 10, 23, 24, 30, 37, 54, 62, 63, 66, 76, 80, 81, 84, 87, 88, 103, 104, 106-108, 113, 116, 134-137, 142, 144, 149, 151-153, 156, 173, 180

Obligations of conduct, 6, 84
Obligations of results, 6, 84
Occupation, 10, 44, 62, 63, 86, 87, 89, 173, 174, 186, 189
OECD Guidelines, 7, 60, 101, 110, 185

P

Paraguay, 4, 5, 41–55, 124
Partnership, 2, 25, 57, 58, 67, 72, 100, 162, 164, 166, 177, 181, 184
Peer-to-peer economies, 76
Piero Foresti & others v. South Africa case, 9, 161–162
Populism, 2
Preferential arrangements, 125
Privacy, 162
Procedures of enforcement, 7, 104, 105, 109, 110
Project finance, 8, 9, 131–140
Protection of environment, 3, 34, 36
Protectionism, 8, 17, 18, 52, 117, 127
Protectionist patterns, 121
Public order, 44, 52

R

Ratification, 4, 5, 7, 28, 42, 49, 55, 57, 104, 109, 127, 164
Recommendation, 4, 10, 30, 36, 44, 52, 54, 87, 105, 115, 152, 172, 179, 185, 186
Regional integration, 2, 43
Regionalism, 15
Regulation level(s), 33
Regulatory chill, 9, 155, 157, 166
Regulatory competition, 3, 4, 16, 18, 21, 33, 35, 36
Regulatory distortion, 6, 72–77
Regulatory framework, 1, 2, 46, 50, 145
Regulatory instruments, 5, 50–55
Regulatory level, 5, 49–51
Remuneration, 28, 62
Resolutory competition, 34

Responsibility, 4, 10, 21, 27, 37, 38, 62, 81, 82, 101, 110–111, 113, 116, 117, 138, 144, 145, 147, 151–153, 174, 185
Right to collective bargaining, 10, 53, 61, 63, 87, 173–175, 187, 190
RLTFA (Regional labour and Trade Framework agreement), 27
RTAs (Regional Trade Agreement), 26, 27

S

Safe livelihood, 41
Safety and health, 187, 188, 190
Salary(ies), 17, 18, 27, 107, 161
Sanction(s), 16, 18, 21, 36, 38, 76, 81, 84, 100–102, 104, 107, 108, 112, 114, 117, 125–126, 175
Scholars, 9, 100, 141, 143, 144, 162
Scorecard, 125, 126
Self-regulation, 81
Shareholder, 61
Small and medium-sized enterprise(s) (SME(s)), 156, 178
Social benefits, 58
Social conditionality, 1, 2, 17, 20, 27
Social dimension, 4, 20, 35, 47, 175
Social Dumping, 16–18, 27, 52, 114, 121
Social Globalization, 31
Social Justice, 10, 19, 24, 37, 51, 87, 102, 121, 145, 171–174, 178–179, 184
Social model, 4, 44, 100, 102, 110
Social obligations, 7, 116, 136
Social partners, 183
Social policies, 11, 143, 147, 166, 176, 178, 181, 182, 184
Social progress, 3, 11, 19, 23, 34, 36, 184, 185
Social protection, 10, 29, 167, 173, 176, 177, 179, 182–183
Social Regulation, 1, 7, 100, 101, 108, 114–117

Social risks, 8, 9, 132, 134
Social security, 5, 11, 43, 53–55, 90, 176, 182
Social sphere, 15, 18
Social standards, 3, 7, 16, 17, 25, 30, 100, 101, 104, 114, 116, 121, 151, 162
Soft unilateralism, 8, 127
Special Incentive Arrangement for Sustainable Development and Good Governance, 7, 121–127
Stabilization clause(s), 2, 6, 10, 81, 89, 139, 141–154
Stakeholder, 7, 30, 88, 115–117, 138, 165, 183, 184
State-Investor Agreements, 10, 141–154
Strikes, 24, 46, 53, 64, 65, 89, 102, 105
Subsidiaries, 37, 113, 133, 144
Supervisory bodies, 51, 64
Supplier(s), 29, 61, 101, 110, 146
Sustainability, 2, 22, 25, 29, 30, 49, 105, 177
Sustainability Impact Assessment (SIA), 29, 105

T

Tariff barriers, 58, 60, 61
Temporary withdrawal, 122, 125
TFUE, 8, 29, 105
TPP, 5, 9, 57–59, 63–68, 100, 103–105, 107–109, 162–167
Trade exchanges, 17, 27, 165
Trade International Organization, 1
Trade relationship, 21, 99–127
Trade Unions, 46, 49, 65, 108–110, 112, 135, 159, 162, 163
Transactions, 2, 83, 147
Transnational, 7, 26, 27, 72, 77, 78, 80, 89, 100, 101, 111, 113, 114, 116, 117, 144
Transnational agreements, 111
Transnational collective agreements, 7, 100, 101, 116, 117

Transnational social regulations, 117
Transparency, 7, 83, 106, 108, 115, 138, 158, 163, 167
Transplanted rights, 43
Treaty, 6– 8, 18, 19, 29, 30, 42, 51, 52, 72, 76, 81, 83, 84, 88–90, 103–108, 114, 116, 122, 146, 153, 156, 158, 160–163, 172
Tribunal(s), 6, 9, 54, 74, 82, 83, 106, 111, 143, 155, 158–160, 162, 163
Tripartism, 11, 173, 176, 179, 181, 183–184
Tripartite, 2, 11, 54, 61, 65, 79, 179–185
Trump, 2, 57, 103, 166
TTIP, 71–91, 162–166

U

UN, 7, 8, 18, 23, 61, 62, 64, 89, 124, 126, 127, 131, 134, 151, 152, 172, 176, 177, 179–182, 186
UN Convention, 8, 124
UNCTAD, 156, 159
Unfair trade practices, 16, 17, 89
Unilateral system, 8, 127
Uruguay, 4, 5, 41–55

V

Value chain, 35, 101
Venezuela, 4, 41–55
Veolia Propreté, 9, 160, 166

W

Wage, 10, 29, 53, 58–61, 77–79, 87, 102, 105, 107, 160, 166, 167, 171, 172, 176, 186, 187, 189
Welfare, 17, 20, 52, 157, 182
Well-being, 5, 26, 140, 175
Work conditions, 6, 73, 188–190
Work environment, 4, 46
Workers, 5, 6, 19, 22, 25, 36, 37, 42, 46, 48, 50, 52–54, 58, 59, 61, 63–68,

74, 78, 79, 86, 87, 89, 90, 101, 107, 108, 110–113, 135–137, 139, 157, 160, 161, 165, 171–174, 176, 178, 180, 182–190
Workers participation, 111
Workers' associations, 53, 65, 174–175, 188
Workforce, 42, 74
Working conditions, 3, 5, 6, 21, 28, 29, 34, 51, 52, 61, 64, 78, 87, 102, 103, 105, 132, 143, 183, 188–190
Workplace, 11, 35, 77–79, 89, 175, 182–184
World Bank, 2, 20, 28, 36, 132
WTO (World Trade Organization), 1, 17, 20, 36, 61, 100, 125, 160

STUDIES IN EMPLOYMENT AND SOCIAL POLICY

1. W. Beck, L. van der Maesen & A. Walker (eds), *The Social Quality of Europe*, 1997 (ISBN 90-411-0456-9).
2. R. Blanpain, M. Colucci, C. Engels, F. Hendrickx, L. Salas & E. De Smyter, *Institutional Changes and European Social Policies after the Treaty of Amsterdam*, 1998 (ISBN 90-411-1018-6).
3. V. Lo: *Law and Industrial Relations: China and Japan after World War II*, 1998 (ISBN 90-411-1075-5).
4. A. Den Exter & H. Hermans (eds), *The Right to Health Care in Several European Countries*, 1998 (ISBN 90-411-1087-9).
5. M. Biagi (ed.), *Job Creation and Labour Law from Protection towards Pro-Action*, 2000 (ISBN 90-411-1432-7).
6. W. Beck, L. van der Maesen, F. Thomése & A. Walker (eds), *Social Quality: A Vision for Europe*, 2000 (ISBN 90-411-1523-4).
7. F. Pennings, *Introduction to European Social Law*, 3rd ed., 2001 (ISBN 90-411-1628-1).
8. J. Murray, *Transnational Labour Regulation: The ILO and EC Compared*, 2001 (ISBN 90-411-1583-8).
9. R. Blanpain & C. Engels (eds), *The ILO and Social Challenges of the 21st Century*, 2001 (ISBN 90-411-1572-2).
10. M. Biagi (ed.), *Towards a European Model of Industrial Relations? Building on the First Report of the European Commission*, 2001 (ISBN 90-411-1653-2).
11. J. Clasen (ed.), *What Future for Social Security? Debates and Reforms in National and Cross-National Perspective*, 2001 (ISBN 90-411-1671-0).
12. A. Numhauser-Henning (ed.), *Legal Perspectives on Equal Treatment and Non-Discrimination*, 2001 (ISBN 90-411-1665-6).
13. R. Blanpain (ed.), *Labour Law, Human Rights and Social Justice* 2001 (ISBN 90-411-1697-4).
14. M.-C. Kuo, H.F. Zacher & H.-S. Chan (eds), *Reform and Perspectives on Social Insurance: Lessons from the East and West*, 2002 (ISBN 90-411-1819-5).
15. P. Foubert, *The Legal Protection of the Pregnant Worker in the European Community*, 2002 (ISBN 90-411-1842-X).
16. M. Biagi (ed.), *Quality of Work and Employee Involvement in Europe*, 2002 (ISBN 90-411-1885-3).
17. F. Pennings, *Dutch Social Security Law in an International Context*, 2002 (ISBN 90-411-1887-X).

18. T. Carney & G. Ramia, *From Rights to Management: Contract, New Public Management and Employment Services*, 2002 (ISBN 90-411-1889-6).
19. R. Blanpain & M. Colucci, *European Labour and Social Security Law, Glossary*, 2002 (ISBN 90-411-1905-1).
20. I.U. Zeytinoglu (ed.), *Flexible Work Arrangements: Conceptualizations and International Experiences*, 2002 (ISBN 90-411-1947-7).
21. J. Berghman, A. Nagelkerke, M. Boos, R. Doeschot & G. Vonk (eds), *Social Security in Transition*, 2002 (ISBN 90-411-1969-8).
22. R. Blanpain, *The Legal Status of Sportsmen and Sportswomen under International, European and Belgian National and Regional Law*, 2003 (ISBN 90-411-1980-9).
23. R. Blanpain & M. Weiss (eds), *Changing Industrial Relations & Modernisation of Labour Law, Liber Amicorum in Honour of Professor Marco Biagi*, 2003 (ISBN 90-411-2008-4).
24. J. Malmberg (ed.), *Effective Enforcement of EC Labour Law*, 2003 (ISBN 90-411-2160-9).
25. M. De Vos (ed.), *A Decade Beyond Maastricht: The European Social Dialogue Revisited*, 2003 (ISBN 90-411-2163-3).
26. M. Sewerynski (ed.), *Collective Agreements and Individual Contracts of Employment*, 2003 (ISBN 90-411-2190-0).
27. R. Blanpain & M. Van Gestel, *Use and Monitoring of E-Mail, Intranet and Internet Facilities at Work: Law and Practice*, 2004 (ISBN 90-411-22-66-4).
28. A. C. Neal (ed.), *The Changing Face of European Labour Law and Social Policy*, 2004 (ISBN 90-411-2312-1).
29. E. Sol & M. Westerveld (eds), *Contractualism in Employment Services: A New Form of Welfare State Governance*, 2005 (ISBN 90-411-2405-5).
30. F. Pennings (ed.), *Between Soft and Hard Law – The Impact of International Social Security Standards on National Social Security Law*, 2006 (ISBN 978-90-411-2491-3).
31. L. Dickens & A. C. Neal (eds), *The Changing Institutional Face of British Employment Relations*, 2006 (ISBN 978-90-411-2541-5).
32. G. Sebardt, *Redundancy and the Swedish Model in an International Context*, 2006 (ISBN 978-90-411-2503-3).
33. A.M. witkowski, *Charter of Social Rights of the Council of Europe*, 2007 (ISBN 978-90-411-2608-5).
34. M. Sargeant (ed.), *The Law on Age Discrimination in the EU*, 2008 (ISBN 978-90-411-2522-4).
35. G. Di Domenico & S. Spattini (eds), *New European Approaches to Long-Term Unemployment: What Role for Public Employment Services and What Market for Private Stakeholders?*, 2008 (ISBN 978-90-411-2614-6.)
36. C. Welz, *The European Social Dialogue under Articles 138 and 139 of the EC Treaty: Actors, Processes, Outcomes*, 2008 (ISBN 978-90-411-2744-0).
37. M. Rönnmar (ed.), *EU Industrial Relations v. National Industrial Relations: Comparative and Interdisciplinary Perspectives*, 2008 (ISBN 978-90-411-2770-9).

38. F. Pennings, Y. Konijn & A. Veldman (eds), *Social Responsibility in Labour Relations: European and Comparative Perspectives*, 2008 (ISBN 978-90-411-2783-9).
39. F. Pennings & C. Bosse (eds), *The Protection of Working Relationships: A Comparative Study*, 2011 (ISBN 978-90-411-3289-5).
40. S. Devetzi & S. Stendahl (eds), *Too Sick to Work?: Social Security Reference in Europe for Persons with Reduced Earnings Capacity*, 2011 (ISBN 978-90-411-3426-4).
41. U. Becker, F. Pennings & T. Dijkhoff (eds), *International Standard-Setting and Innovations in Social Security*, 2013 (ISBN 978-90-411-3233-8).
42. E. Ales (ed.), *Health and Safety at Work: European and Comparative Perspective*, 2013 (ISBN 978-90-411-4661-8).
43. F. Pennings, T. Erhag & S. Stendahl (eds), *Non-public Actors in Social Security Administration: A Comparative Study*, 2013 (ISBN 978-90-411-4917-6).
44. A. Neal (ed.), *Cross-Currents in Modern Chinese Labour Law*, 2014 (ISBN 978-90-411-4763-9).
45. B. Waas (ed.), *The Right to Strike: A Comparative View*, 2014 (ISBN 978-90-411-5007-3).
46. A. Ojeda-Avilés, *Transnational Labour Law*, 2015 (ISBN 978-90-411-5858-1).
47. A. Numhauser-Henning & M. Rönnmar, *Age Discrimination and Labour-Law: Comparative and Conceptual Perspectives in the EU and Beyond*, 2015 (ISBN 978-90-411-4979-4).
48. A. Perulli & T. Treu (eds), *Enterprise and Social Rights*, 2017 (ISBN 978-90-411-8234-0).
49. Dr F.C.A. van Haasteren, *Decent Flexibility: The Impact of ILO Convention 181 and the Regulation on Temporary Agency Work*, 2017 (ISBN 978-90-411-9236-3).
50. T. Dijkhoff & L.G. Mpedi (eds), *Recommendation on Social Protection Floors: Basic Principles for Innovative Solutions*, 2018 (ISBN 978-90-411-8623-2).
51. A. Perulli & T. Treu (eds), *Sustainable Development, Global Trade and Social Rights*, 2018 (ISBN 978-90-411-9235-6).